STREET FOOD
SCOTLAND

A JOURNEY OF STORIES AND RECIPES TO INSPIRE

AILIDH FORLAN

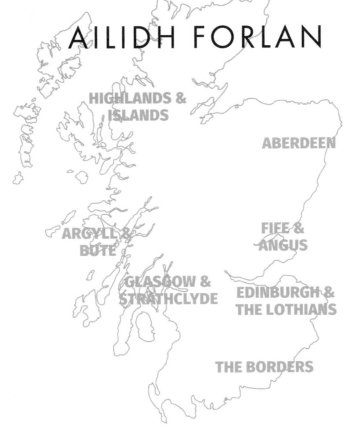

HIGHLANDS &
ISLANDS

ABERDEEN

ARGYLL &
BUTE

FIFE &
ANGUS

GLASGOW &
STRATHCLYDE

EDINBURGH &
THE LOTHIANS

THE BORDERS

BLACK & WHITE PUBLISHING

First published 2019
by Black & White Publishing Ltd
Nautical House, 104 Commercial Street,
Edinburgh, EH6 6NF

1 3 5 7 9 10 8 6 4 2   19 20 21 22

ISBN: 978 1 78530 263 3

While every reasonable effort has been made to ensure the
accuracy of the information in this book, the Publisher assumes
no responsibility for and gives no guarantees, undertakings or
warranties concerning the accuracy, completeness or up-to-date
nature of the information contained herein and does not accept
any liability whatsoever arising from any errors or omissions.

The publisher has made every reasonable effort to contact
copyright holders of images and other material used in the book.
Any errors are inadvertent and anyone who for any reason has not
been contacted is invited to write to the publisher so that a full
acknowledgment can be made in subsequent editions of this work.

A CIP catalogue record is available from the British Library.

Front cover photography © Ellie Morag 2019
Featured on front cover, Chick + Pea, see page 37

Layout by creativelink.tv
Printed and bound in Spain by Estella Print

For my grandad, Kenneth Haxton, who filled my life with love, whetted my appetite for new experiences and would have loved to eat his way through these pages.

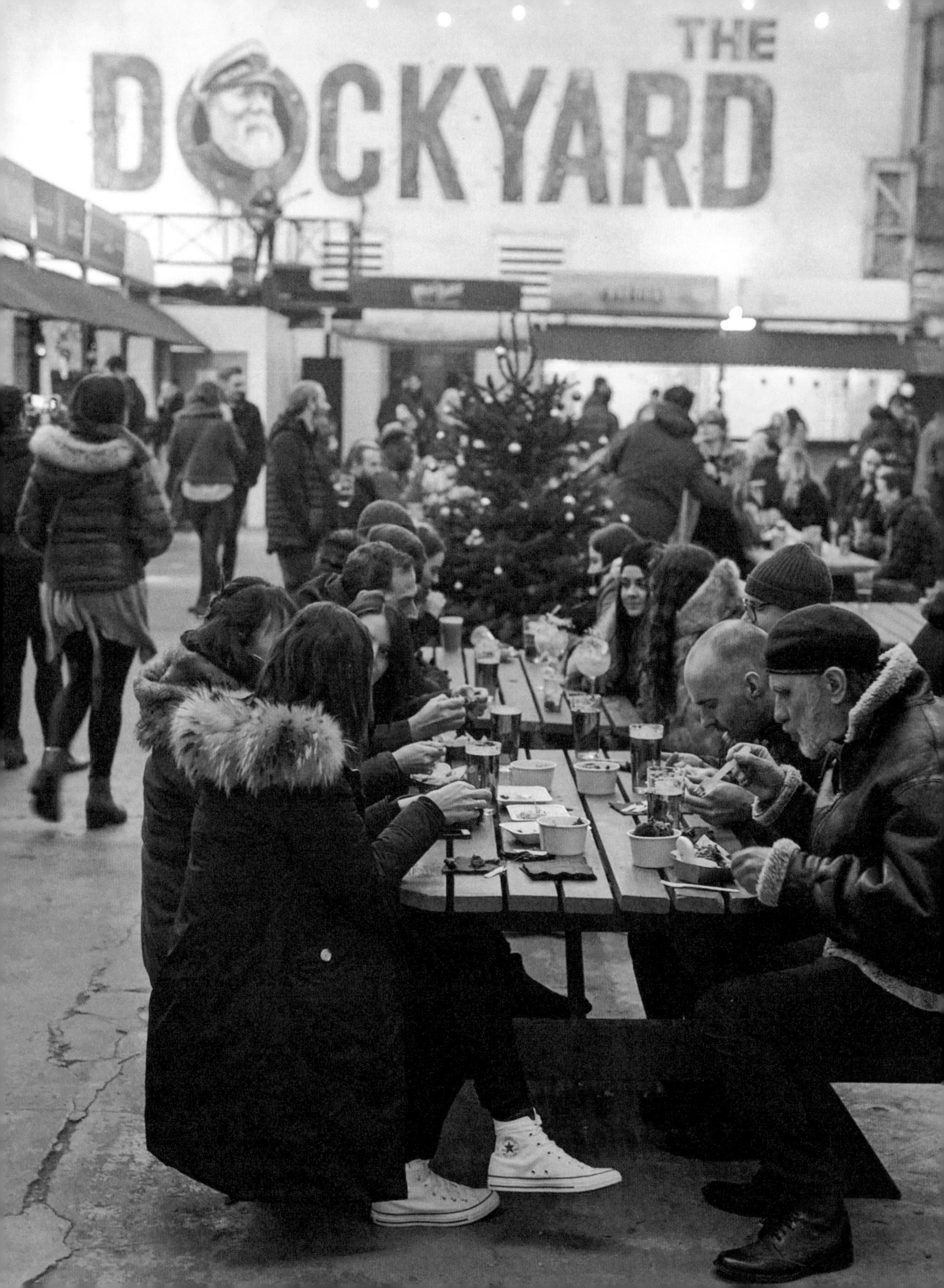
THE DOCKYARD

CONTENTS

INTRODUCTION

I've always believed food is more than just fodder. Even as a two-year-old, chanting 'more ham' from my high chair, it wasn't about being hungry or reliant on honey-glazed ham for sustenance. No, this was my mischievous way of reeling Grandad in, so I could talk baby talk while he pulled faces and blew raspberries on my cheeks. Eating ham together became a powerful connection between us. In spite of the 65-year age gap, there was no doubt that we were at one.

Fast forward to 2019 where food, for me, still extends beyond its basic function as nourishment. As cheesy and as clichéd as it sounds, food is the ingredient that binds us together. It's a vehicle for social harmony, common ground and unity, a universal experience. And I love to eat. My fondest memories were made at a table with friends and family, putting the world to rights while bonding over our mutual love for intense flavours and moreish textures. It's clear we'll never give up carbs or go light on the butter. But what we will do is explore the ever-evolving food scene, opening our minds and taste buds to new cuisines and their cultures.

When you take these joyful experiences out onto the street, be it authentic kerbside dining or in a curated market environment, the whole world opens up in front of you. By stepping out from the comfort of four walls, whether at home or in a restaurant, you're inviting others to join your culinary ride. From the initial bite of moist, blackened chicken tacos, smothered in a fiery pineapple salsa that dances on your tongue, to your first encounter with juicy Peruvian cow hearts, the chances are there's an equally apprehensive stranger nattering away to you, about to share the same delightful gastronomic awakening.

Living in Edinburgh, I've spent umpteen years gravitating towards its street food scene. On a sunny weekend you'll find me bopping to the beats at the Pitt and munching on butter-milk-brined fried chicken, while in my student days I'd regularly take the pilgrimage to the police box on Quartermile for *those* Brazilian crêpes. And now, *Street Food Scotland* has taken me further afield – from beside a seafood trailer in Longniddry, to strolling along Aberdeen's beach boulevard tucking into a hearty vegan chilli. I've hunted for street food up and down this country and had the absolute privilege of sampling real honest cooking from the very best traders. It's been tough, really!

Sadly, most people don't know their local food scene; it's a closed book, or a book with only a few pages turned. Thanks to this delicious project, I've explored Scotland's street food and found it an affordable, adventurous way to delve into those unread chapters. There's something refreshing about getting to know the person who's sourced, prepared and cooked your food, all with a smile on their face while standing open to harsh, unpredictable elements. It's been an incredible, eye-opening and downright scrumptious journey, and I hope as you read *Street Food Scotland*, you'll be inspired to taste it for yourself.

UNDERSTANDING STREET FOOD

WHAT IS STREET FOOD?

Street food is defined as *'prepared or cooked food sold by vendors in a street or other public location, ready for immediate consumption'*.

Hot dog carts in New York or roasted chestnuts at the Christmas market might instantly spring to mind, while in the UK you'd probably struggle to find someone who hasn't succumbed to the late-night temptations of a burger van. But we're no longer talking about the unhygienic greasy offering that makes us feel even more disgusting the morning after a big night out, nor the kind that has traditionally fuelled truckers in laybys along the M8. We're not in limp lettuce or watery tomato territory anymore.

In the contemporary street food scene, there's a genuine, ever-increasing concern for the provenance of the poultry, seafood and meat used – not forgetting the freshness of the bun encasing it, sealing its juiciness in. The traditional condiments have also been overhauled. Vats of ketchup are replaced by flavour-intense homemade chutneys, while mayonnaise takes a backseat when the sweet earthiness of black garlic aioli enhances burgers beyond compare. We're living in the golden age of toppings: chips don't simply come with salt, it's Parmesan and truffle fries, and sometimes not even potato at all with the humble spud replaced by chunky halloumi drizzled in ras el hanout Greek yoghurt and pomegranate molasses.

In recent years, street food has become gourmet. Culinary innovation is happening out there on the streets and there's a huge focus on local and hyper-seasonal sourcing. Don't get me wrong, I'm sure there's still plenty of wholesaler meat and battery chicken floating about (not that anyone will fess up), but there's more of a farm-to-stall ethos than I'd anticipated. Yes, supporting local independent producers might eat away at business profit margins. But, when they reel off lists of Scottish suppliers, local vegetable growers and dairy farmers, as so many street food traders have done, their commitment outweighs any loss of profit and earns them respect from socially conscious foodies. When items can't be sourced ethically and made to work commercially, I've seen traders go the extra mile. An Ayrshire wood-fired pizzeria on wheels ditches canned sweetcorn in favour of pungent wild garlic pesto, homemade and foraged from woodlands beside the owner's home. Margins are tight but quality won't be compromised, so Scotland's natural larder can be a more economic and much tastier option.

TOP NOTCH & HERE TO STAY

Street food has revolutionised the way we perceive good food – a first-class dining experience doesn't necessitate a dish plated with tweezers presented on a linen tablecloth, or even a table at all. Give us a (recyclable) cardboard plate heaped with paella, with its recipe passed down through generations and its simmering chicken stock aromas wafting through the open air, perhaps with an industrial backdrop or gorgeous coastline and a perch

for our pint, and we're delighted. Of course, unless you've been living under a rock, or in a stuffy fine dining establishment, you'll have read even some of the UK's most discerning critics scorning street food. It's a passing fad that won't last, we've had our fill, it's waning in enthusiasm now, it's another millennial trend that's running out of road ... But ten years on and booming in Scotland, there's no sign of this revolution slowing down.

Just look at Singapore! When not one but two street food vendors are awarded the coveted Michelin star, you know it's time to sit up and listen ... or rather, get out and eat!

Hill Street Tai Hwa Pork Noodle and Hong Kong Soya Sauce Chicken Rice and Noodle received their international accolade in 2016. Back then even Chan Hong Meng, owner of the latter, confessed he never knew 'hawker food' could go global.

'Hopefully the next generation will also pick this up,' he said, chatting to Reuters about his concerns over the street food trend fizzling out.

This Michelin-starred recognition alongside its growing worldwide popularity assures me the next generation certainly will. These two stalls achieved what restaurants bend over backwards for, by doing one thing and doing it well ... and that's where street food and restaurant fare differ.

RESTAURANTS vs STREET FOOD

How often do you discuss a restaurant with friends, only to rationalise the awkward lack of consensus with 'Oh, I must have ordered the wrong thing'? In street food, there is no wrong thing.

You won't find an Asian fusion menu studded with rogue mozzarella and tomato salads or a crowd-pleasing pasta section at the end, because street food's not about menus as thick as an Ikea catalogue that need to tick the vegetarian, vegan and gluten-free boxes to appeal to the masses. Restaurant chefs are too often dictated to, or are pigeon-holed into a particular cooking style that's desperately attempting to

fill the market gap or stand out from competitors on a busy high street.

Street food outlets have at their helm a chef patron who'll wake up at the crack of dawn to encompass all the roles within a restaurant: buyer, prepper, sous chef, head chef, front of house, kitchen porter and event organiser. They absolutely are the ship's captain. It's extremely impressive! There's autonomy to cook whatever the chef's passionate about and they can be flexible about dietary requirements because of the presence of other traders. Street food's transitory nature means vendors can adapt their offerings to trial new flavour combinations and meet their customers' changing demands. It's not quite so easy for restaurants to reinvent themselves each week.

Diners looking for a smart or relaxing evening meal tend to instantly dismiss street food – and, granted, there are some occasions where this sort of uber-casual al fresco dining isn't appropriate.

TOP TIP Wrestling a meatball with a wooden chippy fork on a business lunch, only to spill it down your chin and onto your white top, probably won't impress your high-flying client.

Of all the common misconceptions I'm determined to correct, the first is that street food is either fast food or just a quick bite on the hoof. Sit at a picnic table in Glasgow's Dockyard Social and try convincing anyone that the place doesn't warrant a whole day of grazing! Sure, the wait for a batch of zesty chilli and ginger crisped squid may go by in the blink of an eye, but this is far from the insipid fare offered up by franchised quick service outlets. From tasty tempura-battered calamari rings to crunchy onion bhaji morsels or a downright dirty burger, oozing with melted cheese and dripping rebelliously down your arm, street food is defined by quality and freshness.

There's nothing dubious about a four-minute wait in street food because it's all prepared, and cooked to order, right in front of your eyes. In many ways, that's why it trumps restaurant food. Just two minutes too long under a heat lamp on the pass can result in lukewarm, rubbery or congealed disappointment. Now, you won't find one of those infrared bulbs in a Citroën H van.

A FEAST FOR THE SENSES

Places like Platform in Glasgow are veritably the world's best buffets. Perhaps you'll find succulent octopus dumplings or tender beef brisket quinoa bowls, even blackened Shetland haddock roti with fish so soft and flaky you could cut it with a spoon. There's always a fine assortment of multicultural delights. At this street food market, each trader is packaged up and laid before you in cutesy bright pods that almost put Joseph's technicolour dream coat to shame.

When our senses play such an integral role in the dining experience, it's clear to see why street food thrives. Take the gigantic open-air restaurant that is Ho Chi Minh City or the bustle of Mumbai, where a traveller could spend weeks hunting down the very best bun cha or vada pav.

Anyone who's been fortunate enough to navigate the streets of these sense-tantalising cities will return from their journeys waxing lyrical about more than just the depth of flavour. It's the open flames and kerbside woks, the relentless hustle, tiers upon tiers of vivid fruit and vegetable baskets, scooters zooming past . . . all very normal in a place where street food is a part of everyday life.

Of course, in the UK it's totally stripped back. But where restaurants take great delight in shielding the kitchen and masking its permeating smells to create a polished experience, street food celebrates an organic atmosphere with its aromas and sights raw and exposed.

When we eat with our eyes first, it's fascinating to watch the domino effect a downright sexy dish has. I've seen people do a full 360 on their street food choice, based on the amount of cheese oozing out of the toastie strolling past them. I've wandered through a farmers market with no intention of eating, only to smell freshly steamed gyoza and instantly change my mind.

Thanks to the mobile nature of street food, you get a taste for what's on offer before you even think about ordering food; you can't spy on restaurant meals in the same way. (Though zig-zagging through tables on the longest route to the bathroom, I give it my best attempt.)

FOOD FOR ALL

Without being too contrived, there's something blissfully welcoming about street food and this extends beyond the basic argument of 'well, it's mostly outside, anyone can join the queue'. It's inclusive not only in the sense that there's no dress code or imposed formality, but strangers needn't chat to one another, and yet they do. In gatherings like Dockyard Social, Big Feed, Platform and the Pitt it'll often be the case that a long table is shared by handfuls of hungry groups. There's rarely any elbow touching or encroached personal space, but there is every chance the day could evolve unexpectedly with new-found friends.

Everyone typically shares an agenda: to eat quality food and have a good time doing so. With multicultural fare at a pocket-pleasing price, it's beautiful to see people of all ages and backgrounds come together to expand their palates and appreciate street food in harmony.

THE RISE OF UK STREET FOOD

Street food was a thing long before this cool 21st-century revolution. The excavation of Pompeii has revealed over 150 *thermopolia* – the forerunners of fast food restaurants. These open-air kitchens would have served many of the town's residents, most of whom couldn't afford their own private kitchens. In Ancient Greece, small fried fish were sold on the streets; in Cairo, the Egyptians munched on kebabs, fritters and rice; in ancient China, street food fed the poor – who would occasionally be sent to buy some for their masters too, so they could enjoy the delicacies in secret.

Britain's street food tradition dates back to hot sheep's feet in the 12th century, and it's been engrained in us ever since. Do you know the muffin man? Yes, the one who lives on Drury Lane . . . Everyone who's grown up in the UK – or has had the joy of watching *Shrek* – has heard of the street hawker who flogged his baked goods on London's streets before and during the Victorian era. By the 18th century, thick-crusted meat pies and pastries, jellied eels, pickled whelks, pea soup and freshly shucked oysters were on offer. The people of London were spoiled. Then came the Industrial Revolution when the influx of workers into the city and a lack of access to kitchens, meant people relied on market traders for their meals. Street food became the central working-class diet – just as in ancient civilisations thousands of years before – and the prudish middle- and upper-class Victorians looked down on it.

Richard Johnson, journalist extraordinaire and founder of the British Street Food Awards, is on a mission to bring street food back. Chatting away, it's clear we both agree the nation needs to experience how great it is to eat together.

'There was definitely a time when eating was a little bit too carnal,' he tells me. 'It was hidden, done behind closed doors. But from the 1960s, it became much more public thanks to the likes of Wimpy, McDonald's and KFC; everything was "finger licking good" and we weren't embarrassed to eat in public – and out on the street. Gradually we emerged from the darkness and started to eat together.'

The 2008 recession helped our cause, too. When restaurants were struggling because we were all staying in for dinner, entrepreneurial chefs realised their opportunity was out on

the streets. If they could provide food of a restaurant standard with a dose of theatre, at a fraction of the price, then we'd all come running. And we did.

It was a slow start. In 2010, the first year of the British Street Food Awards, Richard recalls three hundred applicants competing for the prize of a food processor. 'But a lot of those were "man with a van" and a frozen burger,' he says. 'We were ahead of the curve – the revolution hadn't begun.'

Wahaca pioneer Thomasina Miers remembers when 'getting anything other than a hot dog or Mr Whippy on the streets was almost impossible'. But then traders upped their game, and by 2015 there were over 3,000 traders, eager to show off the personality of their food. Since then, the scene's taken off, evolving into an eclectic celebration; the quirkier the experience the better.

'These days everything has to be experiential . . . it's not enough to sit in a restaurant, there needs to be something more,' Richard explains. 'People expect experiences and street food chimes with where British society is currently at; we want to escape laptops and computers, to get out and be with other people, to talk, drink and eat.'

On top of that, there's a demand for a change in the monotony of everyday routine. And then there's the food. We're not quite waving goodbye to the nation's favourite generic curries, but we are craving distinctive regional and ethnic cuisine like never before. We want to taste authenticity: a fragrant Sri Lankan curry, Peruvian fare beyond the mainstream, bao buns perfected in Fuzhou and *frittatina di pasta* from the streets of Napoli. Served piping hot from a truck hatch is where we'll find it.

STREET FOOD IN SCOTLAND

Beyond its traditional tartan, whisky and shortbread, Scotland buzzes now with talented fashion designers, ceramicists and artisan bakers. I'd like to throw street food into that mix; granted it's not built into the fabric of our society like tartan (pardon the pun), but we are impeccable at it. There's more to our repertoire than fried food and haggis . . . though a few knockout examples have snuck their way onto these pages. Even our resplendent smoked salmon is the tip of the exquisite seafood iceberg we're boasting from our pristine waters.

In Scotland we have a rare relationship with our land, sea and all the people involved in its farming, fishing and production. Whether it's the plump texture of hand-dived scallops served up at a seafood shack in Ullapool or hearty stovies that showcase the versatility of leftover Scottish lamb and comfort us through Murrayfield's harsh bite. Nowhere else have I experienced such natural, untainted quality, nor such depth of appreciation for it.

Ironically though, Scottish street food is rarely sold on the streets. There's one C word in this industry, and that's 'council'. Gloriously feel-good films like *Chef* – where Jon Favreau tours the streets of Miami, casually mounting pavements to sell his Cubano sandwiches

– tend to romanticise the truth behind selling street food. In reality, nothing quite kills a trader's ambition like a stern licensing board, who can't envision the role street food could play in reviving an area. (A notable exception is Paisley Council who cottoned on and attracted more than 16,000 visitors over one weekend in April 2019 with a Platform pop-up.) Overall, traders wishing to open up shop in public areas are met with resistance. For traders, it's better to make a beeline for one-off events and privately owned markets – not that organising these is a walk in the park either.

Scotland as a whole jumped on the street food bandwagon a little later than London. It's the capital's tycoons, like Henry Dimbleby and Jonathan Downey of Street Feast, now in four locations across London, who are driving the UK's explosion. These hugely impressive large-scale gatherings reel thousands of Londoners into once derelict sites. It's at Street Feast's Dinemera in Shoreditch where I first properly fell in love with long, liberating evenings spent in street food markets.

But it's a fine balance. If street food becomes too commercialised and polished, then it'll lose its appeal. Brand logos on queue dividers and sponsored drink menus, though money-making opportunities, will undermine street food's cool guerrilla vibe. In Scotland the pioneers of street food are working hard to turn the sad corners of their cities into vibrant, inviting areas. And there's nothing corporate about it. Scottish street food markets are raw, and unapologetically so. There are makeshift chairs, donated Christmas lights illuminated regardless of the season, quirky small-batch spirits poured into cardboard cups and not a suit in sight.

Scottish street food warrants recognition and the British Street Food Awards have evolved to reward the growing talent north of the border. 'The awards are ten years old this year,' Richard Johnson explains. 'In the beginning we just had heats for the North and Scotland, but it became clear that, with the change in politics, that wasn't going to cut it anymore. We needed a Scottish Street Food Awards, and Welsh and Northern Irish ones, too. So, we started Scottish Street Food Awards in 2016. Scotland has amazing ingredients and, with its modern culture of food sharing and partying, it was perfect for street food.'

New traders pop up at the awards each year to showcase their best dish. A little friendly rivalry celebrates a larger picture. The demand for these unpretentious and (often) outdoor dining experiences is only increasing, in spite of the dreich weather. We've evolved to become hardy. Those exploring the Arrochar Alps in minus temperatures are assured there'll be a silky latte and unrivalled bacon roll awaiting them at the resilient Top 'O' the Rest Snack Bar. Their colourful, thriving presence demonstrates the 'out-in-all-weathers' attitude Scotland has.

Richard Johnson comments on the initial uncertainty around UK street food. 'People said street food would never work in these islands because it's too cold, but then in countries like South Korea there's snow on the ground and people still go out to track down really good dumplings and soup. I never want to eat that much when it's hot! I would rather eat street food when it's a little bit chilly. The Scottish climate is perfect for it.'

I'd be inclined to agree.

STREET FOOD DOS & DON'TS

DO DITCH THE CAR

Unless it's logistically impossible to juggle dogs and young children with your energetic grandma in tow (all perfectly plausible given the family friendly nature of street food events), then I'd consider hopping on public transport and leaving the car at home. I'm always surprised by the range of quality Smith & Gertrude wines at the Pitt and the impressively stocked pop-up bars elsewhere. With an increasing emphasis on supporting local, it's a delight to swig on craft beers from the nearby brewery or sample the latest artisan spirits – Scottish rum mixed with Bon Accord rhubarb soda is my go-to.

DO TAKE CASH

It's 2019, Square or iZettle have probably pimped out most of the traders. But in the likelihood that one or two have been left behind in the Stone Age, it's best to go fully equipped with some notes. In fact, some markets charge £2 entry and, when appropriate, it's nice to pop a wee something in the trader's tip jar. So, delve into that piggy bank and make sure you've got some loose change in your pockets.

DON'T THROW YOUR RUBBISH ANY OLD PLACE

This isn't one of those supermarket scenarios, where a customer tears the shrink wrap off their broccoli, amid the vegetable aisle, in plastic protest. Nine times out of ten the environmentally conscious trader is one step ahead of us in the save the planet march. The real crime here is seeing stacks of compostable Vegware trays wrongly piled high in a black bin when there's an empty green-lidded one right beside it. Please please *please* check the bottom of the packaging or check with the trader before binning.

DO PERUSE ALL THE MENUS BEFORE MAKING A DECISION

In the heat of the moment it's easy to get carried away. I've seen the eyes of grown adults light up, like kids in a sweetie shop, when entering their food and drink playground for the afternoon . . . only to order the first things their eyes spot: a jumbo hot dog that *probably* contains less than 30 per cent pork (not featured in this book for obvious reasons). I've totally been in that position and felt instant regret when spotting that unctuous short rib of beef dressed in zingy chimichurri, which I simply no longer had room for. Regardless of how ravenous you are, try to check out all of the menus before ordering!

DON'T FILL UP ON SAVOURY; LEAVE ROOM FOR DESSERT

From homemade gelato sandwiched between freshly baked chewy cookies to indulgent crème brûlée that's burnt to order, street food doesn't neglect desserts and therefore neither should you. If you're lucky you may even find a doughnut-shaped, pillowy, vanilla-bean marshmallow smothered in chocolate and buttery shortbread crumbs – now these really are worth saving room for!

DON'T COMPLAIN ABOUT THE PRICE

Street food is much cheaper than the food served in restaurants – there are fewer overheads and less guaranteed seating – but in terms of quality and freshness it's probably of a higher standard than your average establishment. Yet during my adventures, I encountered an obnoxious man shouting '£6 for a burger, are you having a laugh?' (I've rewritten this moment in my head as a sitcom scene featuring Ricky Gervais.) Shortly after giving in to the seeming rip-off he, with his tail very much between his legs, returned to apologise for his rudeness while declaring it to be the best burger he'd ever eaten. I guess hanger affects us all differently; but urgh, I'd hate to be that guy.

DON'T ORDER THE SAME AS A FRIEND

Okay, this is a personal rule that I apply to all types of food; no matter what setting, I'll typically convince a friend to order a variety of dishes and share them. Then once I know what I like I'll re-order that again. If I'm speaking your language and you also live in perpetual fear of food envy, then spread out and try to cover all bases (skipping the dodgy hot dog mentioned earlier).

DON'T FORGET TO TELL THE TRADER WHAT YOU THOUGHT

In the middle of busy restaurant service, how often do you think your server actually relays positive feedback to the chef? If there's one lesson I've learned from chatting with Scotland's best traders, it's that interaction is welcomed and may even be one of the prime reasons for ditching the miserable day job in the first place. Chatting to customers is a highlight of the lifestyle; constructive feedback and new recipe ideas will always be received with a smile.

DO DRESS CASUAL AND LAYER UP FOR THE WINTER

This is Scotland. So, while the weather may be an occasional deal breaker, there's also every chance you'll meet a brave Scot donning shorts and flipflops (a December look that I never could quite hack). Even when the sun's beating down on us in May and we're deluded into thinking it's 'taps aff' weather, if you're out for a proper street food session, you will get cold! The Pitt boasts fire pits, Dockyard Social have invested in patio heaters; the big players are doing everything in their power to ensure that the show goes on. But a proper winter coat wouldn't go amiss and, regardless of the time of year, dress casual and wear your favourite pair of trainers. Street food is more than just good grub, there's live beats, dancing, family-friendly activities; you wouldn't want a blister to spoil all the fun.

DO BE PREPARED TO EAT ANYTHING

By this I'm not insinuating the return of the horse meat scandal – far from it – I'm simply saying street food can be a little unpredictable. Once or twice I've gone to a street food market, in an attempt to track down something, *anything*, containing halloumi, only to be met with bitter disappointment. Plans change, vintage vans break down, the weather stands between a great day of sales and a 'nah, we'll give this event a miss, we'll make a loss' kind of day. If you're craving something very particular you might be better off at a restaurant, but otherwise head out with an open mind and be prepared to taste everything from crispy duck topped fries, to spicy patatas bravas and bowls of Hawaiian poke.

EDINBURGH

From the lingering smell of the hops, which wafts out of Edinburgh's breweries (and always reminds me of cheesy popcorn), to the thriving social calendar where – from the twinkling enticements of the Christmas market to the raucous cultural bonanza of the Fringe, and every day in between – we're spoiled beyond rotten for things to do . . . I love all the faces of this city; it's my home.

And even for those whose emotional ties are less strong, as you'd expect from Scotland's capital, Edinburgh overflows with places to explore. In fact, whether I'm donning my culture-vulture hat, grounding myself in one of the city's many hidden gardens or, more often than not, letting my curious epicurean taste buds lure me into a new eatery, barely a day goes by when I don't discover something new and totally unexpected – and I've lived here for years. In many ways, this comparatively compact capital punches well above its weight; the population sits at around 500,000 and yet Edinburgh attracts over four million tourists a year. To keep up with the expectations of its visitors and residents alike, the city must constantly evolve, adopting and refreshing an innovative global outlook if it's to stay ahead of the curve while retaining its traditional charms. For an example of how successfully it does that, you need only look at our flourishing street food scene.

You might have heard people say, 'Edinburgh's a city of villages,' and they're not wrong. You can stroll or cycle, jog or dog-walk from one unique pocket to another with ease, and the opportunity to sample the tasty wares of our traders and producers en route make these explorations all the more enjoyable. From the four weekly farmers markets in Leith, Stockbridge, Grassmarket and Castle Terrace, to the plethora of charmingly restored old-fashioned police

boxes (which seem to be converted into a new eatery at a rate of what feels like one a month), never before has our city been so punctuated by such diverse and delicious street food.

For me, the Scottish street food scene was born here – in one of Edinburgh's most gallus districts, Leith – from where it continues to seep into the unexpected corners of events and markets, even non-foodie ones such as vintage clothing and flea markets, throughout the city. In the time I've been researching and writing *Street Food Scotland*, four new standout traders have emerged; one Spanish, one Italian, one Middle Eastern and the fourth is 100% plant-based with a Czech twist: all a giant nod to Edinburgh's global perspective.

The outrageous rate of expansion is indicated further by the Edinburgh Food Festival. In 2019, the organisers doubled their schedule, hoping to attract more than 2018's 30,000 visitors to George Square Gardens. Since 2014, every July the university gardens come alive with a huddle of exceptional stalls from across the country. Tummies are lined by the likes of Pablo's patatas bravas and Jarvis Pickle's handcrafted pies. While Beetle Juice's 'Bonnie', the beautiful converted VWT2, joins Poco Prosecco in ensuring that all visitors remain well watered. Really, the festival is a fantastic foodie way to ease locals into the Fringe lifestyle, preparing them for the influx of tourists to follow.

Intriguing, imaginative and international . . . Edinburgh's street food scene is absolutely one to relish. And, given its super-speedy evolution, you'll never be short of choice for traders and cuisines to explore. Which means that now's a great time to get stuck right in!

THE
PITT

It makes sense to start at the Pitt, the first market to pioneer the street food movement in Scotland. For me, it will always be something of a gateway drug: an addictive, stimulating atmosphere I just couldn't, and still can't, get enough of. I ventured down there from Stockbridge, via the scenic Water of Leith walkway on 16 July 2016, seven months after it first opened. (I love how social media fills the gaps in our memory and pinpoints our exact location at any given moment . . . this particular day was always worth shouting about.)

> 'PEOPLE DON'T GO TO THE PITT TO EAT. THEY GO THERE TO EXPERIENCE SOMETHING OUT OF THEIR COMFORT ZONE.'
> – FRANCESCO BANI, WANDERERS KNEADED

What awaited me was a melting pot of Leith and wider Edinburgh, an industrial yard full of like-minded foodies, crowded around wooden pallets repurposed as tables, gently bopping to the folk guitarist in the corner while sipping on wine from Smith & Gertrude, or a craft IPA from Barney's Beer, and sampling the delights of all these street traders, who I'm pretty certain no one had ever heard of. The Crema Caravan, Harajuku Kitchen, the Buffalo Truck, Fire Dog, Babu Bombay Street Kitchen – really, where had all these up-and-coming traders emerged from? It was seriously happening, and I mean bursting with conviviality and flavour. This was the start of something very special.

Back then the Pitt was entirely outdoors. Come sunshine it offered a welcome solution to the dearth of local beer gardens and, as I found out that December, even in the depths of winter when you could see your breath misty in the air, nothing would detract locals from swinging

by. There were cups of silky hot chocolate and piping hot spiced mulled wine, Pinnies & Poppies homemade graham crackers sandwiching cinnamon and smoked caramel marshmallows to form the perfect s'more (if you haven't tried one, you haven't lived) and, crucially, fire pits with roaring flames to keep us warm.

Now, the Pitt has expanded into the neighbouring warehouse to provide year-round shelter for its thousands of regulars. 'From the first day it rained, we always said, "Oh wouldn't it be nice to have an indoor space,"' Hal, one of the Pitt's founders, tells me. The converted space used to be a mechanic's garage and then an insulation business; recently it has been bought by a developer who wants to convert all three adjacent properties into flats. 'But that won't be for another few years, so we're borrowing it for a while,' Hal says with a smile.

'Despite growing, the Pitt has fully retained its soul,' Robin, owner of the Buffalo Truck, tells me. He's now a resident on the Pitt's roster and goes because all his friends work there; the sense of community and support among traders is staggering. But there's more to it than that; the Pitt is a superb place for Robin, and his friends, to trade. 'The punters are our customers, but the traders are our customers too; that's why we charge a percentage of the sales, rather than a flat fee – we've realised that's so much better for traders on rainy days,' Hal explains.

At markets like the Pitt, the whole is much greater than the sum of its parts and by that I mean that each trader lures in their own following, who, while in the buzzing courtyard – a true smorgasbord of enticing aromas and mouth-watering plates – will become

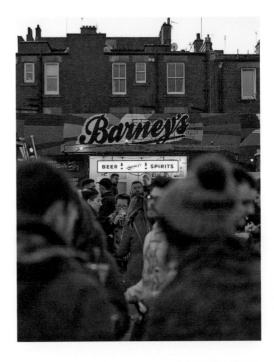

acquainted with the others. From the flowing drinks to the funky tunes, the jovial atmosphere and the careful curation of the best traders in Scotland, pulled in from nearby, from Glasgow and even further afield, it's the weekly pop-up that everyone wants to trade at. It's testament to the Pitt's success and popularity that it plays host to the annual Scottish Street Food Awards.

The Pitt is now home to both Barnacles & Bones and Ròst, but keep your eyes peeled for them elsewhere too. From the Fringe to the Electric Fields Festival down in Thornhill, they've been known to travel individually and as the Pitt on Tour, when the footfall and adventure have been worth it.

It's my pleasure to introduce you to the two chaps behind it all: Hal Prescott of Barnacles & Bones and Scott Kirkham, owner of Ròst ...

BARNACLES & BONES

'STREET FOOD IS POPULAR ALL OVER THE COUNTRY NOW. LUCKILY YOU DON'T EVEN NEED TO MOVE TOO FAR FROM YOUR PATCH. MORE AND MORE, PEOPLE WHO HAVE FOOD AT THEIR EVENTS HAVE REALISED THAT IT NEEDS TO BE OF A CERTAIN QUALITY, SO THEY'RE HUNTING DOWN US INDEPENDENT GUYS. THE OPPORTUNITIES WHEN I STARTED SIX AND A HALF YEARS AGO WERE FEW AND FAR BETWEEN, WHEREAS NOW YOU CAN EASILY FILL YOUR DIARY WITH EVENTS . . . WHETHER THEY'RE GOOD EVENTS IS A DIFFERENT QUESTION!'

– HAL PRESCOTT

It all began with a portion of crab on a bank overlooking the main stage at the Isle of Wight Festival. That's where Hal had his lightbulb moment. With each bite, the tray of fries laden with soft white crabmeat flakes transported him back to Mandal, on the southern tip of Norway, where he used to visit family as a young child. 'In late July there's a crab festival there,' he tells me. 'Everyone is drinking and eating crab on the streets, it was so obviously imprinted in my mind . . . and there I was almost reliving the experience with some friends at a festival.' When Hal returned home to London, he made

it his mission to learn everything about crab; how to source it, the cost, where it's landed, in which parts of the UK it's most plentiful, and even how it's exported out across the continent. Some might say he found the shellfish 'crabtivating'. Apologies.

Hal had worked in the food and drink industry all his life: first as a bartender at Bar 99 while studying Economics and Philosophy at Aberdeen University, then in his home city of Liverpool in a quirky food-focused deli on the Royal Albert Dock. Soon afterwards, he landed a job on the management course at Majestic

Wine in Livingston, before falling for the lure of London as so many tend to do. His obligatory stint in the Big Smoke involved working as a wine importer for a private company that sold into the likes of Marks & Spencer, but Hal soon realised that he was just a tiny fish in a colossal pond and, really, that the wine industry is outrageously fickle.

'After writing this book,' Hal laughs, 'you should write another one on how tough the wine industry is; in the supermarket aisles there's no brand loyalty, everyone just wants a £5 bottle of wine which will contain five or perhaps ten pence worth of juice if you're lucky – I loved my job but there were so many problems,' he confides.

Meanwhile, Borough Market was very much happening; street food was taking off in London and, should the crab concept evolve, Hal had the opportunity to prosper with it. It was taken to the pub to be mulled over with a couple of lagers, as most good ideas are, and there, his friend Fabian who owned a car, a garage and had always wanted to start his own business, jumped at the opportunity. Barnacles & Bones was born.

automatically cuts off about 60 per cent of the potential audience; your customers are either allergic or simply don't like seafood,' he explains.

So, he added meat into the mix and rebranded as Barnacles & Bones, extending his offering to excel beyond a pescatarian paradise. Now there's dishes like delicate, moreish crab and corn fritters, langoustines doused in tarragon butter and those famous paprika-seasoned crab fries all on the menu alongside Hal's signature unctuous short rib of beef which has been braised in sherry, positioned on salted fries and topped with a loud and zingy chimichurri. The stall is a surf and turf lover's dream and, not surprisingly, its discerning customers have sprawled the dishes all across social media.

When Hal arrived back in Edinburgh in the summer of 2015, he opened up shop in the teeny-tiny police box outside John Lewis. It was never part of the plan, but when he strolled past that For Sale sign and realised he had the means to transform it into a mini restaurant, his imagination ran wild.

'My ideas were grandiose, admittedly. It would be like continental Europe with people sitting outside relaxing and eating, I thought. But, actually, it was more difficult than I'd ever imagined. It was a lot colder, and the people, well, it's an unusual part of Edinburgh – people just don't stop for long there. It's a weird mix of commuters, church goers and homeless people,' Hal explains. Which means that the police box was a hard graft. In the conventional sense, it wasn't the success story Hal had envisaged, but little did he know, that among the handful of traders there, he'd meet Scott Kirkham and they'd soon become the godfathers of Scotland's street food scene.

Back then it was known as Claw. The duo took it to various pop-ups across the city and the brand started to gain momentum among the street food scene. It wasn't long, however, before Hal had a yearning to return to Scotland and take the business and its reputable name with him. When it transpired that Fabian's parents were trademark lawyers, there was no point in arguing; best to find the silver lining and use this as an opportunity to adapt. Hal did just that. 'I'd learned that solely doing shellfish

HAL'S GREMOLATA

Hal recommends slathering this on top of anything grilled but, quite frankly, it would be equally superb smeared on a slice of toasted sourdough. Once you've made it, this gremolata should last in a jar in the fridge for ages; just make sure there is enough oil to cover the surface.

INGREDIENTS

Large bunch of flat leaf parsley, washed

Plenty of good oil, such as cold pressed rapeseed or olive

Capers, optional (start with a couple on a teaspoon and add more for extra saltiness)

1½ lemons, juiced and zested

1 bulb of garlic

METHOD

1. Coarsely chop the parsley, then zest and juice the lemon.
2. Blend everything and add some more oil.
3. Leave for a few hours to mix all the flavours.
4. Now slather on any grilled food items of your choice.

RÒST

VERB.
GAELIC FOR ROAST
TO COOK FOOD BY HEATING
IN AN OVEN OR FIRE
VERBAL NOUN: RÒSTADH (ROASTING)

Scott Kirkham has an unrivalled grounding in food. He understands fresh produce and how it's grown like few others; he knows exactly where foragers might find the best wild herbs and berries in unexpected corners of Edinburgh and beyond. Believe it or not, the ingredients us laypeople pluck from the supermarket shelves have had a whole life of their own prior to their purchase.

Scotty's abundance of knowledge stems from his time as a gamekeeper on the Phoines Estate in the Cairngorm National Park. Come the Glorious Twelfth (of August), guests flock there to partake in Scotland's grouse hunting season, while Scotty maintained the land and cared for the game's wellbeing all year round. 'We butchered, cooked and ate our own wild produce and in the summer months we'd grow our own potatoes, cabbages, leeks, lettuce. It's where my appreciation for Scotland's natural larder began,' he says.

When he returned to Edinburgh, Scotty did a catering course at Telford College before earning his stripes as a chef for seventeen years, twelve of which were as kitchen manager at the Scottish group Howies.

'I've always been interested in street food,' he tells me. 'I've really followed it from its beginnings in the States, with the food truck phenomenon.' Scotty's opportunity to test the waters arose when he started working at Whitmuir Organic Farm, south of Penicuik. The farm acquired 'Frank' the food truck to channel their farm-to-fork ethos, with Scott at the helm (or steering wheel). While very successful in the summer months, opportunities dwindled in winter, which made Scotty redundant after a year and a half. Fortunately for us that was just enough time to whet his appetite.

Enter stage right Ròst, the earthy green trailer upon which scenes from his grandma's cottage in Ullapool are doodled along its flanks. The

stunning mural features the Highlands mountainscape intermingled with deer silhouettes and game birds. These artistic enticements are a teaser for what's to come – perhaps a seven-hour smoked venison pastrami slider with pickles, mustard mayo and crispy onions, or the absolutely knockout peanut butter crunch pheasant burger served in a fresh, squishy bun. Who would have thought that buttermilk-brined fried pheasant, served still tender with a coarsely ground brittle coating was a good idea? Scott Kirkham, that's who, and it's beyond delicious.

'There's no rhyme or reason to it though,' Scotty smiles. 'I just cook what I fancy, but I'll always use Scottish produce like game from George Bower and foraged ingredients from East Lothian where possible.'

Scotty's the kind of guy who finds the energy to stand and cook all day and return home to watch cooking programmes all night. Netflix is filled with street food inspiration I'm told

. . . just kidding, I know that only too well. Both Scott and I have been delving into *Street Food*; each episode explores a pocket of Asia where firing up dinner on the edges of an alleyway is the norm.

'Did you watch episode six in Seoul?' Scotty asks. 'Jo Jungja makes this baffle, it's leftover rice put in a waffle machine to act like the slices of bun encasing a burger. She puts the filling in the middle and then dresses it all up, I'm going to trial that soon,' he promises. 'Punters would be confused by it in a restaurant but that's why the trailer works.' He's totally right when he says people eat with their eyes first, and that's why he'll line up dishes along the shelf of his trailer before a day of trading; needless to say, I'm a-lookin' and I'm a-likin'. A lot.

Scotty started off trading at the top of Leith Walk outside St Mary's Cathedral, in 2015. That's where he met Hal. They were both crazily ambitious and craving more than simply joining a cluster of vendors that might, or indeed might not, attract passers-by. Edinburgh was ready for a street food destination and, boy, were they going to give us one.

With Scotty's trailer stored in his friend's yard (what we now know as the Pitt), it seemed like an obvious, cool place to host something. They gave it a whirl and on their first day of trading, 12 December 2015, over 1,200 people showed up. It was Edinburgh's only permanent street food market back then.

The Pitt has been a huge learning curve for Hal and for Scott. From figuring out the logistics, like supplying electricity, gas and water to ten traders in the yard and to its huge neighbouring warehouse too, to battling with the council red tape and tweaking the line-up to keep things exciting for visitors; you've got to admire the gents' tenacity. 'We started with nothing at the Pitt. It was an empty space that we've built up ourselves; it's grungy and gritty, but it's colourful too, that's what's attractive about it. I'm proud of what we've achieved, and we've done it without seeking investment.'

There may have been the odd trader roaming about before, but it's at the Pitt where Scotland's street food movement took off. If you haven't yet been, please rectify that immediately. I'll be the one lingering near the food vans gradually and happily making my way through them all.

Hal and Scott clearly had a vision and we're so lucky it's come to fruition. The Pitt is a thriving hotspot, packed with the city's best traders, but you can also find them else-where should you wish to explore. If you're in the capital, here's some of the traders you might stumble upon . . .

KOREAN PULLED PORTOBELLO MUSHROOMS

SERVES 2-4

INGREDIENTS

6 portobello mushrooms
Bread, slaw and mayo of your choice to serve

FOR THE BBQ SAUCE
1 cup soy sauce
¾ cup dark brown sugar
2 tbsp minced garlic
1 tbsp rice wine vinegar
1 tbsp chilli garlic sauce (such as Sriracha)
1 tsp grated fresh ginger
1 tsp Asian (toasted) sesame oil
1½ tsp ground black pepper
1 tbsp cornstarch
1 tbsp water

METHOD

1. Preheat the oven to 180°C.
2. Mix all the BBQ sauce ingredients together in a big jug.
3. Place the portobello mushrooms face up on an ovenproof tray or dish.
4. Now pour your sauce over the mushroom and roast in the oven for about 40 minutes.
5. When roasted, use two forks to pull the mushrooms apart in a big bowl.
6. Serve! These are beyond delicious on bao buns with Asian slaw and cilantro mayo, or on toasted sourdough.

THE BUFFALO TRUCK

As a collective, Scotland has almost been ruined by the American franchises. Our understanding of good fried chicken has been warped by the Colonel's soggy, battered and cartilage-filled bargain buckets. But then, we've never really had much to compare it to. That is until Robin Strigner strode into town and raised the bar with the Buffalo Truck.

Robin's chicken is life changing. It's the kind that'll render most other fried chicken insignificant, tasteless and imperfectly cooked. There's the Classic served with black garlic mayo and 'hoose' pickles, the Buffalo with tangy hot and blue cheese sauces and the Korean with Gochujang hot sauce, sesame and spring onions. Three simple burgers that are quite rightly perched up on a street food pedestal and praised by those who've had the honour of tucking in. So, what's the secret?

The chicken is left to soak in a buttermilk brine combination overnight, then it's dredged in seasoned flour, gets re-dunked in the brine and dredged again, before being fried. That way it's got a thicker coating, Robin explains. But there's so much more to it than that. Robin tested, tweaked and tested again over forty recipes before he began trading. The batter is crunchy with unexpected flecks of fennel seed, the chicken is succulent and juicy, and the brioche is springy.

When the question 'Have you got Buffalo Truck in the book?' risked sounding like a broken record, I just had to track Robin down to ask him some questions.

THE BUFFALO TRUCK

AWARD WINNING
★ BUTTERMILK FRIED ★
CHICKEN BURGERS
→ CLASSIC
BLACK GARLIC MAYO,
PICKLES ★
★ → BUFFALO Chicken
HOT SAUCE & BLUE
CHEESE CREAMINESS

Q&A

HOW DID IT ALL START?

I was working as a marine biologist in Norfolk, basically I was a researcher. There were things about it that were fun but ultimately a big chunk was just reading, writing and doing reports, like data analysis – I was bored. I'm not very good at sitting at a desk all day; I prefer to do practical things. I was living in this tiny town and it was a pretty isolating place. I was in my mid-twenties and I thought, seriously, is this how I'm going to live out what should be some of my best years?

I wanted to do something else, and I got an opportunity to work in a restaurant called the Kinmel Arms in Abergele (I'm originally from Wales and I knew the owners through a friend), so I left Norfolk and started cheffing. Shortly after I started, the guy who was training me left, so I got thrown in the deep end and got a real quick education in how to cook professionally.

This lifestyle was far too intense. I once again found that I didn't have a life, which is one of the reasons why I left the marine biologist job in the first place. I spotted a truck on eBay, already converted with a kitchen in it, and I saw it as my chance. For a long time, I'd had a pipe dream of having my own food truck. So I went for it: I quit my job and just did it.

HOW DID YOU GET INTO THE PITT?

Back in 2016 I met Hal through my ex-girlfriend, who knew him from Aberdeen back in the day. He'd just started doing Barnacles & Bones up in the police box by John Lewis; we got chatting and he told me that him and Scott (of Ròst) had this idea of doing something at the Pitt. I traded at one of their first street food markets and just took it from there.

WHY CHICKEN?

The truck already had really good fryers, so I thought, what involves frying? Everyone loves fried chicken, I love fried chicken! I thought, if I could do fried chicken but not make it trashy, just something good quality that a proper chef would eat and deem to be good food – that would be great. That was the goal.

WHERE DID THE RECIPE AND INSPIRATION COME FROM?

I didn't go to America for inspiration. I've been there more recently and did try some bits and pieces, but honestly, I didn't find any of it better than mine. I used my short cheffing experience as a basis for some techniques – marinating, brining, that kind of thing. But then I did loads of research and testing; I tried over forty different fried chicken recipes, altering the concentration in the brine, and things like that. All my sauces and pickles are handmade by me too.

WHERE CAN PEOPLE FIND YOU?

I live in Leith, the truck stays in Edinburgh, and I'm now at the Pitt every week. In terms of road-worthiness, this truck is on its last legs; mechanically, it's seen better days. So, this one will stay at the Pitt. In February 2019, I bought a new van – a converted ambulance – that'll travel to events throughout Scotland.

WHY DO YOU LIKE THE PITT?

It's got such a good atmosphere, it feels genuine and not too corporate. The Pitt has character, it's got soul. I like the way they've made it bigger using the warehouse next door, they've managed not to kill its spirit while making it much more appealing in terms of space and weather protection. They've done a great job. I'm genuinely good friends with Hal and the team; it's a nice scene. If I wasn't trading, I'd come and hang out here.

WHAT HAS THE PITT DONE FOR LEITH?

Some people might argue it's part of a wave of gentrification and I can understand that, but I don't really agree – we're doing something positive for the community, loads of Leithers come down every weekend, which is a good thing. And it's not that expensive, I'm selling great quality

food for £6 a portion, it's hardly like we're opening an oyster bar!

I think they've had one or two noise complaints from the neighbours, but it's only on a weekend and it's over by 10 p.m. It's not anti-social, it's no worse than a bar; in fact, it's probably better. Generally, the reaction from the local community is hugely positive.

HOW WELL DO YOU DO AT FESTIVALS AND OTHER EVENTS?

We're one of the most resilient food traders; we genuinely do well. At a festival there's every chance no one's heard of my truck: people come from all over and they're presented with a choice, so it's not like they're seeking me out specifically. But they see a cool-looking truck with fried chicken plastered on it, everyone's been drinking, it's just something you want to eat in that environment.

That's really key in street food as well: a lot

of people try to push a concept, but it's more important to provide something people want to eat. If you can come up with a clear distinctive product that people actually desire, but can also ramp up the quality, then you're onto a winner. Don't push what you want on the public, put your twist on something they'd want anyway.

WHAT DO YOU THINK OF STREET FOOD IN EDINBURGH vs LONDON?

London is so densely populated, it's the cultural epicentre of the UK. Potential success is probably greater than up here in Scotland, but it's probably so much more difficult to achieve. Even logistically – like trying to find somewhere to store the truck! It's much glossier in London, companies like Street Feast are multi-million pound enterprises. In Scotland, it's still much more grass rootsy.

WHAT'S THE DIFFERENCE BETWEEN A BURGER VAN AND STREET FOOD?

That's an interesting question and, technically, there isn't a difference; a snack van on an industrial estate is still street food. But when we talk about street food, we're talking about its modern iteration, which is like the hipster version. If you're talking about *that* kind of street food then the difference is essentially (a) the standard and (b) the marketing. It's marketed as interesting, quirky, romantic and cool. The target market tends to be completely different too.

HAVE YOU HEARD PEOPLE TALKING ABOUT BUFFALO TRUCK?

Yeah, it's got itself a bit of a cult following; my step-brother's girlfriend told me there's a girl in her office, who has no idea who I am, who's started a 'chicken chat' WhatsApp group with the sole purpose of coming down to the Pitt to get Buffalo Truck chicken. It has weirdly gained some kind of legendary status. I couldn't really ask for much more than that.

WHAT'S HAPPENING NEXT?

I don't really want to expand. Part of the reason I got into this is freedom . . . I could get premises, but that would mean settling down. I don't know what my long-term life plans are, so at the moment I'm happy ticking over; if I can make it as big as it can be while keeping it small, then I'll do that until it doesn't make sense any more. Who knows!

MOO PIE GELATO

On Emma's first ever day of trading, she pushed her bike, with its heavy freezer compartment, all the way up Leith Walk. And then she stood on the side of St Andrew Square and sold absolutely nothing. Not a single scoop.

It would have been easy to admit defeat, to brush off the day as a risk that didn't quite pay off and just crack on with her life with the gelato idea parked to one side. But that's totally not Emma Riddell. Three years later, she's the woman who's got half of Leith tucking into gherkin and cream cheese gelato at the Pitt, and, surprisingly, we're all loving it. Yes really, it's insanely delicious!

Hilariously, Emma studied as a nutritionist – all I'm saying is, if gelato is featured on a recommended diet plan, where do I sign up?

'I just didn't want to do it anymore,' she tells me. 'It didn't feel very fulfilling and no one really took me seriously, maybe because I was a wee young thing.' Working for herself with no ceiling

limiting her success was far more appealing. 'I wanted to learn one skill and get really good at it, then I could have the lifestyle I wanted, with full freedom to earn as much or as little as I wanted, with no one capping it.'

Naturally, being a huge fan of ice cream, Emma flew out to Bologna to undertake an intensive course at the Gelato University – seriously, why wasn't this an option on my UCAS form? It was set up by renowned ice cream genius Carpigiani in 2003 and, once there, Emma was taught what would soon form the foundations of her company, Moo Pie Gelato.

'We learned life hacks, but like gelato-style: you should always store your gelato at −14°C so that when the first customer comes in and

you need to serve it (also at −14°C) you don't need to wait for it to thaw,' she informs me. 'Chocolate gelato will always be harder because it's got more fibres in it, unless of course you add a shovel of sugar to it. Ice cream is different to gelato; scientifically it's to do with the quantity of milk fats. Traditionally, ice cream is higher in both sugar and fat, it's served at −18°C, whereas gelato is served warmer, releasing more flavour on your palate. Gelato is then smoother, denser and creamier.'

Essentially, like her outrageous s'more 'freak shake' that overflows with chocolate ganache, whipped cream, sugared doughnuts and the Marshmallow Lady's butterscotch

marshmallows, Emma is brimming with some serious knowledge.

When she returned from Italy, Emma hired out a small prep kitchen area in the Breadshare Bakery on Jane Street, Leith, and took out a loan to help cover the costs of her machinery – the pasteuriser was £9,000 and the batch freezer was £19,000. Fortunately, piggybacking on Breadshare's market licence, she soon set up shop beside the tram stop near St John's Church. 'It was 5th August 2016 and it didn't take me long to realise that the commuter crowd had absolutely no interest in gelato. They were just bombing past me and because I wasn't well known, I don't think many of them even

their converted mechanic's garage, so even though ice cream sales might be volatile in Scotland, she'll always have footfall, and a roof over her head too.

With bold flavours to make even Ben & Jerry's look dull, Emma has become something of a gelato queen. One cone might contain olive oil, ricotta, lemon and bay leaf, another might be rhubarb, hibiscus and spiced crumble, or perhaps caramelised white chocolate, cherry and pistachio. It's all superb. My go-to flavour riffs on the dessert Umm Ali, the Egyptian cousin to our beloved bread and butter pudding. It's a divine combination of cardamom and cinnamon gelato with caramelised pastry, almonds, pine nuts, sesame and rose water, all textured with honeyed shards of pistachio and toasted coconuts, sandwiched between a warm cinnamon sugar doughnut from the Kilted Donut. And just like that, I've died and gone to heaven.

Emma's next step is to invest in a nostalgic soft serve machine to specialise in flavours like pistachio or chai latte. 'Originally, I started out wanting to make the best 99 and then I realised that gelato was seen as the Rolls-Royce of the ice cream world, so I pursued that instead,' she explains. 'But really I'd love to get an old school van, pimp it out and go to festivals all over the UK with my soft serve. I could even pitch up on the street like a traditional ice cream van too.'

Emma picked up the keys to her own wee shop at 26 St Mary's Street on 29 July 2019, where she'll continue to rotate four flavours a day with absolutely no crowd pleasers, just whatever wacky concoctions she wants to trial. She'll maybe even package her gelato in 500ml tubs; now, that's seriously getting dangerous for my waistline.

realised what I was selling,' she reflects. 'In fact, I distinctly remember one day in September, it was 22°C and still I'd only taken £20 for the whole day.'

Not long after, Hal from the Pitt approached Emma and the rest, as they say, is history. From jumping in her white van with the bicycle in the back and shooting off to events, to attending regular pop-ups at the Pitt and even securing a pitch at Big Feed's launch day where there were thousands of customers, Emma has spent the last three years honing her craft to become, for many, the source of Edinburgh's best gelato. In February 2019 her regular appearance at the Pitt turned into a permanent residency inside

THE
PERUVIAN

I have very strong opinions about eating animal products. I've never been a vegetarian, unless you count my early teenage years spent being difficult at meal times then sneaking leftover bacon and sausages out the fridge when no one was looking. I'm not opposed to it – far from it; self-controlled plant-based dieters have nothing but respect from me. But, frankly, I like the taste of meat, believe we've developed sharp teeth that can chew through the gnarliest of steaks for a reason, and want to support Scotland's hard-working farming industry. Having said that, I am working to maintain at least two meat-free days a week.

But for me, what's worse than those who eat meat and selfishly indulge in their carnal pleasures, are those who'll turn their noses up at half of it. If an animal has been killed for my consumption, I'm appreciating every morsel of it, right down to the offal. Crispy chicken skin, paprika-dusted pigs' ears, lamb sweetbreads, whole whitebait, congealed blood marketed as black pudding; wasting precious cuts is criminal. I'm a nose-to-tail diner and so is Carlo Carozzi, the man dishing up cow hearts (*anticuchos de corazón*) under his street food brand the

Peruvian. That's what they eat in Peru, Carlo tells me.

'I've got this T-shirt that says "guinea pigs are lovely" and everyone thinks it's cute until I turn around and on the back it says "stewed or fried". It's natural for us, in Peru we eat guinea pigs!' But let's get back to cows.

The *anticuchos* were originally eaten by the Incas, and Carlo grew up tucking into them at Sunday family BBQs. It's not easy putting their deliciousness into words. First the cow hearts are marinated for 24 hours in white vinegar and spices like cumin, ají pepper, garlic and oregano, before being skewered and grilled. What remains are these yieldingly tender chunks of meat, with a subtle offal flavour and a lingering smoky aftertaste.

'They're a cheap ingredient that you can find on every street corner in Peru from 5 p.m. till 1 a.m.,' Carlo says. 'Street food is a huge thing over there, but for different reasons. In Peru, some people are so poor, they have no choice but to cook on the street.' But Peruvian food is outstanding. In the list of the World's 50 Best Restaurants, Lima, the capital where Carlo is from, features twice. In fact, the restaurants Central and Maido are in the top ten.

Carlo came to Scotland eighteen years ago and it wasn't long before he craved food from his homeland, in particular *lomo saltado* – a bowl of stir-fried sirloin steak and French fries folded with tomatoes, onions, soy sauce and ají amarillo paste, served with rice on the side.

'It's Peru on a plate. We eat a lot, I can't exaggerate it enough,' Carlo laughs, 'though the Scots do finish it all. This big hearty dish is what we're about, all the protein and carbs.' He soon realised that satisfying his cravings was impossible: nowhere in Scotland served traditional Peruvian cuisine. 'You can't imagine what it feels like, I spent over fourteen years thinking about Peruvian food and not being able to have it.' That's when the cook took action.

Carlo has worked in restaurants and bars all his life – working his way up until he was general manager – but he's by no means a trained chef. He learned everything from his grandmother, who lives in Yurimaguas in the jungle.

'I never actually cooked with her, I just stood and stared. I didn't want to touch anything for

fear I'd screw it up,' Carlo tells me. 'The village is only accessible by boat, and because of that I still hate fish. Granny used to cook stews with river fish heads and all their bones; it stank the house out. I can't go near the stuff now, but she helped me learn about balancing flavours, like in my ceviche.'

Starting up, the trickiest part was finding a supplier. Specific ingredients are integral to Peruvian food; it's the tingling sensation you get from Peruvian chillies, the ginormous kernels you can only find from choclo corn, and the choice of 3,800 varieties of potato, which all have their place in Peruvian cuisine. It's all about the flavour.

'In Mexico and Ecuador they make ceviche, but we have ají limo and that's where the flavour comes from. For it to taste the right way, that's what you've got to use,' Carlo explains. After two years, he tracked down the supplier that delivers to the Peruvian restaurants in London, roped in a friend to make his logo and now just needed somewhere to trade. 'I thought, with my contacts in the industry, it'd be easy to get a pitch at the 2017 Fringe. That was stupid of me. I didn't get offered anything in the heart of it all, but I could trade beside the graveyard of St John's Church in Princes Street Gardens.'

And Carlo did just that. With three weeks to order his first pallet, rent out two garages to store the produce in alongside any equipment – fridges, fryers, burners – Carlo spent all of his life-savings and made it happen. He transformed the space into his own little Peruvian corner and stood there ready to cook with massive speakers playing salsa music. Within days news spread through Scotland's Peruvian community. 'I posted about it on Facebook and thousands of Peruvian people came out from, well,

everywhere – Aberdeen, Dundee, Stirling – they all came to eat my food. It exploded! I served one man who told me he lived and worked in Peru for many years . . . then it turned out he'd been the principal of my primary school in Lima. It was amazing,' Carlo tells me.

Then it *really* took off. Carlo's cow hearts sailed through the 2018 Scottish Street Food Awards and earned him a place at the British final in London. There his *Leche de Tigre Ceviche*, a delicate balance of sea bass, fresh lime juice, salt, coriander and those all-important Peruvian chillies, snapped up the award for best snack. Quite right. It's the kind of refreshing food a friend will order, you'll beg for a nibble of it, and just like that it'll be all you can think about until you track Carlo down for a full portion of your own. That's the tricky part. Between the occasional pop-up at the Pitt and the odd one

in Glasgow, Carlo's achieving all this without a means of transport.

'I don't have a driving licence. For each day of trading I have to carry everything down three flights of stairs from my flat, go to one garage to collect produce, then to another to collect equipment. Really, I'm reliant on my friends like Pablo from Mosquito Bites, Ewan from Shrimp Wreck, Robin from Buffalo Truck and the Pizza Geeks guys to help me out,' he says.

'Street food is really tough,' Carlo continues. 'And you need to do a lot of research. I'm blessed because I'm doing something no one else is doing. I want to keep growing, and there's more dishes I want to make so I'm scraping together to bring over new machinery from Peru. The problem is, doing this costs me a lot, and sometimes I don't get much money back from it.'

This isn't the first time a trader has spoken of the difficulty in meeting customers' demands; they want high-quality food but simultaneously it has to be cheap. 'Maybe that's why lots of people churn out rubbish, they just buy a trailer and start up. It's these guys that make everyone else look bad. Customers will eat from them at an event, generalise their poor experience to all street food and assume no one else has passion or knows what they're doing either,' he says.

For Carlo, street food isn't enough. He set out to give Scottish people a taste of what he had growing up and there's so much more to it than the food. 'It's about the alcohol, the beers, the pisco sours, the passion fruit sours, we even have ones made from purple corn called chicha morada pisco sours.' Carlo's stall is the only place we can get our hands on Inca Kola, a bright yellow soda that's Peru's version of Irn Bru, but he's setting his sights higher. 'Peruvian food deserves a permanent spot and I want to be the one who does it. I want to give back to the Peruvian community here so I'm working to save up for a little place; when I finally get there, it'll be amazing.'

Papas a la huancaina is a traditional Peruvian dish. Essentially, it's an orgasmic chilli cheese sauce poured over boiled potatoes and eggs. When Carlo first served it to the people of Scotland, there weren't many takers . . . until he replaced the boiled potatoes with fried chips, garnished it with chopped chives and called the dish 'Peruvian Cheesy Chips'. For an authentic Peruvian experience follow Carlo's recipe, but if you rather opt for the unhealthier Scottish version, Carlo won't judge.

PAPAS A LA HUANCAINA

INGREDIENTS

SERVES 2–4

1 medium onion, chopped
2 cloves of garlic, chopped
¼ cup ají amarillo paste
1 cup Queso Fresco
½ cup evaporated milk, plus more as needed
6 potatoes, boiled
4 hard boiled eggs, sliced
Lettuce, for garnish
Oil, for frying

METHOD

1. Heat the oil in a pan over a medium to high heat.
2. Add the onion and sauté until translucent, about 5 minutes.
3. Add the garlic and ají paste and continue to cook until heated through, about 5 minutes.
4. In a blender, add the onion mixture and all remaining ingredients except potatoes, eggs and lettuce.
5. Blend until thoroughly combined and sauce is an even deep yellow/orange.
6. Add more evaporated milk to reach desired consistency. Taste and add salt if necessary.
7. Serve over the potatoes, sliced eggs and lettuce.

CHICK + PEA

'It's a funny thing, street food in Scotland,' Jeremy Downton tells me, 'in that we're not really trading on the streets; we're trading in clear-cut, defined markets where licences have been applied for long in advance. It's a cloudy version of the reality of what street food originally was, which was pitching up and trading on the street, hawking at anyone who passed by.'

This pre-planning and permission-requesting might not be romantic, but sometimes that's the way it's got to be if you want to turn street food into a thriving business. Jeremy tells me, 'If you want to trade on the street, the person with the trader's licence has to be on site all the time.

A couple of years ago at the Fringe, he had the opportunity to trade in two places at once but, because of these restrictions, it was physically impossible. The council makes it difficult for one-person street food businesses to expand, but that's where curated markets provide a silver lining. It doesn't matter who's at the helm there; if Jeremy wanted to, he could have all three of his brands – Chick + Pea, Kebabbar and Nom Eat – trading at the same time at different events across Scotland.

Jeremy and I are friends who go way back. In fact, he and his fiancée have declared that they dine in my shadows; one day I'll Instagram somewhere new with a nice write-up, the next day that's where they'll head. In the same way, I monitor Chick + Pea's movements like a hawk; it's the stickiness of the pomegranate molasses and the moistness of the freshly made falafel, the way his roasted garlicky yoghurt is balanced so as not to muffle the harmony of his other ingredients – plus it's the fact that Jeremy works with proper squeaky Cypriot halloumi when so

many others use a cheaper replica. I must have eaten Jeremy's food dozens of times over the past three years and yet each individual dish still evokes feelings of awe and contentment, as if it were my first ever bite.

It's all served out of a downright gorgeous Citroën H van. Which is why Chick + Pea seemed an obvious choice for the front cover of *Street Food Scotland*. Not only does the van's royal blue cladding give a subtle nod to our saltire, but Chick + Pea represents everything Scottish street food is about: adventure, cultural experiences, personal journeys from pot-washer to trader with all sorts of tangents in between; local sourcing, flavour, passion, aesthetics, approachable food for everyone and even the trials and tribulations of life on the road.

When we catch a glimpse of that van, we're lured in by the promise of delectable Middle Eastern and Mediterranean delights served from its hatch. When Jeremy sees that van, however, he's reminded of more roadside problems than you could ever imagine. Umpteen hours spent waiting for the breakdown truck on the hard shoulder of the M6, having watched one of his tyres fly off into three lanes of traffic, is certainly up there as one of Jeremy's all-time lows. 'It's beautiful but so impractical,' he tells me. 'Eventually I had to buy a Land Rover and a trailer to tow Albert [the van's chosen moniker] everywhere.' He pauses and then admits, 'That crushes the romanticism of it.'

Jeremy has wanted to work in food for as long as he can remember. 'I feel like my life is such a cliché,' he laughs, before recalling the days of watching Jamie Oliver, you know, back when he was cool and used to slide down the banister before hopping on his scooter to go to Sainsbury's. 'That was a really inspirational thing to see. I didn't understand the recipes, but I'd read his cookbooks and every now and again I'd pluck a recipe out and try it.' When he reached fourteen, his mum marched him down to the local pub where he became the pot-washer. There, he swiftly learned that if you washed up quickly, you could turn around and observe the chefs in action. He soon became *chef de partie*; 'I use that in the loosest sense,' he laughs. 'It was a tiny place and I just made the occasional salad.'

That marked the start of years of hospitality experience. First, Jeremy became a sandwich artist, though not just a lowly sandwich artist: he moved up the ranks to become senior supervising sandwich artist, accredited with a University of Subway qualification and everything. 'All jokes aside, it was a real insight into how a big company standardises and arguably sacrifices quality and flavour but nonetheless expands globally,' he says. Next, he worked in a hotel in France then, during his years studying at Aberdeen University, he was a barista at Costa. Finally, he worked front of house at Wagamama before graduating ready to take on the world.

Jeremy's more than a keen foodie; he has an entrepreneurial mindset that's restrained enough not to let his excitement get the better of him. 'I was so desperate to do my own thing, but knew I had to work for someone else first,' he tells me. 'I found a job in international finance because I needed the money to then reinvest and as much as I thought I knew everything about business, I really didn't.' What Jeremy *had* picked up were the teachings of Eric Ries and his Lean Startup methodology that features the minimum viable product approach.

The *what?* Yes, I was stumped too. It essentially means if you start a new innovation you should do it on a shoestring then if it's rubbish you can change it and keep on changing until it's 100% right. That way you're not compromising huge amounts of money or time because you're 'pivoting' (as Ries terms it), until you've worked out exactly what's successful and what isn't. Jeremy originally wanted his own restaurant, but street food is the epitome of MVP (an acronym looks business-savvy, right?) – so that was his plan B.

In April 2016, Jeremy took the plunge and bought the Citroën H van, renovating it every evening and weekend for months. When he'd learned how to do things like build a cabinet to support the deep-fat fryer, he booked into his first event. 'I missed the first day of trading,' he confesses. 'The van didn't have hatches, so the ventilation cut out – the worst moment in my street-food career to date. I turned up at the Pitt (where I'd been storing the van), in proper fat rain and asked the welder, Howie, to cut two circles out of the roof. He did, but then he covered them with masking tape. With no chimney stacks on, water gushed into the van, forming puddles everywhere. I'd managed to cut my hands, so the rain was exacerbating the bleeding. I had to call Edinburgh Food Festival to apologise and start the following day instead.'

Okay, so it wasn't the prettiest of starts, but once Jeremy got stuck into the street food scene, it soon materialised that he never needed an MPV after all. Chick + Pea was a hit from the off; it brought freshness and flavour via a cuisine we'd never quite fully experienced in Edinburgh before. There were Middle Eastern restaurants, sure, but they all seemed to be those fusty ones where not a single dish delivered bold

experimental spices intermingled with sweet sticky fruits. As Jeremy explains, 'I wanted to show how Middle Eastern food can be so much more than harissa spice.'

It was *Honey & Co: Food from the Middle East* by Sarit Packer and Itamar Srulovich that gave him the idea. Jeremy was gifted this glorious cookbook by his fiancée back in 2015, and each turn of the page brought more fascination. 'I wanted to eat everything in it and that very rarely happens. Typically, I'd open a cookbook and be like, "Oh, they've put chicken with a different sauce and a different carbohydrate. How revolutionary!" But this one made me realise that this kind of cuisine wasn't everywhere yet. It wasn't in Edinburgh and I wanted to change that.

'I started experimenting with the recipes, adding my own tweaks; I went to London to their sister restaurant, Honey & Smoke, where I met Itamar Srulovich and he couldn't have been nicer. He even gave me tips on the perfect falafel technique!' Jeremy tells me.

And, joyfully, Jeremy's food was a mighty success. So much so that in August 2018 Jeremy launched its meatier counterpart Kebabbar, where juicy East Lothian chicken thighs meet tzatziki and fries to form a majestic souvlaki. Then in July 2019 he started experimenting with plant-based fare under his brand Nom Eats.

'People see me, they see the Chick + Pea van, and there's that association with halloumi fries. They're all over Instagram, so really, Ailidh, it's your fault,' he laughs. Jeremy's right. The halloumi dish has almost overtaken even the popularity of the falafel flatbread. 'It's a great dish, but it's the falafel that I've slaved over, and I hope that's what sets me apart,' Jeremy explains.

Oops! On that note I'll leave you with some new advice: order a portion of falafel flatbread and ask for halloumi in it too . . . now you can enjoy the best of both worlds!

'A MAN CAME UP TO ME WHEN IT WAS RAINING AND SAID, "YOU CAN'T EXPECT STREET FOOD TO BE SUPREMELY SUCCESSFUL IN SCOTLAND BECAUSE YOU'RE CONTENDING WITH THE WEATHER," AND TO AN EXTENT HE'S RIGHT. WHEN WE'VE TRADED OUTSIDE, WE'VE RETROSPECTIVELY ANALYSED THE SALES TO SEE THE CORRELATION OF DIPS AND TROUGHS WITH RAIN AND SUNSHINE. BUT THAT SHOULD NEVER BE A DETERRENT; IT'S THE EXACT SAME AS BRICKS AND MORTAR BECAUSE PEOPLE DON'T TEND TO LEAVE THE HOUSE ON A RAINY DAY FOR RESTAURANTS EITHER. LIVING AND TRADING IN EDINBURGH, AUGUST IS SO IMPORTANT. IF YOU HAVE A BAD FRINGE, THEN YOU'RE DONE FOR IN THE WINTER.'
– JEREMY DOWNTON, CHICK + PEA

MIDDLE-EASTERN STYLE FLATBREAD

SERVES 4

INGREDIENTS

FALAFEL
250g dried chickpeas, soaked overnight
1 onion
A handful of chopped parsley
A handful of coriander
2 tbsp ground coriander
2 tbsp ground cumin
1 garlic bulb
2 tsp salt
Vegetable-based oil

HUMMUS
1 small tin of chickpeas
2 tbsp tahini
1 tsp minced garlic
A pinch of good salt
1 lemon, juiced

ISKENDER-STYLE SAUCE
Tomatoes, fresh
1 tbsp of harissa (and more, to taste!)
Sugar
A pinch of good salt
Vegetable-based oil

TO SERVE
Cypriot halloumi, in slices 0.5 cm thick (use the real deal; don't skimp!)
Flatbreads, 4 or more

METHOD

1. Drizzle the tomatoes with oil and salt and put in the oven at 140°C for 2 hours. Remember to check on them every half-hour.
2. Blitz the falafel ingredients together in a blender until smooth.
3. Drain the tinned chickpeas and keep the water to one side.
4. Blitz the chickpeas, tahini, lemon juice and garlic until smooth. Add chickpea water until desired hummus consistency is achieved.
5. When the tomatoes are soft and shrivelled add to a blender with the harissa and a pinch of sugar, blitz until smooth. Taste and adjust salt / sugar accordingly.
6. Heat a pan of vegetable-based oil to circa 180°C (be careful!) and use a falafel press or a dessert spoon and drop the falafel mix in. Work in small batches and cook until golden.
7. Remove from oil, place on kitchen roll, then sprinkle with kosher salt.
8. Griddle the sliced halloumi in a pan.
9. Add your hummus, iskender sauce, halloumi and falafel to a flatbread in a frying pan on medium heat, fold and grill on both sides. Serve hot, eat quick.

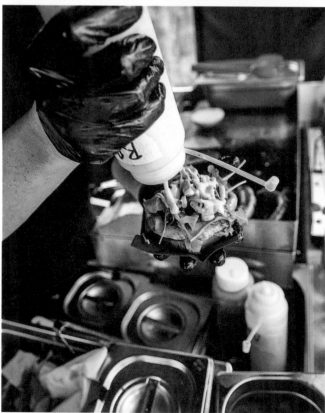

THE
SAUSAGE MAN

While working for Barnacle & Bones he was 'Crab Guy'; at Ough! Bagels he was 'Bagel Boy' . . . now with a street food business of his own, Liam Gardiner has promoted himself to 'Sausage Man'. Though that won't stop other traders calling him 'Sausage Boy'. It's a term of endearment, I'm assured.

When Liam and I met, we strolled through Stockbridge market, picked up an avocado bowl from Mana Poke and found a cute spot by the Water of Leith to chat. Back then, he'd only traded four times. So, including him in this book was a bit of a gamble, but knowing his experience and the quality of produce in his offering, I was sure it would pay off.

Liam first got a taste for street food when he moved to Barcelona after university. A couple of markets had just opened up, including the monthly Paolo Alto, tucked away in the residential neighbourhood of Poblenou.

'It was better than anything you'd typically find on the street, it was a real destination, a curated market of street food filled with local artists and musicians,' he explains. 'I really liked it there, so when I moved back to my hometown, Edinburgh, I reached out to Hal from the Pitt to see how I could get involved.' He started working for Barnacles & Bones, which was then about a year old. This enabled them, with Liam's help, to be in two locations at once – the Pitt and the (temporary) Food & Flea market. A year later he connected with Ewan from Shrimp Wreck and began working at his new Ough! Bagels pop-up in Thistle Street Bar, taking it to the Fringe Festival, too. And before he knew it, Liam felt experienced enough to get out there and do his own thing.

There was no question of what his street food business would serve. Back in Barcelona, Liam had joined a multicultural football team and they'd always eat choripán after the match: 'It's a fresh, really well spiced chorizo sausage in a roll, topped with garlicky green chimichurri. Really, it's incredibly simple but nothing like we get here, even the sausages, aren't cured like how we know them,' Liam tells me. In Scotland when we might have a soggy microwaved pie at a football match, in Barcelona choripánes are the staple. That's what Liam aspires to. If he had it his way, they'd be served everywhere from friendly knockarounds at Inverleith park to Scotland matches at Hampden.

On his menu, the parsley-smothered juicy paprika sausage rolls join otherworldly delights – like Barry, a spiral pork, haggis, chilli and Irn Bru sausage. ('One for the tourists,' Liam admits.) Or there's the smoky sausage topped with red eye gravy. 'In the southern states of America, when they're cooking country ham, they'll brown slices in a cast-iron skillet to render the fat and then deglaze the pan with coffee, so it's got a bitter, acidic edge but with the salty smokiness of the pork; it's a great combination. That one's proving popular.'

The meats are all made in collaboration with George Bower, Stockbridge's finest butcher. Liam makes his own seasoning and takes it to the team at Bower's and together they decide what texture to create; the chorizo is minced for longer while others might be coarser. It's all prepared in natural hog casings, ready to be grilled at the Pitt and served up in a bespoke light and fluffy rectangular roll by Glasgow's Seb and Milli Bakery.

Scrumptious and thought provoking –

seriously why has no one else thought to elevate the great sausage bap? There's also a bean and gluten-heavy vegan roll, and as Liam's street food journey unravels, he'll introduce more Catalan inspirations. 'In Barcelona, there's a spring festival called Calçotada, basically a party dedicated to celebrating the harvest of the calçots. They're a type of spring onion that are charred over an open fire before being wrapped in newspaper, just like fish and chips. I love food from the Iberian Peninsula, so I'll always try to riff off that,' Liam explains.

So, what are the positives of street food? For Liam, that's being your own boss and developing amazing ingredients with local suppliers. The negatives? Well, naming your brand the Sausage Man is probably going to attract some characters. 'One bloke said I should have called it "Sausage Fest" and began talking about orgies. I was grilling his food, so I couldn't run away: it was pretty uncomfortable,' Liam laughs.

ROLLY'S ICE CREAM

When you line up for a Rolly's ice cream, know that you'll always get more than you've bargained for. There's no pulling that lever to dispense Mr Whippy here, nor the traditional ice cream scooping we're accustomed to. No, this is a fascinating theatrical performance where a base of sweet Graham's Family Dairy milk is rolled out on a -20°C steel surface, to be chopped up with chocolate bars and fresh fruits, scraped and aerated, frozen and rolled right before your very eyes. Oh, and the attraction's owner, Michael Notarangelo, can talk the hind legs off a donkey, so be prepared for the story of its inception while you wait.

Given the choice, I'd always opt for a dining experience where I could see my food being cooked versus one where I couldn't, so surely that preference can apply to ice cream, too? Just roll with it. My first encounter with Rolly's was at the Secret Herb Garden, nestled at the foot of the Pentland Hills; Michael had pitched up to make some bespoke creations using their Old Curiosity camomile and cornflower gin. The guests gathered in awe and the faces pulled by the patient, salivating onlookers, reaching for their phones to document the spectacle on social media, will always remind me of sitting at a teppanyaki table. Indeed, many know the sensational dessert, originally from Thailand, as 'stir-fried ice cream'. That's where Michael first came across it. He was walking through Chiang Mai, having just graduated in mechanical engineering and saw traders chopping up the ice cream on the side of the streets.

'It looked cool, but I didn't really think much of it,' he tells me. 'It wasn't until my contract on the Queensferry Crossing was coming to end that videos of ice cream rolling kept popping up

on Facebook. I was being made redundant and I didn't really want to be a mechanical engineer, so I was in limbo. I chatted it through with my girlfriend during a rubbish film. The next day I went on Alibaba, like eBay for catering equipment, found a steel unit and went for it.'

Ice cream runs in the family: after emigrating from Italy to Edinburgh, Michael's grandad operated an ice cream van. 'That probably inspired me, too,' he confesses.

Michael could write a sitcom on the trials and tribulations of getting that machine shipped over from China; needless to say, once he'd hired a shipping agent, paid for it to be transported, waited six months for it to arrive and then tracked down the gas needed to make it work, he was determined to make it a success. From launching with a smashed Tunnock teacake flavour in Portobello in 2017, and selling out in two hours, to boasting options like 'the golden nugget' made with Ferrero Rocher and indulgent, boozy Kahlúa custard to appeal to adults too, Michael's become an ice cream expert.

'I am a perfectionist and I am really self-critical: after every event I reflect on how we can make the operation slicker, reduce queue time, improve the flavours and now I'm smart about events, only selecting ones where I'm guaranteed footfall,' he tells me.

In the winter, it's tricky. When the sun's beating down, Rolly's Ice Cream reels in the crowds but, being such a seasonal product, Michael has had to branch out with more street food brands. 'It's not that Rolly's is unsustainable; it's an excellent business idea and it'll continue to be my focus. But in this inclement weather I needed something else to keep me ticking. My second street food company is called

Dog n Bon and it's all about gourmet loaded hot dogs and haggis bonbons. You should try them sometime!'

I recently fell down a YouTube rabbit hole and discovered thousands of videos posted by tourists in Phi Phi Don, Vietnam, and Santiago, Chile, where skilled craftsmen line the streets with their scrapers geared up for action. You no longer need an international flight to witness them but, in Scotland, Rolly's Ice Cream is still one of a kind. In the likelihood that Michael's snapped up for a wedding, the internet is full of DIY tutorials for you to experiment at home. Have a go at Michael's recipe . . . though, having seen the aftermath on my kitchen cabinets, I should reiterate that Michael's mastered the art so we don't have to.

RE-CREATE ROLLY'S ICE CREAM

FOR 10 ROLLS

INGREDIENTS

CUSTARD
4 eggs
300g sugar
800ml milk
500ml double cream
50g plain flour, sifted
10ml vanilla essence
Pinch of salt

HOT FUDGE SAUCE
340g granulated sugar
85g brown sugar
100g cocoa powder
30g plain flour
½ tsp salt
1 x 410g can evaporated milk
250ml water
30g butter
2 tsp vanilla extract

METHOD

CUSTARD
1. Beat the eggs and sugar together for approximately two minutes until pale and creamy.
2. Add flour and salt then continue beating.
3. Heat the milk in a saucepan (do not boil).
4. Slowly add hot milk to egg mixture, constantly whisking.
5. Return mix to saucepan on a low heat until it's thickened and coats the back of wooden spoon (NB: stir constantly).
6. Strain the mixture into a container, leave to cool slightly, then add cream and vanilla.
7. Place in the fridge for a minimum of 4 hours.

SAUCE
1. Place the sugars, cocoa, flour and salt into a saucepan.
2. Add the evaporated milk, water and butter and bring slowly to the boil, stirring constantly. Once boiling, cook for five minutes.
3. Remove sauce from heat and allow to cool slightly and stir in the vanilla extract.

The good news is, it's not too late to turn back! If you're a messy cook, you could churn the ice cream in a machine for 30 minutes, scooping to serve in a sundae glass with warm fudge sauce drizzled on top.

Alternatively, place a couple of ladles of your cold custard in a big frying pan (that fits in the freezer), swirl with a few spoons of fudge sauce and perhaps mix in chocolate chips or crumbled flake bar. Now place the frying pan in the freezer for 4 hours. Be patient, it must be fully frozen. Next, place the bowl you'll serve the ice cream in with the scrapers you'll use in the freezer for 30 minutes. (I used the one that scrapes ice off my car; it went in the dishwasher first!)

Now you must act faster than the speed of light. Take everything out the freezer and scrape the ice cream into rolls by placing the scraper at an angle against the edge of the pan, pushing forward away from you. Roll up all the ice-cream, place it vertically in your frozen bowl, add any extra toppings and tuck in. Or do what I did: head to @rollysuk and find out when Michael's next trading. You can't beat the real deal.

NORELLI

Surely there's an unwritten rule that goes: If you get the opportunity to eat a pizza or any other Italian delight, cooked right in front of your eyes by a man called Luigi, you have to say yes. It's the same with eating Spanish tapas cooked by a man named Pablo. Their names alone are a good indication that you're in safe hands.

Norelli serves the kind of food that transports you to a bustling street in Naples. You'd probably have a deep orange Aperol Spritz in one hand, and a hockey puck of *frittatina* peeking out of a brown paper bag in the other – a ball of béchamel-coated bucatini pasta, dotted with prosciutto and wild mushrooms, all coated in flour and fried – yet not remotely heavy. One of these might gently expand your tummy in preparation for one of Norelli's typical Neapolitan pizzas, layered with San Marzano tomatoes, mozzarella and salami all imported from Italy, with its soft, almost chewy centre and tall bubbly crust. Alternatively, there's the rich tomatoey pork, beef and pancetta meatballs with mince so moist

your teeth slide through them. And just like that you suddenly find yourself in Luigi's mother's kitchen, observing their creation intently.

'My mother never followed a recipe, she just measured ingredients by eye. It was my mum's auntie, Rosalea, who taught her to cook,' Luigi explains. 'She learned how to make the most delicious sauce you'll ever taste – just tomato, garlic, butter and nice olive oil, and it all comes together beautifully. It's the simplicity; that's what makes it a signature Italian recipe.' Luigi would come home from university and, out of necessity, linger in the kitchen and question his mum's every move.

Since learning his way around the kitchen, for

a long time Luigi's plan had been to open his own gelateria. He bailed on his law degree early to pursue the dream of becoming a professional chef and trained at one of the best schools in Italy, Università dei Sapori in Perugia, before undertaking a three-month gelato course and then moving to Edinburgh.

'On our first date he actually threw business papers on the table and asked me to look at them. We'd already exchanged some chat, so he knew I was a commercial manager,' Dagmara, Luigi's girlfriend and now business partner laughs.

Wow, Luigi, that's a first! He was so eager to open his own place, but as is so often the case, life got in the way. Luigi and Dagmara's relationship is built on a mutual appreciation for food,

later to be filled with copious experimental dinners, BBQs hosted for friends and trips abroad to experience the aromas and chaos of both Neapolitan and Vietnamese street food.

'I'd been to Vietnam before, and it's in Hanoi and Ho Chi Minh City that I fell in love with street food; I loved the idea of people sitting outside, being in the fresh air. When I came back to Scotland, I even drew up a proposal for "Flamingo Street Food" that would have been the name of my Thai stall . . . but I just put it in a drawer and concentrated on my day job,' Dagmara explains.

They were both harbouring a burning desire to launch their own street food business, and in February 2019 it finally happened. They'd recently moved in together, and Luigi would

three-wheeled motor became theirs. Now behind the wheel of a beautiful vehicle, Luigi's attention turned to the food. He nipped back to Italy to spend time with his childhood friend, owner of the best pizzeria in the local area, to find out everything he could: from how the yeast works, to the concentration of stone milled flours and even what conditions best help the dough to macerate.

'I'm still learning every day,' he admits. 'Some of my friends have twenty years' experience in the kitchen, whereas mine's more like eight' – though, I can assure you, you wouldn't think it from trying his food.

They are still so new to the scene, this is just the beginning of Norelli's adventures. 'So far we've brought the most scrumptious savoury things that we've ever tasted in Napoli to the people of Scotland,' Dagmara tells me. 'The feedback has been amazing, but what would be the cherry on top of the cake, is if customers get to try Luigi's ice cream too.'

That's certainly something for us all to look forward to.

Their attitude holds great promise; some traders like to guard their recipes with their lives, but Luigi is most obliging! 'I've always been taught that the recipe isn't the secret,' he tells me. 'Food is just chemistry and, in many cases, like gelato, it's an exact science. The secret, as clichéd as it sounds, is love. It's the passion, the research that goes into the ingredients and the love you pour into your own product.'

Of course, joining that love is glugs of olive oil grown in Frasso Telesino, Luigi's hometown in the province of Benevento city, which his mum brings across regularly. Love is all you need, but you can't beat proper Italian olive oil!

use his afternoon kitchen break, from Scottish bistro Howies, to scroll through furniture on Gumtree.

'He rang me up excitedly and shouted: "I've seen a really, really nice Piaggio, you're going to love it, it already has a pizza oven . . . are you thinking what I'm thinking?" And, of course, I was,' Dagmara explains.

Dagmara met Michele Civiera – owner of three superb pizzerias in Edinburgh: Civerinos, Civerinos Slice and the High Dive – to exchange the keys and in that moment the slick, black,

FRITTATINA DI PASTA NORELLI

INGREDIENTS

500g bucatini (pasta)
200g prosciutto cotto (roasted ham), cubed
150g wild mushrooms, cubed
200g smoked mozzarella, cubed
150g peas, fresh or frozen
Olive oil, to fry

FOR THE BESCIAMELLA SAUCE
100g plain flour
100g butter
1 litre hot milk, full fat
Salt and pepper
Nutmeg

FOR THE BATTER
½ litre cold water
300g flour

METHOD

1. Cook the bucatini in a pot of boiling water. Once cooked, drain and leave to cool.
2. Fry the mushrooms in a frying pan with a spoon of olive oil and the garlic, and set to one side.
3. Make the besciamella sauce. Melt the butter over a low heat before adding the flour. Stir for 2 to 3 minutes before whisking in the hot milk and the rest of the ingredients. Continue whisking the mixture until it takes on a gravy-like consistency.
4. Combine the bucatini with the mushrooms, 200g of the besciamella sauce, ham, mozzarella, peas, parmigiano and a pinch of pepper.
5. Pour the mixture into a shallow baking dish, making sure the ingredients are evenly distributed, cover and place in the refrigerator for about two hours.
6. After two hours, heat some oil in a frying pan.
7. Remove the pasta from the fridge. Take a biscuit cutter or a small cup and cut the pasta into small round 'fritters'.
8. In a large mixing bowl, make the batter by simply mixing the water and flour together.
9. Now, heat some oil in a frying pan.
10. Submerge the pasta rounds in the batter, so they are fully coated, and fry in the hot oil until golden brown.
11. Remove from the oil and drain on kitchen paper.
12. Serve warm or at room temperature.

MOSKITO
SPANISH BITES

When a Glaswegian friend first asked if I wanted to pop over to the Big Feed to 'drink a few cocktails and get some mosquito bites', my immediate response was no. I'll be honest, that just didn't sound like my idea of fun.

It was moments later, when reading the play on words, that I instantly backtracked. Pablo Moscardó's friends call him Moski and these are his traditional Spanish tapas; there'd be nothing itchy about it, but there was every possibility his bites might leave a lasting impression. How right I was. Having realised that Pablo's based in Leith but does the rounds between my usual haunts – including the Pitt, Canteen at Archerfield and the occasional Bowhouse Market – his *patatas bravas* have since become a staple in my diet.

Rather than using frozen ones, Pablo peels and hand cuts at least forty kilos of potatoes himself, and yes you can tell the difference. They're first blanched at 130°C and then again for good measure at 180°C until they scream

'Eat Me' with their suitably crispy coating, generously dusted with sea salt flakes and sweet paprika. Pablo then douses them in his own *All i Oli* (garlic and oil in Valencian dialect) with a further sprinkle of a fierier paprika, this one not so forgiving. His croquetas are equally fabulous. I like the vegetarian ones that marry together a gooey centre of alliaceous leek and salty blue cheese in a crunchy panko encasing. Though, don't get me wrong, I wouldn't turn down the creamy chicken and béchamel sauce ones either.

Pablo was wasted as a barista; I'm sure he rustled up a mean Frappuccino but really, addressing Edinburgh's severe lack of proper Spanish fare was his calling. He came to Scotland in 2014 with his girlfriend, a suitcase and a little money, with the intention of learning English for a year. It was challenging.

'I didn't have a flat or job or anything when I arrived, so we were living in a hostel,' Pablo says. 'We started looking for jobs where only a low level of English was needed, and I managed to get a job as a kitchen porter in Malvarosa in Portobello. We moved into our own flat but then the job was given away to the owner's friend. It meant we had to move into a youth hostel, but I managed to find more jobs, first as a housekeeper, then as a kitchen porter and then a commis chef.'

When his English improved and he landed a job at Starbucks, everything fell into place; from a flat of his own in Leith, to serving lattes to bankers and electricians who would soon offer their support when he bought and needed to renovate a horsebox; Pablo even enrolled in a cooking course at Edinburgh College and is set to do level 3 in 2020.

'It took a while, but now life is better here,' Pablo tells me. 'It's easier to study and open your own business and there's daily flights to Valencia so if we wanted to see family we could. So, we decided to stay. Here, I'm happy.'

Pablo borrowed money from his family, found a slightly shabby horsebox online and spent eight months juggling Starbucks shifts while slowly renovating it. His first event involved competing with a succulent rolled pork loin dish elevated by roasted peppers, onions and green aioli at the Scottish Street Food Awards in May 2018. Talk about jumping in at the deep end. Rubbing shoulders with some of the more established traders, his street food journey quickly turned from emailing every festival and market, to maintaining a hectic balance of college three days a week, prepping on Thursdays and Fridays, then shooting off to an event practically every weekend.

'I've made so many friends and learned so quickly,' he says. 'I've realised lots of organisers aren't organised – when you arrive, there's no power so the fryers keep blowing, or even worse there's no people. I paid £250 for a day at an event in Dundee and they'd only sold 2,000 tickets. I've realised that trading at places like the Pitt, where you're charged a percentage, is so much better. If the weather's horrible, you aren't giving away money out of your pocket.'

Pablo is ambitious; he saw a gap in the street food market and worked hard to take it. His food might not be the most eye-catching and even he'll confess that between portions of calamari, diced potato and this superb crusty roll he makes filled with chorizo, gouda, grilled onions and chimichurri, it all looks a little beige, but I'm okay with that. The food has to taste good and, as Pablo points out, 'Some people do food and it looks amazing, there's colour on top and it draws you in but then the flavours don't explode in your mouth.' His food certainly does explode, and hearing customers' feedback is the best part of the job.

'I love travelling all over Scotland, meeting new traders and customers,' he says. 'Working in a kitchen you'd just pass the food out a window and that would be that. Here I get people telling me it was amazing and sometimes I get pointers on how I can make it better; it's great, then I know how I can improve.'

It's tough out there on the streets, but Pablo's prepared to hustle his way to the top. He's eyeing up a second set-up, because what's

PATATAS BRAVAS

INGREDIENTS

FOR THE PATATAS
200/300g of potatoes (Harmony, Nectar or Cultra)
Hot paprika
Oil, for frying

FOR THE ALL I OLI (MAKES 1 LITRE)
4 garlic cloves
300ml whole egg or pasteurised egg
700ml sunflower oil or half olive oil and half sunflower
Sea salt

an authentic Spanish experience without sangria, right? He'll open a cute trailer, prop up some oak barrels beside it and get the red wine flowing alongside Agua de Valencia, a bright and citrusy cocktail that you might sip on the Mediterranean beaches of Valencia – if only our Scottish weather could take the hint. The big dream is to open an intimate space, where Pablo can demonstrate his tapas flair, but for now here's a teaser, should you be looking to add Spanish charm to your next soirée . . .

METHOD

1. Wash and cut the potatoes into cubes.
2. Poach them in a pan with abundant frying oil or in a deep fat fryer at 130°C for 10 minutes until soft. Remove from the oil.
3. Increase the oil temperature up to 180°C and place potatoes back in for 1 or 2 minutes more until golden and crispy.
4. Season the potatoes with sea salt and hot paprika.
5. Prepare the *All i Oli*. Blend all the ingredients together with a hand blender, starting at the bottom of the mix slowly going up with the hand blender, until everything is mixed with a creamy texture.
6. Add the *All i Oli* sauce and a bit of hot paprika to the potatoes and serve.

STOCKBRIDGE MARKET

Whenever I'm asked, 'What are your plans this weekend?' my response will most likely include a trip to Stockbridge Market. The cluster of fifty independent stalls in Jubilee Gardens started off as just a handful in September 2011 when it was launched by husband and wife team Beth Berry (owner of the Olive Stall and Au Gourmand Bakery) and Jeff, more formally known as Jean Francois Toulouz (owner of Creperie @ The Market).

The market's a happy, special place. I moved to Edinburgh just after it opened, stumbling upon it almost immediately. It's more than a destination to pick up groceries from Ovenstone Organics and Peelham Farm, or source a weekend treat – *burrata* from Unknown Italy, a chocolate brownie from Bad Tempered Baker, a Scotch & Co chorizo scotch egg eaten on the hoof. The market has fostered my appreciation for quality local produce and my street food curiosity.

Beth and Jeff have curated a foodie heaven that you can't find anywhere else. From Casa Roble cooking proper Spanish paella from scratch, with its wafting aromas teasing the rabble of lingering souls, to Christina Knight's ugali pie – a polenta base with plantain, spinach and tomato sauce. And not forgetting Glasgow's Babu Kitchen, which Beth and Jeff brought right to my doorstep. I'm eternally grateful!

Every Sunday, it's Stockbridge's beating heart and my weekly stroll wouldn't be the same without a portion of *those* juicy, medicinal gyozas from core trader, Harajuku Kitchen. In the depths of winter, few other delights could lure me out of bed; when your toes are numb and your ears are close to falling off, these steaming hot pork and cabbage dumplings are just what the doctor ordered.

HARAJUKU KITCHEN

Keith and Kaori Simpson were on the street food scene long before there was one. Kaori was resident chef for the Consulate General of Japan, when her friends Cameron Bell and Rikki McCowen came to her with an idea. It was 2009 and they wanted to organise a market in Stockbridge on Portgower Place. They knew Kaori cooked up some mean Japanese dishes so her involvement seemed an obvious choice.

Picture this: Kaori stir-frying udon noodles on an old BBQ propped up on the back of their car and Keith breaking the market's awkward silence by strumming on a bouzouki one week, a mandolin another. These were simpler times, with fewer rules and regulations and no gazebos launching in the wind.

'Artisan Roast started up there with a coffee van, they now have four cafés! The market was a logistical nightmare, though, so it didn't last long,' Kaori recalls. But the village wanted something in its place, so two years later Beth and Jeff got in touch and Stockbridge Market was reborn in its new home.

Kaori grew up in Hong Kong and Manila. Her father was an international tuna trader, her mother and her Samurai great-grandfather both

restaurant owners. It was perhaps inevitable she'd end up as an amazing chef. Her mum's from Fukuoaka, where tonkotsu ramen is served with hand-crafted gyoza as if it were as inseparable as fish and chips. 'I spent my childhood making gyoza with my mum. We'd make hundreds for the Japanese community in Manila, so after experimenting with dumplings, we tried Mum's recipe at the market,' Kaori says. 'They were so popular, and now everyone's doing gyoza. Gyoza bars are everywhere … maybe it's all connected.' 'Yes,' Keith chips in with a laugh, 'they all came to Stockbridge Market and ate yours!'

These bite-size morsels contain free-range pork from Shaw's Fine Meats in the Borders. 'That's the secret,' Kaori tells me. 'Some people get their meat from the cash and carry – it

tastes and smells horrible.' The minced pork joins Chinese cabbage and garlic, folded inside slightly thicker pastry, to ensure they don't break on the hot griddle, good for cooking en masse. They're seared with oil then splashed with water and covered in a metal cloche to lightly steam before being topped with Kaori's chilli garlic sauce, spring onions, coriander and pickled ginger. The latter is normally reserved for noodles, but customers keep requesting it.

'You've got to find a balance with letting the customer lead. If you give them too much leeway, they'll ask for tomato ketchup,' Keith laughs. 'I've eaten the dumplings every weekend for ten years. It's ridiculous, but a lot of street food traders won't eat their own product.'

Harajuku Kitchen started because Kaori missed Japanese street food, little did she know it would result in an award-winning restaurant beside Bruntsfield Links. It's a prime example of the evolution of street food. Here's the story …

Richard, a chicken farmer, approached the Japanese consulate in search of a Japanese chef because he wanted to open his own restaurant. 'From there it all happened,' Kaori says. 'We'd scrimped together so we could put in money too, and when Richard left we bought his shares.' It's in this unusual space with a tiny dining area and two spacious kitchens that the team gathers to relax and fold gyoza. 'I'm happy we still keep the traditions and Japanese ingredients,' Kaori tells me, and it's clear the Scots are happy too.

Under Kaori, the AA-rosetted restaurant has won accolades including Best Restaurant in Scotland at the prestigious Golden Chopsticks Award 2019. And Keith takes their pop-up stalls to boutique festivals across the country.

'Street food is boom or bust,' he says. 'On a sunny day it goes like the clappers, but on a rainy day it can be dead.' He takes the gazebo to Stockbridge Market each Sunday and to the Grassmarket fortnightly. 'The business is every waking hour; I jump out of bed and panic! You've got to have passion. It's hard work, it's endless.

'I'll be honest, it's difficult,' Keith continues. 'Sometimes, street food sucks!'

MANA POKE

Mana Poke's journey into street food was a little unconventional. Roddy Kennedy and Wis Jantarasorn met while working in the sales team at iZettle, the payment solutions platform that empowers small businesses. A typical day was about more than just acquiring new accounts; they spent hours chatting to their customers, predominantly food and drink start-ups and wannabe restaurateurs, helping them launch their own businesses.

'We caught the bug from them,' Roddy says, 'listening to those small independents within the food and drink community speak so enthusiastically about their ideas and what ignited their passions, that's what got Wis and me talking.' With no foodie background of their own – ahem, though Wis's parents do happen to own Dusit, arguably Edinburgh's best Thai restaurant – they were going to be smart about it. 'Street food is perfect because you can test the market before you jump in and commit to a bank loan. If it doesn't work out, there isn't a huge financial loss. It's better than going all gung-ho, putting £30K in and watching it fall on its ass which

so many people do – we've seen it first-hand,' Roddy explains. So, that was it decided . . . and they were going to boast multiple USPs too.

When the street food revolution is so often perceived as just 'fried things' – and that's before we address Scotland's affinity with the deep fat fryer – Roddy and Wis weren't even going to tiptoe along the lines of that stereotype, instead they'd do the opposite and serve up raw fresh goodness. With thirty more traders to go on my street food mission, my cholesterol levels are truly grateful.

Since 2015 poke has been making a name for itself, first in southern California, then in New

York and now in the European capitals of the world. Except for Edinburgh. In fact, until Wis and Roddy threw on their aprons in July 2018, poke was practically unheard of in Scotland, so let's go back to the basics. It's pronounced poh-kay (don't worry, you won't be the first to have said poke, like the kind you used to give your crush through Facebook ten years ago). The dish starts with a foundation of sushi rice (Wis and Roddy's is teased to its full fluffy potential), then it's built up with an Asian-style slaw (theirs is made with basil, mint, coriander, ginger, fish sauce, lime, sesame oil), spring onions, shallots and your choice of avocado or sashimi-grade blast frozen salmon (Scottish, of course, from Something Fishy on Broughton Street) or Sri Lankan yellow fin sashimi-grade tuna. (Apparently it comes with a QR code that tells you the exact square mile in which the tuna was caught. That's pretty neat.)

Wis and Roddy then add their own light Japanese-style pickle of cucumber, radishes, rice wine vinegar and sugar, followed by a tamari and sesame oil dressing and a sauce, perhaps Hawaiian chilli pepper water, their zingy ponzu dressing or a drizzle of sriracha mayo. There's monthly specials too, such as the 'pineapple express' with its fiery topping that dances on your tongue and goes great with local Edinburgh Fermentarium or Aye Pickled kimchi. And voilà – that's Mana Poke.

Mana is an indigenous Pacific islander concept that means (something like) moral authority and prestige. It's the power of the elemental forces of nature embodied in an object or person and its source is understood to be supernatural. Just like the Danish word *hygge*, there's no literal translation into English.

'Hawaiian food is completely unrepresented in Scotland,' Wis explains. 'The thing we feel is missing in Edinburgh is a really phenomenal cultural experience – we looked to see which cuisines and cultures around the world we could do justice to using Scottish ingredients. Then we spotted that gaping Hawaiian hole.'

Their salmon is vibrant orange and of unwavering Scottish quality but, with plenty of Asian influences, many of their other ingredients are grown a little further afield. 'We try to keep it as local as possible: we buy a lot of fruit and veg through Edinburgh Community Food,' Wis tells me. 'They redistribute the profits to provide education on healthy eating for underprivileged areas in and around Edinburgh,' Roddy chips in. In theory, their support will come full circle. 'Hopefully the next generation will be more clued up on international cuisines and healthy dishes like poke, perhaps we won't always need to explain its origin and flavour combinations to every customer,' Roddy says.

Right now, it's an educational piece that typically starts with 'Do you like sushi?' followed by a response like 'Yes! Actually, I've seen it on Instagram once, but never in real life.' Now, if you're of that ilk, you won't have a reference point. So, take it from me, it's hard to not speak in superlatives when tucking into their food. It's the lightest, freshest, most exciting, tangiest, moreish, flavoursome dish I've encountered, possibly ever, and it'll leave you most thankful for choosing to order it. If I were forced to name just one dish that I had to eat day in day out until I leave this world (most likely with gout), I'd undoubtedly choose an item off Mana Poke's blackboard.

'I really dislike the word authentic,' Wis tells

me, 'unless you're serving poke on the beaches of Hawaii, there'll always be a unique spin on it.' Many of the eateries in Europe's poke community – London, Berlin, Milan, Stockholm – adopt the Subway method, where customers are free to select their protein, vegetables, pulses and extras. But the boys work with a limited menu to guarantee a simplified scrumptious experience for newbies. For Wis and Roddy, street food is a stepping stone. It fulfils two goals: first, they can engage with customers and test the waters, finding out what flavours people like and don't like, while spreading the word about poke and encouraging a younger audience to eat fresh fish. And second, street food is a platform to raise revenue until they can open their own place.

'The dream is to have a tap room with pacific Hawaiian food, hot and cold, and Hawaiian beer. It'll be a casual hang-out space for meet-ups, hopefully in Stockbridge,' Wis says. 'We do the farmers market at Leith, occasional pop-ups at the Pitt and at Platform in Glasgow, but Stockbridge Market has to be given a lot of credit. So many people that started here went on to open their own restaurant. I mean, look at Harajuku Kitchen, we want to emulate their incredible success story,' Roddy says.

The duo's food hero is Andy Ricker. He opened a northern-style Thai restaurant in America when multiple professionals warned him against it because people wouldn't be able to take the unusual flavour combinations or spice levels. He stuck to his guns, and against all odds, it thrived. His restaurant Pok Pok is now a kingdom of six, and this is how Roddy and Wis plan to keep expanding the community's palates in pursuit of making Edinburgh's street food offer that little bit more tropical. Really, they're revolutionaries.

THE PONZU POKE

INGREDIENTS

1½ cups short-grain sushi rice

600g sushi-grade yellowfin tuna or salmon

4 tbsp tamari gluten-free soy sauce

2 tsp toasted sesame oil

1 tsp grated ginger

1 tsp minced garlic

3 spring onions, white and green parts, thinly
  sliced

3 blood oranges, juiced

3 limes, juiced

FOR THE SLAW

4 carrots, grated

½ red cabbage, sliced

2 tbsp coriander, chopped

2 tbsp mint, chopped

2 tbsp basil, chopped

2 limes, juiced

1 tbsp honey

2 tbsp fish sauce

1-inch piece of ginger, grated

FOR THE PICKLES

300g radish

2 cucumbers

3 tbsp rice vinegar

1 tbsp caster sugar

Salt to taste

EXTRAS

2 large, ripe avocados

Black and white sesame seeds

Handful of coriander

METHOD

1. Rinse the rice in a fine-mesh strainer.
   Cook according to instructions or in a rice
   cooker.

2. With a sharp knife, cut the fish into 1-inch
   cubes. In a large bowl, mix together the
   soy sauce, sesame oil, ginger, garlic,
   vinegar, blood orange juice, limes to taste.
   Add the fish and green and white of the
   spring onions and stir gently to combine.
   This much can be done up to an hour in
   advance. Keep chilled.

3. For the Asian-style slaw: grate the carrot
   and slice the red cabbage in a bowl add
   fish sauce, honey, coriander, mint and basil,
   ginger and mix together.

4. For the pickles: slice the radish and cucumber and pickle with rice vinegar, sugar and
   salt.

5. Before serving, pit and slice the avocados.

6. Arrange your poke bowl with a generous
   scoop of rice, yellowfin tuna, avocado,
   slaw, cucumber and radish pickle. Sprinkle
   sesame seeds on top.

7. Serve with coriander and more soy sauce
   on the side.

THE
HAGGIS BOX

If street food is about doing one thing and doing it well, it makes sense to see our national dish celebrated out on the streets. For Scots, the holy trinity of haggis, neeps and tatties needs no introduction; though cousins Laura and Peter Sutherland have perfected their spiel for visitors. And here it is . . .

'Haggis is the national dish of Scotland, it's made from sheep meat with oats and spices, some lamb and beef fat, and onions. It's a traditional peasant dish that uses up all of the sheep, so there's the meat and also the sheep's heart, liver and lungs too, all encased in the sheep's stomach. When it's served traditionally, it comes with neeps and tatties which are the Scottish words for turnips and potatoes.'

The uptake is superb. Curious tourists wandering down Edinburgh's bustling High Street are eager to try Scotland's delicacy. 'We heard it was a bird,' one North American lady said. 'No, it's a furry wild animal with one side of legs longer than the other,' another chipped in. It's

easy to laugh, but since importing haggis into the US became illegal in 1971, it's natural that a few people have bought into the fictitious creature of Scottish folklore, with many yet to try it.

I know what you're thinking: Haggis? On the Royal Mile? Groundbreaking. But bizarrely, there are few eateries doing our savoury pudding justice. It's either made unnecessarily posh with jus, tempered against its will with the likes of curried pineapple chutney and potato bhaji, or served up unenthusiastically in a beige mound, with haggis I'm convinced plopped out of a can.

However, the Haggis Box are becoming increasingly unique in their approach. Laura and Peter treat the humble dish with the respect it

deserves; there are no thrills or unnecessary extras. It's not moulded into bonbons or crumbled onto a pizza – as scrumptious as that is – no, this is honest, unpretentious street ·food in the heart of Edinburgh's Old Town.

'You know when you think of a business idea and then later you're like no, that's rubbish, it'll never work? This one stuck with me for a while – surely someone is offering haggis, neeps and tatties on the streets of Edinburgh and they're doing it well?' But, to Laura's surprise, this wasn't the case. So, in August 2018, she finished up her office job and hatched a plan with her cousin Peter to set the wheels in motion. They secured the police box in the Grassmarket, owned by Lucy Bergius (Over Langshaw Farmhouse Ice Cream), and from their first day of trading, the punters rolled in thick and fast. Even the winter drizzle wasn't a deterrent. The Sutherlands enticed solo travellers with chit-chat and offered them a welcome escape from sitting awkwardly in a restaurant by themselves.

Then it exploded. 'New Year went absolutely wild. People were desperate; they'd come for the Scottish Hogmanay experience and we slotted into that. We kept having to go back to my flat to cook more, transporting containers back and forth to the police box. We couldn't cook the stuff quick enough,' Laura recalls.

When haggis sales soared on Burns Night, they took the opportunity to give back to the community. 'The Grassmarket is a hub for people in need,' Laura explains. 'All through the winter, we gave away quite a lot of haggis. If people have money, they won't always spend it on food; and proper, hot meals aren't easy to come by.' So, they created an open mic afternoon, encouraging customers to stand on a podium and recite one of our national bard's famous poems. And in return the Haggis Box would pay forward a hearty plate of haggis, neeps and tatties at a Grassmarket Community Project drop-by dinner the following Monday.

'*Some hae meat and canna eat, and some wad*

eat that want it; But we hae meat, and we can eat, Sae let the Lord be thankit.' Needless to say, when helping to nourish the vulnerable is offered up as a side to your Burns Night Supper, it's less sleekit, cowran, tim'rous beastie and more, 'Hold my haggis, I'm up!'

In April 2019, the Haggis Box relocated to join the rich heritage of Old Tolbooth Market. We sat in the cobbled courtyard and marvelled at its history. It opened as a Magdalene Asylum in 1807, providing a halfway house for 'reformed prostitutes'. By 1817, it neighboured Edinburgh's colossal Gas Works, a building that met the demand for gas lighting right into the 1900s. The site became a bus depot in 1928, then a car park in the 1990s – and to think it's now briefly been home to the Haggis Box's forest green hut. Like all traders, Laura and Peter will be on the move, but they'll never roam too far.

'What we're doing is simple; it's quality haggis, neeps and tatties with a vegetarian option and two sauces. We'll never be a destination for lunch every day, because the menu doesn't change. We have people who come regularly, but because it's a touristy offering, we'll stay in this central area, where there's plenty of footfall.'

They're not exactly reinventing the wheel, but of all the overpriced experiences I've begrudgingly forked out for in that part of town, the hour spent tucking into a generous £6 portion of the good stuff, in its moat of creamy whisky sauce, is up there as one of my favourites.

THE HAGGIS BOX'S TOP TIPS

HAGGIS

- Great quality haggis is essential; we use Findlay's of Portobello, though a lot of Scots will have their own favourites.
- Zhuzh it up with a dash of balsamic vinegar!

NEEPS

- We get our swede from Perthshire or Berwickshire for the best taste.
- Add a little turmeric to make that already bright orange swede that bit more vibrant.
- Seasoning with salt and pepper is essential.

TATTIES

- For mash that celebrates the taste of potato, we use Maris Pipers from East Lothian.
- Double cream, butter, salt and a thoroughly good mash is all you need.

WHISKY SAUCE

- We chose Auchentoshan American Oak as the perfect base for our sauce. The Lowland Single Malt is rich with vanilla and coconut, yet still smooth and delicate, allowing the spiced haggis to take centre stage.

TUPINIQUIM

Have you ever wondered, when strolling through Edinburgh, where all the wee boxes, just two square metres in size, positioned on street corners and intersections, originated from? Ebenezer MacRae designed 142 of these historical landmarks and installed them in 1933 as part of the new Edinburgh police box system.

Nowadays, you might see one, with its siren fitted on top, and think of *Doctor Who*. But my mind instantly jumps to a scoop of luxury strawberry and coconut ice cream from Over Langshaw in the Grassmarket, a delicious Five Guys-style vegan burger and milkshake from Lazy Lettuce on Melville Drive or a crispy Brazilian crepe filled with shredded chicken at the top of the Quartermile. I guess I'm just programmed that way.

The police boxes shut in the 1980s and it wasn't until 1995 that Edinburgh Council decided to sell a batch of them. Savvy entrepreneurs snapped them up, realising the abandoned huts could be converted into thriving business ventures. 'This one was bought for Charlie, a boy who studied politics at the university, by his dad,' Fernando Miranda, owner of Tupiniquim, tells me with his head poking out of the one on Lauriston Place. 'He was the first guy to have that vision. With the Royal Infirmary right there,' he points, 'this was the busiest corner in Edinburgh. He sold magazines and flowers to nurses, doctors, visitors and patients, then when it was time to graduate, he leased it out to Gordon and Vincent who were pioneers of quality espresso.'

The two gents started California Coffee and rolled it out to 39 other Tardis-style boxes, back in the good old days before Starbucks; but

when the hospital moved, passing trade rapidly ceased. 'Someone else took over the box, but they couldn't make it work,' Fernando continues, 'so it was shut for three years until we stumbled upon it in 2010.'

At that time, Fernando was studying environmental management at Edinburgh University, where he met his partner, Gardenia, who had come to Scotland to study English. 'She got pregnant – whoops,' Fernando laughs, 'so we decided to get married.' They'd already bought a bicycle set up with a giant coolbox, planning to sell freshly squeezed juices, but it was when Gardenia got toothache and had to go to a nearby dentist, that the police box was spotted. 'It was the most fortunate toothache ever! We never come to this side of town normally: it was sat there with a big £500-per-month sign, staring at us.' After much deliberating, they phoned Charlie, pitched him their idea and committed to it. 'I don't regret anything; the police box is iconic, you start off small and it

can trigger something magical, the business can explode.' Indeed, it was in a police box at the top of Leith Walk where Hal, now owner of the Pitt, first started Barnacles & Bones.

Nine years later, with his son Noah running around and dipping into the conversation, Fernando and I sat in the sunshine outside the Tupiniquim police box. I'd been there dozens of times for a crepe, and if I was early enough, a hearty bowl of Feijoada – but never before had I experienced them with a side of cultural history. 'Feijoada is our Saturday dish,' Fernando explains. 'It's the national dish of Brazil made with black beans and pork, with a side of rice, greens, toasted cassava and slices of orange. You've got to eat it, drink lots and then rest. Historically speaking it was created by slaves, they'd take scraps of leftover pigs' knees, trotters and ears and put them in a pot with beans.'

At this point, Noah yells, 'Papa, we use ears to make the Feijoada?' but you – and he – might be pleased to hear that it didn't quite work

with the locals and so Gardenia uses smoked pork ribs, belly and sausages instead. In Brazilian cooking, there's no need to cook with spices, or as Fernando reiterates, 'Salt and the fat from the meat is all you need.' Though they might enhance its colour with annatto seeds from the urucum tree. They're what we use to dye Red Leicester cheese, and in Brazil, the indigenous people use it for body paint, I'm told.

From out of their green hut, with its vibrant orange awning, comes many delights: gluten-free crepes filled with piri piri chicken thighs, avocado and mozzarella or vegan Pumpkin à la Papai with roasted butternut squash, crunchy seeds, spinach and tomato. They're light and crispy on the outside, so utterly moreish and yet filled with nourishing ingredients; you won't find anything else quite like them in Edinburgh.

'From 2003 to 2006, I worked down at Camden market for a French lady doing organic juices,' Fernando tells me. 'We were at the notorious Camden Lock by Regent's Canal and there were about eight stalls on the patch – now there's thousands. I got the idea of crepes from her boyfriend, Dan. He was doing crepes like ham and cheese, or chocolate, and I went to Glastonbury to help him serve. I used to plead with him to do healthy crepes, but he kept saying, "No man, we need to do something simple to make money." He was so sceptical of my ideas.'

Maximising the space available, Gardenia and Fernando had the chance to celebrate Brazilian cuisine exactly how they wanted, deconstructing their favourite dishes, like braised beef called *carne louca*, onto four hot plates wrapped up in a *panqueca*.

'Of course, there are hot dog burgers in Brazil,' Fernando tells me, 'but what defines the street food of Brazil is the thin crusted *pastel*, with its dough made with beans, deep fried and filled with seafood and some purées. I don't even know what's in it, but the ones in Salvador are delicious.' These, and the chewy tapioca pancakes that you might find in Sergipe, where Gardenia is from, inspire the Tupiniquim menu. The couple's crepes are made with rice, corn and tapioca mixed with either almond milk or milk and eggs, and what's inside them tends to come from Gardenia's mum. 'She's a very natural cook, her food is distinctive but still simple, she keeps the original taste of the ingredient whether that be root vegetable or meat, and she's passed that unique ability down to Gardenia.' There's no denying it, each individual ingredient sings.

But their little operation down at Meadow Walk is so much more than simply Brazilian street food, fuelling university students in their lunch break. Fernando has taken it on himself to do up the public garden behind the hut. He's shipping bamboo from China and converting the previously hostile environment into something welcoming and safe. 'The council has no money to do it up and, being so close to the public toilets, it's popular with street drinkers. So, I'm going to transform the garden into a stage for storytellers and performers. It's a community effort with Union of Genius, and Thomas J. Walls coffee chipping in too.'

With the greenery starting to bloom and blues from Cape Verdean singer Mayra Andrade on full blast, I can picture it being a charming spot indeed. My top tip is to get there early on Saturdays before that gorgeous Feijoada runs out!

TODAY'S MENU

MARGHERITA : POMODORINI SAUCE, £5
FRESHLY CUT MOZZARELLA,
BASIL

KALE IS THE NEW BLACK : MARINATED KALE
GUANCIALE, PARMESAN £7

NEVER TOO LATE TO BREAK BAD : SCAROBA,
40H SLOW-WOOD FIRED £7.5
PULLED PORK, FRIARIELLI

DON'T TELL THE COUNTRYMAN : (WHITE BASE)
PEAR, GORGONZOLA, WALNUTS £7

DECONSTRUCTED (GUAC : AVOCADO ONION) £7.5
CHERRY TOMS, CHILLIES, LIME
CORIANDER

TO THE MOON AND BACK : 'NDUJA £7
GORGONZOLA DOLCE, ROCKET

SURF & TURF : GUANCIALE WRAPPED
KING PRAWNS, PESTO £7.5

♥→ ADD PEPPERONI
£2

WANDERERS KNEADED

Not all those who wander are lost. That's certainly true of roaming chef Francesco Bani, whose marriage of flavours and masterly sourdough skills certify that he knows exactly what he's doing. For many, pineapple chunks on a pizza are morally wrong. Fruit has no place on this Italian delicacy, right? Well, if you're of that mindset, it's about to get uncomfortable . . . Francesco's wacky concoctions challenge that debate even further. On any average day you might find roses of parma ham and fresh caprino cheese doused in – wait for it – passion fruit pulp.

'I may have let the passion fruit swim in a bottle of local Lind & Lime Gin for an unspecified period of time,' Francesco jokes. 'I call it: Loves Ya Only When He's Drunk.'

Another pizza, the Boozy Duck à l'Orange, features crispy-skinned duck breast with orange and Edinburgh Gin jam, garnished with bay leaves, charcoaled orange and a big buttery ball of creamy *mozzarella di bufala*. Or there's my personal favourite, Don't Tell The Countryman, which is laden with fresh juicy pear, gorgonzola dolce and the harmonising texture of honey-caramelised walnuts. Bizarrely, it all just *works*. In fact, at the Scottish Street Food Awards, my fellow judge Ben Reade, director of the intimate gastronomic success Edinburgh Food Studio, exclaimed, 'I lived in Italy for four years and it's better than anything I've ever eaten.' Francesco is doing a lot right.

Francesco left Bergamo in 2012, at the age of nineteen, to pursue his career as a pizza chef in Edinburgh. With him he brought that fabulous Italian flair, which simply can't be taught. As you might expect, he got snapped up quickly. If you're an advocate of the wood-fired goods, you've probably eaten Francesco's food without even realising. He was the head chef at La Favorita in Morningside before working with Robin Gardner to open Dough, now widely touted as one of Edinburgh's top pizza take-aways. It's here that Francesco experimented with seawater pizza dough, putting Dough on the map as the first in Scotland to do so.

'The recipe took me six months to develop,' Francesco explains 'I had to continuously measure the salt content and tweak the ratios to perfect it.'

The result is this wonderful artisanal base, that's softer and less crispy than the Neapolitan style and, thanks to the chemical reaction between the minerals, flour and yeast, is lighter and easier to digest. There's far more to his food than just chucking ingredients on some dough and seeing what sticks. Francesco gets scientific and creative; armed with a pizza peel, he is a force to be reckoned with.

Francesco isn't here to sit comfortably among Edinburgh's top five pizzerias, though. He has a higher purpose. 'I wanted to be one of the first to do street food on the actual streets of Edinburgh,' he tells me. 'The city's not quite there yet, and I knew the council would be tricky, but when so many other cities are doing it, we've got to catch up.'

In March 2018 Francesco snapped up an old-school converted 1998 LDV Convoy off eBay and began building a pizza oven in the back of it.

'At the time I wasn't sure if it was idiotic or genius, but I wanted to make sure the street food game in Edinburgh would never be the same again.' He hyped up the masses with photos of his black hipster truck on Instagram

and, while waiting patiently for his street trader licence, he debuted at the Pitt. Then he got lucky. After filling out a lengthy application form – which included asking permission from neighbouring houses and mapping out exactly where he planned to park – Francesco spent five months calling the council until permission for the two highly sought-after slots he'd requested, was granted. What a triumph.

The first pitch would be fuelling young families and students beside the Meadows, at the bottom of Jawbone Walk (where the mobile fromagerie Cheesee Peasee trades on a Saturday), and the second would be supplying pizza to the good people of Portobello during their breezy strolls along the promenade. 'They wanted me to request a specific location, but I couldn't reiterate it enough – I just wanted to trade, it didn't matter which street I was on,' Francesco explains. 'Finally, I got given the end of Brunstane Road North.'

In Glasgow, we've seen traders try and fail to make it work on the streets. Without the promise of a regular footfall or a concentrated audience of hungry foodies at your disposal, it can be pretty tough if your offering isn't worth travelling for. Luckily, Francesco's is. After working 90-hour weeks since the age of seventeen, he's realised that oscillating between the two pitches is what works for him.

'I'm used to restaurant life, waking up in the morning and knowing exactly where to go; at events you wait to be confirmed for a line-up or wait for the next call to come in – it's stressful and it's really not my thing,' Francesco tells me. 'When some traders spend their Fridays prep-ping for an event on the Saturday and then take the Sunday off because they're burnt out, that would be me losing two whole days of trading.'

So, Francesco wakes up at 5 a.m. every morning to put his body straight with a little yoga, before getting the tram out to his prep unit at Saughton. There, he'll make his dough and reunite with the shoulder of pulled pork or dripping beef brisket that had been left to slowly melt in his wood-fired oven for twelve hours at 150°C overnight. Once teed up on Meadow Place or beside the seaside, this juicy, shredded meat arrives on its bubbled and blistered hybrid dough base, accompanied by rich creamy cheeses from Unknown Italy in Stockbridge, and, knowing Francesco, there'll be some kind of quirky alcoholic reduction or unpredictable seasonal fruit on there too.

With food like that, Francesco has no problem finding customers. Between his moreish elasticated sourdough, and the unorthodox toppings smothering it, us judges just had to crown him champion of the 2019 Scottish Street Food Awards. Wanderers Kneaded is Francesco's ride or die. It's no longer a business, it's a creative outlet that Francesco's having a whole lot of fun with.

'It's a wacky extension of my personality really,' he explains. 'By 2020, I'll probably introduce more street food trucks, but there's no way I'll ever go back to working in a restaurant.'

THE LOTHIANS

If you've spent any considerable time in Edinburgh – long enough for the temperature to reach a dizzy height of double digits and the sun to reluctantly peep out from behind its thick cloudy blanket – you'll have noticed a sudden surge of movement. Not only do its residents hot foot it to the Meadows for a frenzied 'taps aff' barbecue (or a slice of happiness from Wanderers Kneaded), they'll also jump on the train or hop in a car, making a beeline for East Lothian's idyllic coast. To eat indoors on a day like that would be criminal. The goal is to inhale the fresh air, soak up the sunshine and perhaps even say *adios* to that pasty winter complexion, made all the more possible when dining al fresco.

CANTEEN
BY ROGUE VILLAGE

'Our idea is to take the interesting cultural things that are typically associated with cities and create these out in more rural locations. That's the whole ethos behind the name Rogue Village,' Peter Maniam explains. After an eight-year stint in London, Peter and his wife Jenny, a theatre producer and a fashion and visual media specialist respectively, returned to Scotland and sought to bring a little more culinary diversity to East Lothian.

'In rural Scotland the options for world food are pretty minimal and when they do exist, they're pretty poor. Out here we're restricted to Indian and Chinese really, there's nowhere to enjoy cuisines like Mexican or Japanese, so even to try and bring that to our county was a pretty advanced, exciting project for us. I think we've achieved it?' Peter contemplates.

He's being modest. On any given pop-up, the fare might range from Cuban to Lebanese, travelling further east towards Thailand, casually stopping off at a country en route to grab a snack for the journey. It's a cultural explosion that gives the locals a chance to stay put in their coastal paradise, blissfully avoiding that monotonous commute to Edinburgh or Glasgow, while itchy-footed city dwellers like myself are offered a lovely day trip destination just twenty or so miles away.

Don't let the name 'canteen' put you off – it's unlike any canteen you've previously been to. For me, the word conjures memories of clinical hospitals and bland food eaten by staff wearing lanyards . . . not to forget that one boy who sat in the corner of my school cafeteria dipping his chocolate muffin into a bowl of ketchup (each to their own, I guess?). No, this is worlds apart and there's nothing ordinary or

muted about it. Canteen Street Food Festival is just one of the many strings to Rogue Village's bow, and alongside the other pop-ups in their portfolio – Hobo Cinema and the illuminating immersive Christmas fairy trail – what better setting for it than Archerfield's 18th-century walled garden, where the grit of street food is juxtaposed with vegetable plots and blossoming sunflowers. When most street food markets opt for industrial environments, perhaps an abandoned factory or a dockside ware-house, there's something rather special about Canteen. It takes the best of urban, combines it with beautiful rural scenery and then glues the whole thing together with the soundtrack of resident DJ, Four Corners. 'Oh, good music is so important,' Peter tells me, 'it appeals to a hugely diverse demographic with music from the 1950s straight through to the 1980s; there's Latin, soul, reggae and blues, lots of global music that reflects the nature of the food our traders are selling without isolating anyone.'

It was here, in 2017, on a glorious August afternoon, that I first clapped eyes on Mama Bross's legendary bagels with their healthy ratio of filling (pastrami, Monterey Jack cheddar and pickles) to chewy bread, which naturally I had to wash down with a NB Gin Salty Dog cocktail. Sinking my teeth into one of (okay, two of) the Marshmallow Lady's pillowy mallow doughnuts immediately followed. These are self-taught marshmallow specialist Nicole's vanilla bean,

fluffed-up sugary goods that she's formed into doughnut shapes and smothered in melted chocolate, which is left to solidify before being dusted with local shortbread and a drizzle of white chocolate – what a time to be alive!

Between hosting these Scottish producers and regulars like Crema Caravan, Chick + Pea and the Cheesy Toast Shack, Peter and Jenny are also working hard to put Newcastle traders on our doorstep.

'We'll always support local and we hope it's a place that traders will aspire to be, but, in addi-tion to that, there's some amazing street food in Newcastle that no other markets are tapping into,' Peter explains. 'In East Lothian, we're almost as close for Glaswegian traders to get to as we are for Newcastle ones, so we thought let's get them up here. Of course, we keep to a high standard that we'll never deviate from.'

Since launching in 2017, Canteen has become a renowned highlight of the summer months for both children and adults alike. As parents them-selves, Jenny and Peter know only too well how hard it is to find an event that caters for both. The good news is there's not a bouncy castle or synthetic chicken nugget in sight, but with ice cream, bubble wands, giant board games and even the occasional skateboarding lesson, a mere stone's throw away from Archerfield's own brewery, Canteen might have just found the golden ticket to an epic family day out.

Venturing that little bit further down the coast, you'll find North Berwick's stunning beaches – a prime spot for picnics and dog walking – and beyond that, there's a harbour so pictur-esque it belongs on a postcard. It's home to an unassuming grey clapperboard hut and from it, phenomenal Scottish shellfish is served up with unrivalled views over the Forth. If you're in that neck of the woods a visit is highly recommended. In fact, no, it's obligatory.

NORTH BERWICK
LOBSTER SHACK

You don't need to be beside the sea to enjoy fresh fish, but it sure does help. Perhaps that's why the Lobster Shack has, if you'll pardon the pun, muscled its way into seemingly every 'best of' or 'top 10' list on the internet. Or maybe it's because, quite rightly, their half and whole grilled lobsters, generously brushed with garlic and herb butter, are more than deserving of every accolade and should be flaunted for the world to see.

Larry sits on his perch of proper double-dipped chips and he's everything you'd hope for in a freshly caught lobster – succulent, fleshy and sweet. With quality like that it would be a shame to leave remnants in the shell, so contraptions like the lobster cracker and pick are provided. Still, it's a handsy affair that'll most likely result in butter-smeared cheeks and white flakes under your fingernails. I'd typically say not first-date fodder, but with a sunset like that coupled with the romanticism of strolling barefoot along soft squishy sands, you can lob that date night etiquette rulebook straight out into the sea.

This is Scottish street food in its simplest form. The Lobster Shack champions provenance and freshness, all served out of a plain-looking hut that's small in size but big on flavour, with just a stone wall dividing it from the home of its catch of the day. Local fisherman Jack Dale delivers the crustaceans daily. His Firth of Forth Lobster Hatchery first nurtures the eggs from berried hens (or pregnant lady lobsters to you and me), then moves the eggs through a system of tanks, separating the now cannibalistic baby lobsters to be reared in their own container until they become juveniles. If you're going to eat the stuff, you've got to know where it's been, right? The process uses filtered seawater directly from the Forth and lasts three months, before the lobsters are released back into the sea. They'd typically have a 0.05% chance of survival in the wild, so lobster ranching gives these critters a fighting chance.

Follow the smells and it's in this spot, on the southside of the harbour breakwater, that you'll find cups of chunky chowder, intensely flavoured dressed crabs and Shetland rope-grown mussels with any spare shells begging to become makeshift spoons, used for slurping up any remaining white wine broth. It's all good, but I'm of the mindset that you can't go and not order one of the huge whole lobsters that Jack and his team of fishermen have hauled out of nearby creels that morning. It's all yours for £39.95, though there'll be a queue for it and it's likely that you'll have to fend off the occasional scavenger too – by which I mean seagulls and dining companions attempting to snaffle your chips.

When I first visited the shack with my cousins back in 2009, it was a much shabbier affair. News of its appeal was yet to spread across Scotland, so it felt like our little secret: you know, the kind of place you want to tell everyone about, but selfishly want to keep to yourself at the same time. Now there's no need.

On Saturday 28 July 2018, they achieved a Lobster Shack record by serving 430 takeaway meals in one day – not bad for a hut that's just two by four metres in size. Where a handful of flimsy metal table and chair sets used to shuffle around in the wind, in 2019 a large glass awning was installed to shelter umpteen proper ones. It'll mean those portions will continue to fly out regardless of the weather, but in many ways, the shack is slowly morphing into a restaurant experience, mirroring Stirling Stewart's other glass-walled venue, the Rocketeer, positioned on the other side of the harbour. With crisp and lemony Picpoul de Pinet wine and even the Lobster Shack's own branded lager, brewed by Edinburgh Beer Factory, it's the most polished incarnation of street food I've recently encountered. Thankfully, a little rustic charm is preserved by cardboard boxes and disposable cutlery – and not plastic ones either, it's all biodegradable stuff made from corn starch.

SEAFOOD CHOWDER

SERVES 4–6

Here is Stirling Stewart's interpretation of this delicious, rich and creamy soup that goes down well on any occasion. It tastes best served with crusty bread down by the harbour in North Berwick!

INGREDIENTS

A knob of butter

1 medium onion, diced

1 leek, finely chopped

¼ tsp fresh thyme

450g East Lothian Paris Piper potatoes, peeled and cubed

½ cup sweetcorn

800ml fresh fish bouillon

140g North Atlantic cod, cut into chunks

140g Scottish salmon, cut into chunks

140g North Atlantic haddock, cut into chunks

320g North Atlantic prawns, peeled and deveined

400ml double cream from Yester Dairies, East Lothian

Sea salt and pepper for seasoning

A little gluten-free flour for thickening

½ lemon, juiced

METHOD

1. Sauté the leeks, potatoes and onion in a pan until tender. Add thyme and simmer for 2 to 3 minutes.
2. Add the fresh fish and bouillon and bring to the boil until the potatoes are nearly cooked.
3. Reduce heat and simmer for 10 minutes.
4. Stir in the fish, prawns and the cream. Cook until the fish is fully cooked and flaky, and potatoes are tender. This will take about 8 minutes.
5. Add the lemon juice and seasoning.
6. Thicken with a little gluten-free flour.
7. Serve with crusty bread, and plenty of sea air!

ALANDAS
SCOTTISH SEAFOOD

If you've toured East Lothian before, you'll know that a trip isn't complete without checking in with the Black family. Named after Jason and Dorothy Black's eldest daughter, Alanda, the company began as a humble chippy in 1991, when she was just one year old. Twenty-eight years later and it's still a proudly Scottish family-run business, now largely under the management of Alanda and her sister Valentina, with the third Black family daughter currently at university. With two more brands and a fleet of four street food trailers, I guess you could say it's grown legs.

'Our family's first fish and chip shop was named Alandas, so, when I started going on the road to seafood events, I thought: We've already got that brand and it's famous for fish and chips, so why not stick with it?' Alanda explains. 'As we're well known in East Lothian, we decided to call our next venture, an ice cream parlour, Alandas as well. That's when the company split into three – Alandas Gelato, Alandas Fish and Chips and Alandas Seafood. I think my sisters have got used to it being named after me,' she laughs. 'It's all any of us have known!'

If you stumble upon one of their trailers, perhaps roaming around the local area or pitched up at the Edinburgh Fringe, you're in luck; anything born of the Alandas pedigree is going to be good. It was at the end of 2013 that Alanda first introduced her seafood street food concept, at the Edinburgh Christmas Market.

'I wanted to showcase the best of Scotland's seafood because obviously we've got some of the richest waters and some of the best seafood in the world,' Alanda says. 'But eating seafood is traditionally associated with prestigious, almost

stuffy restaurants. It's an uncomfortable eating experience and it's not accessible for everyone. So, it got me wondering how we could showcase our seafood in a fun and approachable way that would appeal to all different demographics. That's when I bought the first trailer.'

After an overwhelming response from both Edinburgh locals and tourists, Alandas Scottish Seafood took off. Alanda sought permission to position the trailer in one of the car parks on Longniddry Bents, amid patches of coastal grassland and stretches of shingly sands, and since then – on Saturdays and Sundays during the summer months at least – it's become a magnet for foodies and seagulls alike.

I've often opted for the scenic route back to Edinburgh and miraculously found room for a soft-shell crab burger or a skewer of garlic butter and chilli king prawns en route. Can you blame me? On a clear-skied day, it's a stunning spot to tuck into fresh Scottish seafood. And, even when it's raining, I have no qualms fogging up my windows and leaving a distinctive fishiness lingering in my car for days, when the rewards are so tasty.

When the family started to do more custom with street food than in the shops, they invested in four trailers. Securing that slot at the Edinburgh Fringe was the real game changer, that's where most of the group's new customers are reeled in. The profitability of the prime George Square Gardens spot during August even encouraged Alandas Gelateria to jump on the band wagon – or on the street food trailer, I should say.

It was in 2014, a few months after Alanda

spatula-full proves that frozen sweet treats needn't be synthetic or aerated.

Now, in one direction you'll see kids in George Square coating their noses in the chocolate cone, getting sticky hands and weeping as their tub accidentally falls to the ground, while in another direction there's adults strutting past flaunting their mound of white crab meat-loaded aioli fries; it can be a cruel place to people watch if you haven't got time to join the queue.

When the chippy's menu remains stationary, featuring all the staples you'd expect, the trailers act as an outlet for experimentation. 'Recently I've noticed that we're a nation of foodies; people know good food. The days of people selling cheap rubbish are over and our customers are becoming increasingly more open to trying new things. When we first started at Edinburgh Christmas Market, we had lobsters on display and people would come up and say, "Are they real, what are they? I've never seen a lobster before" – whereas now, the lobster roll is a best seller,' Alanda explains.

I'll admit, I've probably had more than my fair share. It's a contentious debate whether the legendary New-England lobster roll ought to be served hot with butter or cold with mayo, but Alandas lends itself to the latter, known as the Maine-style. Containing Eyemouth lobsters and a generous squeeze of fresh lemon, all held together in squishy brioche rolls, they're a suitably scrumptious handful-sized snack for devouring on the move between Fringe shows. If only there was a suitably sharp Chablis on hand to wash it down with; now that's a serious contender for #firstworldproblems.

started her seafood venture, that Valentina branched out from the family's traditional chippy offering and set up the micro ice cream factory and parlour in North Berwick – where our favourite chocolatey treats like Kinder, Ferrero Rocher and the heavenly Creme Egg are playfully delivered in indulgent ice cream form. Alandas Gelateria is the place to live out your filthiest dessert dreams. 'A scoop of lemon meringue pie?' Sure. 'Another of rhubarb crumble?' Oh, go on then. 'What about a third of cherry cheesecake or cranachan, which is a blend of whisky, fresh raspberries, cream and Scots oats?' Just you try and stop me. 'And would you like a fudge stick with that?' What is this place!

It's unbelievably naughty and, made with East Lothian cream and fresh ingredients, each

ALANDAS SCOTTISH LOBSTER ROLL

SERVES 4

INGREDIENTS

2 cooked Scottish lobsters
2 large celery sticks
½ cup of free-range mayonnaise
1 large lemon for squeezing
Hebridean sea salt
Freshly ground black pepper
4 brioche finger buns

METHOD

1. Halve the lobsters and remove the meat, chop into generous bite-size chunks and finely dice the celery.
2. In a bowl add the lobster, mayonnaise and celery. Mix until there is an even coverage.
3. Halve the lemon and squeeze it all into the mix. Add sea salt and black pepper to taste.
4. Place your lobster mix into the fridge for 5 to 10 minutes, this allows it to absorb all the flavours.
5. Lightly toast your brioche buns, split the tops and load with your lobster roll mix.

THE BORDERS

The Borders has a bit of an undeserved reputation for being boring. The scenery is stunning, with vast open countryside and emerald rolling hills intermingled with pockets of cottages and rural neighbourhoods that are lucky enough to have their milk delivered in glass bottles. But food and drink wise, it's not quite a hub of culinary street food choice.

LINTON & CO

Whether you're shipped off to an event to represent work or you're bouncing around a festival making the most of your weekend, there's nothing worse than being handed an insipid or inedibly bitter polystyrene cup of coffee. Ex-policeman Alex Linton-Critchley and events manager Lara Wilson have had more than their fair share of disappointing caffeine kicks, but from years of hardship comes one ingenious solution. And so, in November 2015, Linton & Co was born.

Roaming the breadth of Scotland in the rather handsome Bernard – a stylish black Citroën H van born on 17 November 1976 in Lanvallay in France – the couple set out to rectify the gross injustice performed on our indispensable sweet nectar of the gods. We shouldn't have to sacrifice decent coffee just because we're outside. It's these tiring days, often bookended by early starts and long drives, that necessitate a hot mug of dark caramel-toned stimulant . . . and preferably one that's seen a coffee bean.

'People go to the Scottish Game Fair year on year and pay a fortune for appalling coffee and bland wholesale cakes,' Lara explains, but if Bernard's on site, visitors are given an ethically sourced, flavour-packed alternative.

Their core blend is Glen Lyon's red stag espresso roasted in Aberfeldy, a delightful town on the banks of the River Tay. The blend is fruity with a lingering chocolate aftertaste, bold enough to shine through a latte or stand alone in a killer espresso. Described as a 'dynamite blend' combining the best beans from Latin America and East Africa, it's the kind of coffee that'll take your taste buds on a journey with every sip, revitalise you to power on through the morning and warm your body to its core on a miserable winter's day. Or, in my case, an unexpectedly nippy April weekend in Paisley.

Glen Lyon Coffee Roasters was set up by Fiona and Jamie Grant in 2011. While working as a journalist, hitching along dirt roads in Bolivia on the back of a motorbike, Fiona became fascinated with the small-scale coffee farms perched on steep mountains and the farmers' dedication to nurturing their beans. Instantly, Fiona knew this was the industry for her, only further cemented by a family road trip down the west coast of America. 'We came across a micro-roastery in practically every town we travelled through and realised this was something we could do back home in Scotland.'

It all began in a bothy at the top of beautiful Glen Lyon in the Highlands, with a pre-loved Turkish coffee roaster and three bags of beans. After travelling to the origin of their coffee and forging relationships with the producers, their speciality coffee company began to grow, and several years later it was time to advance from winters spent digging lorry deliveries out of snowdrifts on their single-track road. The team of five now roast some of the world's finest beans on a Probat in Aberfeldy, and pride themselves on still tracing each bag back to the individual farmer or co-operative that grew it. In an industry where social responsibility is often neglected, it's amazing to hear that Fiona and Jamie have been sourcing from the same co-operative in Rwanda for four years now.

'The income of the co-operative members we buy from in Rwanda has doubled and this year every member received a cow. It's important for us to know that not only is our coffee ethically sourced but that we pay our farmers substantially over fairtrade prices for their amazing beans.'

So, when you're ordering a coffee from Linton & Co, know that you're supporting Glen Lyon in changing lives in East Africa. It didn't need the backing of an incredible story to make the coffee taste delicious, but it sure helps.

Lara and Alex are passionate about sourcing from Scottish independents, and that extends to their loose-leaf tea. After much deliberation, they chose to support the Wee Tea Company, a team of three who blend their tea in Dunfermline. With an impressive range of over sixty teas, and a biodegradable teabag offering, they provide tea for leading tourist attractions like the V&A in Dundee and the National Portrait Gallery. But what's particularly impressive are their disposable paper cups, fitted with mesh lids. Linton & Co's loose-leaf cherry and raspberry herbal infusion was served in one of these, allowing the tea to continually brew, releasing as much flavour from the leaves as possible, all while slowly warming my hands up. A quality tea-drinking experience.

But what really sets Linton & Co apart from other mobile coffee bars are their gooey chocolate brownies. These are lovingly made at Alex and Lara's home in the Borders, adapting the top-secret recipe passed down through Alex's family with twists like salted caramel sauce or peanut butter and strawberry jam. Trust me, I tried (rather unsuccessfully) to get my hands on the recipe. What I did manage to secure are a few pieces of the puzzle, which may help us to recreate these scrumptiously moist brownies at home:

- The eggs are organic, from Kelso's Ednam West Mains Farm.
- The butter is from the award-winning dairy enterprise, Stitchill Jerseys. Four decades ago, Brenda Leddy started with just one Jersey cow, now she's a stalwart of the Borders food scene, with a herd of over one hundred. Real Scottish farm-made butter is hard to source these days, but paying that little extra for churned and hand-shaped butter from Brenda, and her daughter Susan, takes these indulgent brownies up a notch.
- For the salted caramel ones Lara uses the unrivalled natural Isle of Skye sea salt, from the clean waters of Loch Snizort.
- For the raspberry brownies, when in season, the couple pick fresh berries from their garden . . . it's probably best to get approval before scaling the fence for this ingredient.
- Newsflash! Thanks to a few persistent customers, the brownies are now available to buy online.

Like fish and chips or bangers and mash, coffee and brownies are a match made in heaven. But if you're looking for a smaller nibble to accompany your coffee, turn to Lara's Isle of Skye sea-salted caramel bites. These chewy morsels of sticky salty goodness are fortunately soft enough to keep any fillings intact. Lara and Alex kindly shared this recipe without too much of a fight – though I would have fought them for it!

ISLE OF SKYE SEA SALTED CARAMEL BITES

INGREDIENTS

MAKES 25

1 tsp vanilla essence
160ml double cream
60g salted butter
160g caster sugar
160g golden syrup
1 tsp Isle of Skye Sea Salt

METHOD

PAN 1

1. Add sugar to pan, then add syrup.
2. Put on low heat on a small ring.
3. Stir sugar and syrup together & keep on low heat to melt and combine.
4. Turn up heat slightly once sugar is dissolved.
5. Use sugar thermometer to test heat. Take it up to 125°C. Also judge by colour: it should be a deep brown caramel.

PAN 2

7. Don't turn on the heat for pan 2 until pan 1 is almost ready.
8. Put half of the butter in the pan with all of the cream and all of the vanilla.
9. Add salt into the pan: can taste to add more later once sauce is ready.
10. Melt on a low heat to combine ingredients.

TO COMBINE

11. Slowly add pan 2's butter and cream to pan 1.
12. As it bubbles add the second lot of butter.
13. Take temperate back up to 110°C.
14. Test in jug of cold water for consistency. (It should be chewy.)
15. Taste: add more salt if required.
16. Pour into baking tray lined with parchment paper.
17. Cool for 20 minutes.
18. Scatter Isle of Skye Sea Salt on top.
19. Cool for 3 hours, then cut into chunks.
20. Wrap in parchment paper to keep fresh.

THE
CREMA
CARAVAN

While the majority of the world's traders are focusing on their savoury offerings, Borders-based Mel Duncan and her boyfriend Callum McDougall are leading the street food dessert movement from the front. They've got to be incredibly confident, or bizarrely self-destructive, to welcome criticism with the tagline 'not all desserts are created equal'. But slide just one teaspoon of that silky custard into your mouth, with its crackle top melting on the tongue and ambrosial strawberries bursting amid fresh chewy meringue, and it all makes sense. Truthfully, not all desserts are created equal and the Crema Caravan's brûlée, served in its adorable tin-foil pot, paves the way as an exemplary pud.

That's right. Crêpes – yes. Churros – sure. But crème brûlée? No one (including Mel and Cal themselves) quite knew what was in store when Florence the Renault Estafette parked up at the foot of Edinburgh Castle, for a farmers market, in September 2014. It's in these early days that an important lesson was learned, the popular salted caramel brownie-topped crème brûlée could never ever come off the menu.

Mel and Cal knew that they were taking a punt in pioneering something so globally unheard of, but with little tying them down, Mel was optimistic that they'd make it a success.

'No one else was doing what we're doing and we knew that if it didn't work up in Scotland, we could just take the mobile business anywhere we wanted . . . we would've been prepared to pack up the van and move to London or go to Manchester, we would've gone wherever there was work.'

This free-rolling, free-spirited nature is what encouraged the couple to first venture into

street food. After years of working abroad as private chefs and chalet hosts for ski seasons, nipping back and forth to France, it was time for a change. Mel and Cal originally had their heart set on opening a café until, as Mel explains, 'We went travelling to New Zealand, and met a lady there who was a chef, but in the winter she'd go and park her van and serve food at the bottom of the mountains to people off the slopes, and then in the summer she'd do the same but for people coming in from the surf. We soon realised that this really was an idyllic lifestyle; she became our inspiration.'

Spotting a gap in the refined dessert market and knowing how well their crème brûlée recipe had gone down – week on week continuously trumping the freshly baked lemon and chocolate tarts – this was clearly the route for them. Of course, a French classic executed well is one thing, but how could the Crema Caravan's crème brûlée stand out against the offer from high-end restaurants?

Market research revealed that most were garnished with a sprig of mint or fresh strawberry, but no one had dared to embellish the already superb dessert with a topping. And so, the Crema Caravan's USP was born. Chocolate fudge brownie and forest fruit cherry compote, peanut butter blondie and salted caramel sauce, fresh rhubarb and golden crumble; each dessert would be elevated to perfection with the addition of a tried and tested flavour combination.

Little did Mel and Cal know – after investing in a gorgeous retro Renault in May 2014, and fixing her up with a mousy-grey lick of paint that summer – that just a year later they'd win the Best Dessert Award at the British Street Food Awards. The second their gingerbread and

chocolate crème brûlée with Scottish heather honeycomb stepped into the arena, it was game over for fellow the North and Scotland contestants. Here, the unique deliciousness of the Crema Caravan's offering opened up a huge international door for globetrotting Florence (that's the van, remember!), who was soon shipped all the way over to the United Arab Emirates for Eat The World DXB and Love Food Festival. Rubbing shoulders with fourteen of the UK's finest purveyors including London street food legends the Cheese Truck and Oli Baba's (the original creators of halloumi fries), Mel and Cal battled through weeks of scorching sunshine to serve their exquisite desserts at room temperature. 'It felt like a once in a lifetime opportunity ... but the people of Dubai, Abu Dhabi and Al Ain rather took to our crème brûlées and we were back again the following year.'

In 2017, the Crema Caravan family grew, acquiring Percy, another 1970 registration-plate Renault Estafette. Percy's a little bigger than Florence, with room for a coffee machine to keep tired Edinburgh Fringe performers alert and meet the demands of events like the Borders Book Festival. Doubling their business overnight meant that Mel and Cal could split up to work multiple events at once. 'There might not be much happening in the Borders, but with equal distance between Newcastle and Edinburgh, it's the perfect home for us busy traders.'

Mind you, maintaining two vans while busting a gut to whisk hundreds of egg yolks late into the evening doesn't come without its challenges.

'There's never been a time where the vans haven't needed fixing; whether it's a little rust or a whole new engine – behind the scenes it isn't all that glamorous.'

In 2018 Percy broke down just days before a wedding, but thankfully their incredible mechanic understood the importance of delivering crème brûlée to the people. Percy will go to the ball . . . even if he has to be towed there; truly, not all heroes wear capes.

Having started trading in farmers markets back in 2014, before Scotland's street food scene had even taken off, Mel and Cal have seen plenty of traders come and go, with many ambitious ones failing to pass muster. So, what's their secret? Why has the Crema Caravan stood the test of time?

Well, that's simple; it's an original idea with a quality product. Each crème brûlée is scattered with sugar and blowtorched in front of the customer's eyes; it's perhaps the only time the phrase 'burnt to order' can be seen as a good thing. This theatre prepares the long line-up for that all-important snap as the thick caramelised layer cracks with the tap of a teaspoon. And the fact that you can't get one anywhere else? That just makes the whole experience special.

'If you've got a burger van and you apply for events, you'll often hear "we've already got a guy that does that", but with a crème brûlée van, you're never going to get knocked back for having the same offering as somebody else.'

Now when I tell you I'm busy on a lunch date with my friends Percy and Florence, you'll know where to find me.

CREMA CATALANA

SERVES 4–6

INGREDIENTS

500ml double cream
100ml whole milk
1 orange (zest only)
1 lemon (zest only)
1 cinnamon stick
1 vanilla pod
6 large egg yolks
60g caster sugar (plus extra for topping)
Pinch of salt

METHOD

1. Preheat the oven to 140°C or gas mark 1.
2. Place ramekins into a deep roasting tray.
3. Put cream, milk, orange and lemon zest, cinnamon and salt into a heavy-based pan.
4. Split the vanilla pod and scrape out the seeds, adding the seeds and pod into the cream mix. Set aside for a minimum of 20 minutes to infuse.
5. Place the cream mix on a medium heat, stirring occasionally. Keep a very close eye as when it reaches a gentle simmer, then take it off the heat.
6. Put your egg yolks into a medium-sized heatproof bowl.
7. Gently whisk yolks to break them up, add the sugar and whisk gently to incorporate fully.
8. Now strain ¼ of the hot cream through a fine sieve onto the egg and sugar mix, stirring gently to temper the egg mix.
9. Strain the rest of the hot cream onto the egg mix, stirring well to combine.
10. Any bubbles on the surface can be removed with a quick blast of a blowtorch or you can skim them off with a large spoon.
11. Strain mix again into a large jug and fill the ramekins with the mix.
12. Carefully fill the tray with boiling water until the waterline is a third of the way up the ramekins.
13. Cover loosely with tinfoil and carefully place in the oven for 30 to 40 minutes (less if using shallow ramekins).
14. To check they are ready tap the ramekin side: they should wobble like a set jelly.
15. Carefully remove tray from oven and place the ramekins on a cooling rack.
16. Leave to cool to room temperature, cover with cling film and put in the fridge to set overnight.
17. When you are ready, sprinkle with caster sugar and place under a hot grill or blow-torch the top until sugar caramelises.

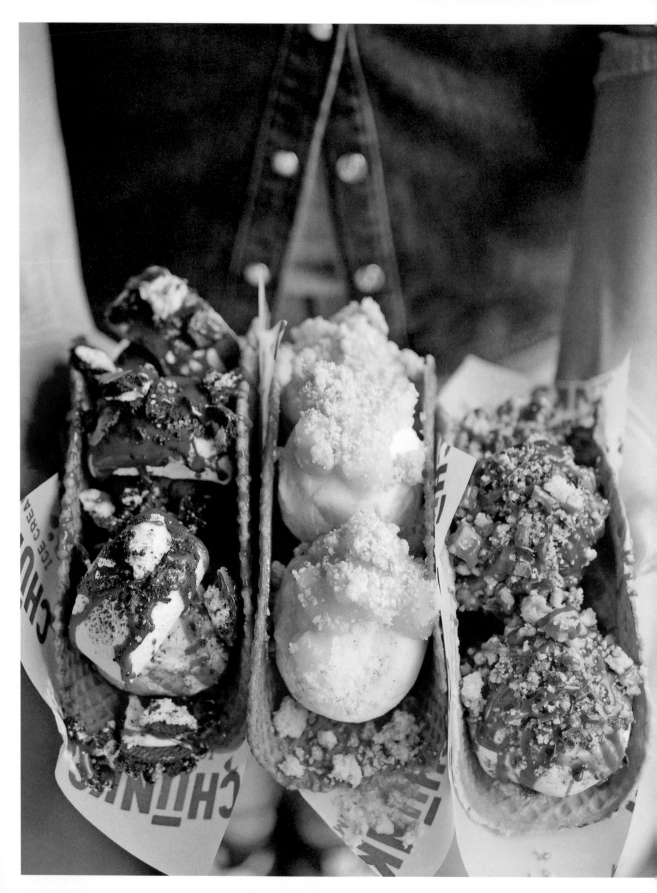

CHUNKS

There's always room for another dessert in my opinion. Thankfully, Platform at Argyle Street Arches are of the same mindset and set aside space for two dessert stalls back in March 2018 when they first launched.

That's when Chunks, the baby brother of the Crema Caravan, was born. Mel and Callum had dabbled in ice cream at the Edinburgh Fringe in 2016, but a rebrand was in order. Glasgow's discerning foodies were worthy of something more, something playful; they didn't just deserve quality ice cream, it needed a crunchy vessel and lashings of naughty toppings too. Of course, Platform only had a concept to go by, but anticipating great things (as you would given the Crema Caravan's pedigree), Chunks was a worthy choice for the much sought-after second dessert slot.

The name Chunks refers to the little boy in *The Goonies* who stumbles upon a freezer in an abandoned kitchen and shouts excitedly, 'I smell ice cream.' It's a reference for the 1980s kids, but also a nod to the chubby kid inside us all, the one who'll sniff out ice cream in any given situation . . . during a lazy afternoon at Platform, for instance. Sign me up!

As you'd expect, Mel and Callum have their hands rather full, but there's absolutely no shame in sourcing from an esteemed local supplier when they don't have time to churn ice cream themselves. They chose Porrelli, a luxury gelato company who've been producing Italian style ice cream in Paisley since 1925, when Gerardo Porrelli came to Scotland from San Biaggio in southern Italy. The ice cream is proper. It's packed with lumps of joy like fresh strawberry, chewy cookie dough or millionaire shortcake; then there's the seasonal specials like Creme Egg and Jaffa Cake ice cream; all of a benchmark quality to complement the homemade components of the dessert. It's assembled in front of the customer. First are Mel's burnt caramel-flavoured taco shells; they make an impressive *snap* sound and boast a perfect thickness to hold the weight of the ice cream. Then there's three generous scoops of Porrelli gelato or sorbet (yes three, I'm telling you this colossal dessert constitutes a meal in itself). And finally, a whole host of toppings, like homemade hot fudge sauce or toasted marshmallows, blueberry pie or homemade

pineapple salsa. The latter is made with pineapple juice and pulp, fresh ginger, lemongrass and lime zest; it's delightful atop of Porelli's mango and coconut vegan ice cream with shavings of toasted coconut.

Growing demand for these frozen gems is almost a blessing in disguise. I'm with Mel on the idea that 'a balanced diet is an ice cream taco in each hand'; but these ones are outrageous, requiring at least two sweet-toothed appetites to tackle them. Chunks are now on the move throughout Scotland and thank goodness! The allure of an ice cream taco on every Platform visit really could have been dangerous.

GLASGOW & STRATHCLYDE

My mum is a Glaswegian. Or a Weegie if you prefer. She grew up in Maryhill and spent her student days dipping in and out of the many curry houses on Gibson Street, sampling the delicately battered vegetable pakora. Back then, street food as we know it today didn't exist in Scotland. But given that these crispy golden fritters have been flogged on the streets of Kolkata for decades, you could say Glaswegians were ahead of the times. In the 1970s, pakoras and other Indian street food delicacies were exclusively enjoyed in flock-wallpapered restaurants. And, oh boy, were the queues long.

'I'd stand for hours, often in the pouring rain,' my mum recalls. 'But the aroma inside was worth it. A portion of pakora was 23p, so two of us could eat a three-course meal and get change from £3. That was far better than Mum's mince and tatties.' Now, you only need to track down Rachna of Babu Kitchen (page 153) for an authentic Indian street-side pakora experience.

I have my own fond memories of Glasgow, visiting my grandparents as a child. Grandad loved a good walk, so many of our days out included a trip to the park – not that I complained! It was never too difficult to persuade Grandad to buy me an ice cream cone, or a wee pokey hat as it's known in Glasgow, from the van parked outside the gates. Maybe that's what sparked my love of street food.

Fast forward to 2019 and Glasgow is teeming with quality traders. It's moved on a great deal from 99 flakes on a kerb by the Botanic Gardens. Like Edinburgh, this section isn't made up of what traders are in Glasgow, but more a curated list of those it seemed only right and proper to include. People make Glasgow. That's the slogan branding this dynamic cosmopolitan city. Glaswegians are renowned worldwide for their friendliness: everyone is welcome, and the concept of a stranger doesn't exist. Is it any wonder that the city is well suited to the convivial nature of street food? While the capital has one buzzing market, Glasgow's sociable population warrants three. Between them, you'll find the freshest on-trend foods the city has to offer. But first, you've got to know where to go.

BIG FEED

If you're unfamiliar with the riverside district of Govan, you could easily stroll past the unassuming industrial warehouse that is home to Glasgow's first street food playground. Big Feed is the brain child of Jonathan Stipanovsky. The capacious warehouse started off as a labour of love, born out of his frustrations with the Scottish weather.

'Seventy to eighty per cent of the time we're attacked by harsh rain, snow and winds; it was about time someone weatherproofed Glasgow's street food experience,' he tells me.

From the outside Big Feed doesn't look like much – I have to admit, I drove straight past it on my first visit. But inside, the cold, corrugated space has been transformed into something warm and inviting.

'The warehouse is run by Glasgow The Caring City, a charity supporting young people in crisis,' an employee told me as we squeezed through the crowds. 'There's two old red double decker buses, and we were given Christmas lights. Then there's arcade machines and pallets dividing it all – anything we could find really.'

Letters illuminated with multicoloured bulbs spell out 'Kit Kat Klub', joining a 'Welcome to Hope Falls' sign in utter randomness. But the whole thing works; even on a bad weekend Big Feed will draw in over 3,000 punters: 'The hot dog truck really grew arms and legs,' Jonathan laughs. Yeah, you could say that.

Big Feed began with Firedog in 2015 – that's Jonathan's bright red gourmet hot dog Citroën H van where you can find 'the UK's tastiest XXL smoked pork dogs' drenched in liquid nacho cheese, crispy bacon and BBQ sauce. They're channelling that whole 'New Yorker mustard and ketchup squeezy bottle' vibe: but, 'The product inside is proper, I spent months blind-tasting sausages, until I found an epic place in Germany

that do the best in the world. I can't disclose the name, though,' Jonathan says.

Back then he found Glasgow's lack of street food events difficult for business, so, naturally, he created his own. Good Food Glasgow was formed after a city council survey revealed that thousands wanted more street food events. It was a pilot project that Jonathan and his fellow operators, including Rachna at Babu Kitchen, had to crush if they wanted to do more. So, after spending summer 2016 trading at Merchant City's Brunswick Street, followed by six weeks in the Broomielaw ... well, you can guess where this is going.

Jonathan was granted permission to move the market inside, and he flung open the Big Feed doors on 4 March 2017. Wow. He'd optimistically briefed the traders to prepare for 1,000 guests, but no one expected to see a queue of 3,000 ravenous faces by 2 p.m. 'Through no fault of their own the traders quickly ran out of stock, though most of them heroically ran back to their units to get more food,' Jonathan recalls.

Big Feed has a real family focus, lit up with string lights and energetic children rushing to the face painters and balloon twisters. But there's something for the adults, too, with a long bar backed by global spirit producers, and a handful of vintage vehicles to impress the most discerning of petrolheads. Since launching, Jonathan's been inspired to open more brands of his own, from plummy fries loaded with shredded duck, to sticky chocolate drizzled churros, burritos, and Salt 'n' Chilli spiced everything. He's taking tips from everyone along the way and is trying his hand at the lot, but it does mean there's a colossal waiting list for any new kids on the block.

PLATFORM
AT ARGYLE STREET ARCHES

The adjoining arches under Glasgow's Central Station are legendary. They've housed some of the biggest names in dance music: Carl Cox, Jeff Mills, Richie Hawtin, Sven Väth and Derrick Carter, to name a few, and indeed it was in this iconic setting that Daft Punk chose to perform their first ever UK gig. But the arches are more than just a nightclubbing mecca.

The not-for-profit organisation subsidised its theatre, a magnet for emerging talent, and drew a broad demographic into its buzzing arts venue. That included Banksy, who in 2001 visited his own 'Peace Is Tough' exhibition and left three poignant works: Mona Lisa surrounded by an ornate frame, a gun-toting monkey sporting a tutu, and between them the words: 'Every time I hear the word culture, I release the safety on my 9mm.' A moment of silence, in awe of such talent, please.

When its doors closed in 2015, it could have been turned into a car park or left abandoned but Hilary Goodfellow, who played a huge part in reviving the arches, argued that, 'It's a space

that deserves so much more than lying derelict.' I wholeheartedly agree. I couldn't think of a better use for the institution, which will continue to resonate with those who thrummed to its rhythm, than transforming it into the foodie haven that is Platform.

Platform champions the independent traders. 'It's giving an affordable platform to genuinely authentic traders that all have their own backstory, in a postcode they ordinarily wouldn't be able to afford,' Hilary explains.

The place is atmospheric and inviting, with exposed brick vaulted ceilings sheltering its lucky visitors from all the generic massproduced foods out there. Each resident trades

five weeks on, one week off, in a line-up of vibrant purpose-built jumbo noodle boxes. That's genuinely what they remind me of. From the eye-catching stalls, wafting aromas of Fujisan's aromatic katsu curries, to the pile-up of Tiny Dancers' dripping burgers and rows of punters getting stuck into the local craft beers, with a play area for kids and biscuits for the pooches; the whole thing's electric.

'Glasgow's been served well in terms of one-off events; the gastronomes can have their appetites satiated occasionally,' Adam, Platform's market manager, says. 'But Platform is the first weekly market: rain or shine, every week there is a street food presence; it's not working off temporary licences and we don't close the doors if we don't feel like it.'

Platform's now fiercely independent beyond just street food. On Sundays, their walls welcome food producers and vintage market stalls. 'There's Freddy & Hicks, Shwarmarama, Tiny Dancers, Fujisan, Ginger & Chilli and so many other great traders, intermingled with the Kitchen Farmer with his own beef lamb and mutton. There's the Kedar Cheese Company with their own herd of brown Swiss cattle — they sell this incredible, creamy mozzarella alongside organic non-homogenised milk that they bring up in churns every week so people refill their own bottles of milk. And we've got the Strawberry Shop with all their fresh produce. So, there's a connection between the food that people can buy to take home and cook themselves, and the quality street food that people eat there.'

The Argyle Street Arches are open till midnight on Fridays and Saturdays, and till 6 p.m. on Sundays, but the best part is Platform isn't just restricted to that space. Limp fries and questionable pork hot dogs are a thing of the past when Platform go on tour with the mission to revamp festival fare. I'm talking sumac and cumin marinated chicken drizzled in fresh mint yoghurt at one in the morning. I went to TRNSMT Festival purely for it. Step aside Stormzy, I've come for the burgers.

DOCKYARD SOCIAL

The truth is, I've never been to Dockyard Social. But truly, that's not for want of trying; my Glaswegian friends assure me it's their favourite hangout in the city.

'You have to try Berto's Brownies at Dockyard! I always get a few to take home – an original, a salted caramel brownie, a peanut butter one and a flavour of the day, literally one of each – then heat them up in the microwave and eat them with ice cream. They are Mike and my favourite brownies ever; they're so gooey!

'Smokey Trotters do incredible burgers. Then Fritti at Dockyard has fantastic arancini, oh and if you like chewy sourdough pizzas then Pizza Hawker is the place to go. Also, you have to check out Honu. Get their Buffalo tempura cauliflower poke bowl and apple-stuffed gyoza, they're topped with roasted crushed peanuts and spiced honey, it's seriously tasty.'

Yes, ma'am. Generally, any advice that Evalyn, blogger Glasgow Gourmet, gives ought to be strictly followed. But, sadly, I couldn't.

Dockyard Social, which first launched in November 2017, has had a rollercoaster of a journey. The huge unit on Haugh Road in Finnieston, founded by Scott van der Hoek, Chris Gibson and Kyle Steel, has one powerful ethos at its heart: 'Eat well, drink well, do good.' Think modern-day adaptation of Robin Hood, but set in the hippest area of town, by protagonists who know what decent food tastes like and who, oh, probably aren't foxes.

'We're taking money from people who are quite affluent and giving it back to those who aren't,' Kyle explains. Dockyard Social wasn't done with deep pockets or to financially benefit the founders. 'It's about helping people by putting on an incredibly immersive experience

where people are passionate about what they do.' Dockyard Social is a local start-up, for local start-ups. The plan was to open for business every fortnight for a couple of days, to raise enough funds to develop the Dockyard Social School. But for some competitors, it was a little too popular. Anonymous noise complaints from a singular source came thick and fast, even on the days when they weren't trading. On 23 November 2018, after numerous battles to get occasional licences, Dockyard Social traded for the last time. The end.

Except it wasn't the end, and everyone loves a happy ending, right? Within those eighteen successful street food events, Dockyard Social had helped numerous small street food entrepreneurs follow their dream and provided vital supplies for Glasgow's homeless community. All that with a backdrop of phenomenal food, it's no wonder they won *The Scotsman*'s Best Street Food in Scotland 2018 award. It wasn't their end goal, but it was certainly enough for the council to grant them a permanent licence on 18 January 2019. That's right, they're back for good and with huge thanks to an altruistic private investor.

When Dockyard Social reopens, they'll be collaborating with Urban Market, purveyors of independent crafts. There'll be room for up to twelve traders – seven in fixed pods, one in a converted shipping container and three or so in their own vehicles – plus four bars with specialist drinks and even an indoor gin garden. But, most importantly, within the warehouse

will be the training and development school, giving a foundation of learning to the homeless, long-term unemployed kids who have come through care and people who have been made redundant.

'Here they'll learn everything from health and safety, food hygiene level 3, how to look after their accounts, branding, business set-up and marketing,' Kyle says. 'But they won't just be trained and kicked to the kerb. We're going to support them throughout and who knows, they could be Scotland's next emerging traders.'

Hospitality is in Kyle's blood. He's the man behind Section 33, named after the eviction notice served by the council to those about to lose their home. He's always been about using food and drink events to change lives.

He's pushed the boundaries with restaurants in swimming pools and fed thousands in a pop-up dinner in the world's oldest music hall, the Panoptican on Trongate, to raise money for its restoration.

'All this was done because my grandma told me not to. Back in the day she said I needed to get a real job, to be a plumber or a plasterer, I couldn't just be in hospitality. So, I feel that, by helping people, whether they've fallen on hard times or they just need an opportunity, I'm able to do my gran proud.

'When we're back up and running, I'll be engaging with the local community on a wider front, hosting events like pensioners' tea dances to get them out the house. It breaks my heart to think there's people sat in their homes with

nothing to do and no one for company.'

Dockyard Social is a non-commercialised experience for the socially conscious. Global comfort food with plenty of options for those with dietary requirements is their vibe. 'These chefs are putting their heart on a plate; they're not following spec books that are done in a commercialised kitchen to meet a certain gross profit margin,' Kyle reiterates. 'They're doing it because they love it and it tastes amazing, and they want to pass that on to others. You've got to try Noi's Café, she isn't anywhere else. Her homegrown authentic Thai is ten out of ten

on the chilli scale and literally evokes emotion, there are so many different flavours in your palate, her story is conveyed through her food. It's outrageously good.'

I, for one, am working up a serious appetite.

'Abandon Chips do some seriously tasty loaded waffle fries,' my friend Chris from Chris Eats said when we were discussing where to eat in Glasgow. That's Kyle's own brand, and he's been kind enough to share the recipe.

Warning: you'll need to lie down after this one!

ABANDON CHIPS' SMASHED BIG MAC

SERVES
4

INGREDIENTS

640–800g waffle fries (crinkle cut
  fries make a good substitute)
4 x 160g good quality burger
  patties (e.g. a blend of brisket,
  short rib and chuck steak)
Ketchup
American mustard
Gherkins

CHEESE SAUCE

225g extra mature cheddar
225g red cheddar
1 tbsp corn starch
1 tin evaporated milk
Franks hot sauce to taste
Chopped jalapeño for nachos

BURGER SAUCE

130ml mayonnaise
60ml ketchup
2 tsp sweet pickle relish
2 tsp white wine vinegar
Salt and pepper

METHOD

TO MAKE THE CHEESE SAUCE

1. Grate the cheese then mix it in with the corn starch.
2. Place in a high-sided pot and cook on a very low heat,
    stirring constantly.
3. Add all other ingredients and cook until smooth.
4. Take off the heat and adjust the seasoning with a little
    salt and pepper. Add more or less hot sauce as required.
5. Enjoy over some Abandon Chip waffle fries or on nachos,
    dirty fries, hot dogs, burgers, or pretty much anything.
    This sauce is amazing.

TO MAKE THE BURGER SAUCE

1. Just mix everything in a bowl and set it aside.

TO ASSEMBLE

1. Heat your deep fat fryer to 180°C.
2. Add waffle fries and cook until golden brown. Drain and
    season.
3. Heat a frying pan or griddle.
4. Season the burgers with salt and pepper and add them
    to the pan, pressing down to ensure as much contact
    area as possible (this will get all the awesome crispy
    bits).
5. Once coloured nicely, flip the burgers over and do the
    same to the other side.
6. Once cooked break up or smash the burger into large
    chunks and serve.

FREDDY & HICKS

Anyone who believes that vegetarian food must mean virtuous salads comprised of kale and avocado, or bland tofu, mushroom burgers and couscous stuffed peppers, clearly hasn't eaten from Freddy & Hicks. Anna Robertson is a knowledgeable stalwart of the street food scene. She's hustled at London's formidable Borough Market for fifteen years, handing out tasters and promoting her wares until the crowds dissolved and even until her voice resembled a rasping goose call. But she doesn't need to hawk at passers-by anymore. Not only is vegetarian food, once on the fringes of our consumption habits, now entirely mainstream but her scrumptious burgers – jammed with deep purple beetroot rosti and slabs of halloumi, elevated by the garlicky heat of sriracha sauce – quite simply speak for themselves.

Less than twenty years ago, meat-free burgers were a concept that was hard to swallow. Even now I've got uncomfortable flashbacks of leftover platters at kids' parties, smeared with indistinguishable fawn patties where unspeakable things had been done to a bag of carrots. But fast forward to 2019 and, wherever Anna is, you'll find a queue of punters, signing up to forgo meat and embrace a more environmentally friendly diet.

'There is no way this burger can actually be vegan . . . that's the best burger I've ever eaten and I'm a meat-eater!' Overhearing sentences like this from nearby tables has you instantly lining up to get in on the action.

Borough Market is the same today as it was in the early 2000s; it speaks for diversity, quality, honest pricing and, crucially, only those who pass the strict four-tiered vetting process can trade there. That's where Anna and her husband

Adam first met. It's a love story of the most delicious kind; he was selling organic bread for the Flour Power City Bakery and she joined them for a weekend job, having just graduated from the University of London with a business degree.

'From that moment I was in love; I loved the history of the market, the fact that you could just turn up with a table and sell what you've got. I loved that you could be outstanding with just one or two simple items, and then be part of a bigger picture, a whole institution of excellent food and this amazing, unbeatable camaraderie.'

Anna soon realised that her passion for street food was taking over from her photography day job and, having fallen in love with a vegetarian man and becoming stepmum to two vegetarian children, it was time to rustle up some decent veggie food of her own. In 2006 the couple decided to try their hand at running a Borough Market stall. They sailed through the first three stages of the application (expression of interest, detailed application and face to face interview) only to be rejected by the tasting panel. But they persevered and went home to tweak their recipes, receiving a unanimous verdict on the second attempt . . . with one small caveat: the products were only allowed to be sold as a chilled retail offering.

There were burger patties, vegetarian sausages, quinoa and hummus pots for customers to play with at home, but with only one other vegetarian offering (a falafel stall) at the meat-centric market, customers didn't stop requesting the products hot. So, in true Anna style – and trust me, you'll witness the same persistence when watching Anna trading in blustery winds while attempting to keep her bright yellow gazebo grounded – they mounted a campaign, filmed a YouTube video and got their customers to sign a petition, lobbying the management committee at Borough Market. Eventually, in 2008, they'd convinced the prestigious institution to let them sell their food hot. This was just the beginning.

Back then they were called the Veggie Table, 'but I didn't want to be pigeon-holed into a niche or tied down to a particular style of food,' Anna explains. 'I will never be preachy about what we're doing either. My diet has changed over the years and Freddy & Hicks is my journey with food – we went vegan in 2015, so we started working with more vegan products, introducing dishes like the seitan burger; vegans go wild for it, there's nothing quite like it for the texture they're missing from not eating meat. But I'm coeliac and found veganism far too restrictive, so I moved back to being a vegetarian. I wanted a name that meant something and allowed the food to evolve with me. Trends may come and go but I'll always offer a range; people are at different stages on their journey of being vegetarian or vegan. Some people have never tried halloumi, others might refuse to eat honey; people go backwards and forwards along that line, so I want to offer everyone something, no matter where they are on that journey.'

When Anna had her own children, using their middle names – Frederick and Hicks – seemed like a perfect fit for the company's identity, and besides, it does have a great ring to it.

After years of borrowing a friend's jam kitchen when it was unoccupied at night, slaving away in the early hours to improve London's vegetarian burger game, Anna and Adam relocated to Swansea to open their own café. 'I spent much more time managing people,' Anna recalls, 'when you have a café you move further away from the food and your relationship with it gets diluted. But with street food you keep the menu small and you can do everything from beginning to end. It's also much more flexible.'

When Anna and Adam moved to Glasgow in 2016, it seemed natural to get back into street food. 'It just worked better for how my life changed, having kids and changing cities. I wanted something that I could dip back into while looking after them.'

Needless to say, Glasgow's street food scene was an anticlimatic awakening for the newly rebranded Freddy & Hicks. There was the odd farmers market, but this was before the days of Big Feed. So, Anna started off with monthly pop-ups in the wee Bakery47 in southside before getting a temporary residence at a citizenM hotel. Once again, they were ahead of the curve – doing street food, eating vegetarian food and even grilling halloumi long before it became cool.

'Because of the weather, the window for outdoor street food was so tiny. It needed warehouses and places like that, it took a bit more infrastructure to get going than we'd expected. When Big Feed launched, we started trading there once a month, then it grew to twice a month and then Dockyard Social started up, too. But, really, it's Platform that changed my life.' Anna secured a residency at Argyle Street Arches from day one, giving her a sheltered spot for loyal customers to find her every Friday, Saturday and Sunday.

In spite of this, Anna's eager to do more. In

2019, she launched a crowdfunding campaign to afford her an upgrade from gazebo to horsebox.

'Street food in Scotland is hard. Even on a sunny day, it takes five hours of preparation before we can serve one single burger. We've been through sub-zero temperatures, driving rain and even gale force winds that have literally launched the gazebo into the air.'

This horsebox will be 'her vehicle for change' and not just in terms of less physical work. Freddy & Hicks has moved on from broadening her own children's horizons on food and making vegetarian food exciting for kids to eat. It's about the bigger picture; making vegetarian food accessible for everyone, no matter the weather. Not once in our conversation did Anna utter the words 'plant-based' and, my gosh, that's refreshing! In an era of marketing stunts and careful phrasing, Anna keeps it honest and fresh, right down to the loaded fries. I'm rarely satisfied by sweet potato fries; they're often soggy, under-seasoned, and beta to Maris Pipers. But Anna's are proper. They're impressively crispy and loaded to the high heavens with ingredients that work: black olives, jalepeños, red onion, tomato salsa, fresh coriander, wedges of halloumi, moreish lemon tahini sauce and sriracha mayo. The flavours just explode in your mouth.

'The adrenaline that you get from doing a great street food event is like no other, when the music's playing, the customers are all around and happy, the steam is coming off the food, everybody's laughing, it's great to be a part of. Whatever we do in Glasgow, no matter where we are trading, it's the people and customers that make it great – they'll turn up rain or shine – they make this scene a pleasure to be a part of.'

MEXICAN QUINOA BURGER

SERVES A PARTY!

INGREDIENTS

250g dried quinoa, cooked in water at
ratio 1:1.75

1 cup kidney beans, drained

¾ cup tinned sweetcorn, drained

200g cheese (vegan or dairy), grated

1 tbsp coconut oil

1 large onion, diced

3 garlic cloves, minced

1 tsp cumin

2 tsp smoked paprika

½ tsp chilli powder

1 tsp salt

1 cup fresh coriander, chopped

1 tbsp tomato paste

1½ tsp liquid smoke

50g plain or gluten-free flour

METHOD

1. Cook the quinoa in water until it's absorbing the
   water, then put the lid on, turn heat off and leave
   it to finish by itself. The quinoa should be slightly
   undercooked and definitely not mushy.

2. Fry the onion and garlic in the coconut oil until
   soft and fragrant, then add the cumin, paprika,
   chilli powder and salt and cook until dispersed.

3. In a large bowl combine the quinoa, kidney
   beans, sweetcorn, onion and spices, coriander,
   tomato paste, liquid smoke, cheese and flour. Mix
   thoroughly and allow to cool in the fridge.

4. Form into 130g balls, squeezing them between
   your palms into a burger shape. Fry in coconut oil
   until browned on both sides and a bit crispy.

FRITTI

If you own a restaurant and spot a man lurking outside for numerous days on end, there's every chance he'll turn out to be Paul Henderson, waiting for inspiration for his next street food brand. That's what he did for Fritti.

'I found my suppliers by hanging around outside my favourite Italian restaurants, watching who delivered their produce and noting down their numbers, then contacting them. I work in the city centre, so it was easy to do.'

That's how he found Carnevale, a family-run business who've been importing cured meats and tomatoes (that actually taste like tomatoes) since 1966, while also manufacturing their rich and buttery Great Taste-awarded *Mozzarella Fior di latte In Palla Carnevale*, in central London. These flavoursome Italian ingredients are combined with Paul's discerning palate to form a fried menu of antipasti delights. I guess you'd expect that, given *fritti* means fried in Italian. From impressively delicate, crispy balls of

saffron risotto filled with soft smoky nduja and mozzarella, to crunchy panzerotti teeming with grilled aubergines and courgettes with sweet San Marzano tomatoes grown in the ashy soil of Mount Vesuvius, my family has had the privilege of visiting Italy on numerous occasions, and Paul's fare trumps the lot.

Paul's a born and raised Glaswegian who's been working in IT for the past twenty years; his partner, Kasia, is a trained psychotherapist with a Polish background. Prior to meeting each other, Kasia had done a couple of pop-up cafés, but Paul had only dipped into the industry in part-time roles while at university, and had once tried to experiment with a clay pizza oven in his back garden, only to watch it collapse

after two Scottish summers. Given there was little professional cooking experience between them, and not a bone of Italian heritage in their bodies either, I'm absolutely blown away by their offering.

'We just love the way Italians eat, wandering around the streets, getting food and drinks to nibble while they wait for a table at a restaurant. We absolutely love the Italian culture and knew that we wanted to replicate it in Glasgow for our first venture.'

It all began after a holiday to Naples. One Sunday morning they saw a queue for one of the famous pizzerias that they'd failed to get into the night before. 'People were coming out

of it with big brown paper bags, we thought that looks interesting, so we got a couple of espressos and joined the queue,' Paul recalls. 'At the end of it they were cooking panzerottis, so we got one between us – they're practically deep-fried pizzas, so what's not to like!? That's where our idea came from.'

The couple then went to Sicily where they gorged on extravagant *fritto misti* platters studded with golden calamari rings, followed by the famous Palermo street food *panelle*. These are chickpea fritters often eaten between slices of bread. In a way, they're like a refined chip butty that you'd get down your local chippy, except much healthier – that's how Paul describes them. Once drizzled with a squeeze of fresh lemon and seasoned with salt and pepper, they're scrumptious.

Their three-wheeled vehicle is a cute Piaggio Ape decorated in the il Tricolore colours, and you can't help but feel affectionate towards it. If it was a puppy, you'd give it a cuddle.

'The story behind the van is interesting – we'd come back from Naples and had decided to go down the fried pizza-arancini-calamari route,' Paul explains. 'We were sitting on the couch one Saturday morning watching a travel programme, and on it a little Piaggio Ape van like ours pulled up in an Italian coastal town, and it was serving fish and chips to the locals there. We paused the programme, got the name of the van and looked them up online. They're a company called VS Veicoli Speciali based in Turin, who specialise in converting Italian vehicles, like the Ape, into street food vans.'

They took the plunge. £30,000 was much more affordable than committing to bricks and mortar. 'You're at the mercy of people coming to you if you have a static place; with a van I could take it out to the people and keep exploring until I found somewhere it worked.'

Erm. Not at 25 mph you can't, Paul.

When he first told the manufacturers that he wanted to drive the Piaggio back from Turin they burst out laughing. Ape means 'bee' in Italian – they were designed to buzz around Italian cities.

'We soon realised that our speed limit restricts us on how far we can go!' Paul admits 'We travel with a fully loaded van, so we stay mainly around Glasgow – the furthest we've been is Darvel in Ayrshire, about twenty-five miles away. It took us a while to get there.'

In June 2018, they pitched up at Sagra Italiana, Glasgow's inaugural Italian Festival in George Square, for their first day of trading. It was just four days after their daughter was born – talk about bad timing – and three days of back-to-back prepping, cooking, serving and washing up was more exhausting than anticipated.

'Nobody tells you beforehand how much work is involved, but, as my sister says, "You chose to do this, no one asked you to do it." It's days after the event before you actually finish, but seeing customers' faces once they've tried the food, it's worth it, I really love it.'

Paul and Kasia have future-proofed their business with the name Ape Street Food. Fritti's the first, but there's every chance of growing their fleet with food from Kasia's Polish roots or South America. Now that they've realised it's a viable business, who knows which direction they'll be buzzing off in next.

NDUJA AND MOZZARELLA ARANCINI

MAKES
18

Fritti's tasty arancini are made using a saffron risotto, stuffed with different fillings then rolled in breadcrumbs, before being deep fried.

....

INGREDIENTS

500g Arborio rice
¼ bottle white wine (Sicilian if you can)
Pinch of saffron
90g onion, finely chopped
120g celery, finely chopped
1–1.5l vegetable stock (hot)
40g unsalted butter
Splash of light olive oil
Vegetable oil, for deep-fat frying

FILLING & COATING
80g nduja (soft, spicy pork sausage)
140g Fior di Latte Mozzarella
Golden breadcrumbs

METHOD

1. Heat the butter and oil in a heavy-based large pan, add the onion and celery and soften for 2 to 3 minutes.
2. Ensure the stock is hot in another pan on the hob, add the saffron to the stock.
3. Once the onions and celery have softened add the rice. Heat until the husks crack, then add the wine. Turn up the heat a little to burn the alcohol off from the wine, and keep stirring the rice, onions and celery.
4. Once the wine has been absorbed, gradually add the stock, stirring all the time. Repeat until the rice is just cooked, you want it to be a little al dente.
5. Put the risotto into a large flat container, to allow it to cool quickly, and then refrigerate.
6. Now prepare the filling. Portion the Nduja into 18 equal-sized balls and do the same with the mozzarella.
7. Take the chilled risotto out of the fridge and use a mould or your hands to shape the rice into balls or cones, making a space in the middle for the filling.
8. Place one nduja ball and one mozzarella ball in each arancino, then complete the shape with more risotto. Roll each arancino in breadcrumbs ensuring it is fully coated. Repeat until all the rice is used.
9. When ready to serve, heat enough vegetable oil to deep fry the arancini, either in a wok or a deep fat fryer. The oil should be 180°C. Fry them in batches for 5 minutes, ensuring they are piping hot in the middle.
10. Serve with marinara sauce and a salad of rocket with olive oil and balsamic vinegar.

TINY DANCERS

The test of a good burger is one that can hold its own in a plain bun, perhaps with a little cheese, some gherkins, a lettuce leaf and a slice of tomato. That way, it's got nowhere to hide. Each ingredient is exposed to scrutiny and can be judged on its own merits, without a ladle of chilli con carne, say, masking the crime scene. Don't get me wrong, I like a sloppy joe as much as the next girl, but that lumpy beef stew is rarely a generous add-on to good quality meat. It's used to inject much-needed moisture to a desiccated patty or to conceal one that's never seen a cow. That's possibly how you know after one small bite of Paula O'Rawe's burgers, or even while perusing her menu, that she uses only the best ingredients.

Paula uses the family-run Cumbernauld-based Bavarian Bakehouse for her buns which feature real butter and milk, not powder. For patties with a good meat-to-fat ratio, it had to be William Cranston's in Pollokshields. Paula's been buying their meat for years and has worked with them on her bespoke burger recipe, made predominantly from shoulder of grass-fed cattle from Finlay Farm in Wishaw.

Then there's the cheese. Anyone with a genuine appreciation for cheese in Glasgow will tell you there's only one place for it: I. J. Mellis on Great Western Road. Kilos and kilos of Keens vintage cheddar go into Paula's Gochujang sliders, while the Blue Swoon one just wouldn't be the same without Mellis's Colston Bassett.

'Stilton cheese from a supermarket can be very young and taste sort of bubble-gummy, but when you buy it from Mellis it's older and has a more sophisticated flavour,' Paula says.

The goal was that all of these real, authentic, genuine ingredients would come together to

elevate a simple burger into something world-class. And as resident (ahem, self-proclaimed) burger expert, I can confirm that they do.

'In street food, it's that passion and interest and care that makes it different from anywhere else,' Paula tells me. 'I care so much about getting the recipe right. When I started with Tiny Dancers, I put it out there and people liked it, so I tried to keep the price as low as I could despite the cost of the ingredients, and I've been trying to get it better and better, and simpler and simpler ever since. It's easy to do stunt burgers and load them with all the mad, bonkers stuff, but I wanted to be the polar opposite of that trend. I want to be simple and transparent – good bread, good meat, good cheese.'

In most situations, less is more, but Paula's street food journey didn't start off that way. She'd always been an enthusiastic home cook and had dipped in and out of kitchens in part-time gigs as a student; so, knowing she wanted to start her own food stall, when her twins were old enough to go to school, she waited for the perfect opportunity to present itself. Back in 2000, she'd lived in New York for a couple of years, with many evenings spent tucking into the takoyaki in Otafuku x Medetai on 9th street.

'I loved it, and when I was thinking of all the elements of street food that matter – interest, taste, flavour and an element of theatre – that jumped into my head,' Paula recalls. I'm sure any Platform regulars will fondly remember the steaming hot octopus dumplings from Paula's first brand Mimi's Takoyaki. How could you not? They were wee attention-seeking things that started off like gloop in the takoyaki moulded cast iron pan and transformed into tasty spherical balls out of nowhere. They were topped with Paula's own beni shoga (beetroot-infused

PAULA O'RAWE'S THROWBACK TO 1995

'I went to I.J. Mellis cheese on Great Western Road on the first day it opened, I must have been 21 or 22 at the time. I walked in, having always loved food, and asked, 'Can I buy a pound's worth?' and the guy said, 'Yes, yes, yes.' He was wearing wellies, so it was super fancy. Well, I'm from Belfast so it was super fancy to me. I asked for a pound of this and a pound of that and kept pointing at cheeses in excitement. What I didn't realise was he was giving me a pound in weight of each, but I'd wanted a tasting portion, a quid's worth of each! My bill came to £27 and I nearly died. I didn't know what to do, but it was a friend's birthday so I just panicked and put it all on a card I had. Oh my goodness, we ate cheese for weeks and weeks. I served it at the little party for my friend – everyone thought I was very posh and must be incredibly rich – I'd spent about £100 in today's value on cheese! I've been going in there ever since, Pauline the manager is fabulous and . . . well, the quality is second to none. But what an expensive mistake.'

pickled ginger) and, with the katsuobushi (dried, fermented, smoked skipjack tuna) flakes on top, were made to wriggle from the wafting steam. Looking back, Paula admits it was too niche to pay the bills; the people of Glasgow weren't ready for octopus balls.

That's when Paula turned to hamburgers, you can't go wrong with a proper crowd-pleasing hamburger. 'Although ostensibly quite ordinary, when you get into the simplicity of bread and meat and cheese you realise the world's your oyster.' And that's better than octopus!

So, what's the secret to a show-stopping burger? In Scotland, we've had the pleasure of pink, medium rare burgers taken away from us, presumably by a 'well done' kind of man on the Food Standards Scotland board, who thought cooking burgers to 75°C would do us all a favour. It didn't. But, in the right hands, this isn't an obstacle. 'The key,' Paula says, 'is the fat-to-meat ratio, that's what keeps the burgers moist, even with the latest legal requirements.' She rolls her mince into the size of large golf balls then smashes them down, giving the thin patties full intense contact with the grill. It gives burgers that caramelised crust, achieving what's known as the Maillard reaction (when you brown meat to release a whole new whack of flavour). At first, Tiny Dancers was all about the sliders, the smaller the burgers are, the more you can eat, right? But now Paula's sizing up for speed and economic reasons, ensuring a shorter wait in that inevitable queue.

Paula is 48 years young this year and eager to encourage more people to get into street food. She reflects on the burgeoning scene. 'When I was younger, I just didn't get the opportunity – not that it wasn't there but it was tougher.

In those days you had to open a restaurant, there were no stepping stones, no street food opportunities, it wasn't easy to try things out for a £2,000 outlay of equipment.' Markets like Platform are more than a line-up of huts, they're hugely supportive communities for anyone looking to try their hand at street food and Paula has had a great experience of that.

'I owe Anna at Freddy & Hicks a lot of thanks,' she says. 'My children go to school with hers, and so I asked her about Platform. I'll be honest, I didn't have a clue, but she showed me the ropes and let me watch her work. She was so generous with her time. I'd say she was my mentor even though she's younger than me, and eventually when I launched, I was never prouder than being set up side-by-side next to her. There's an ageless element to street food, it's so welcoming. I'm living proof that it's never too late to do exactly what you want in life.'

FATBOYS

Joe and I spoke on the phone for almost three hours. He reminisced about being seventeen years old, when he often helped his mum out at her Erincroft bakery stall at Glasgow farmers markets (they're still going strong; get a cheddar and leek plait or a beetroot and black pepper boule, you'll thank me later).

'Next to our stall was Rachna,' he told me. 'She would be there with a massive drum just cooking away. All her food was served straight out of a huge pot, like how you'd typically get it on the streets of India.'

We spoke about mental health, the tough 90-hour weeks, 42 weeks in a row when his parents forgot what he looked like and his love life suffered, the pitfalls of packing up in the rain, and the highlights of being creatively unrestrained, cooking whatever the hell he wanted. He even offered to take me on a food tour of New Orleans and North Carolina (it's in print now, Joe, no turning back). Apparently, I've got to meet Elliott Moss of Buxton Hall BBQ, he's

doing some serious things with wood-smoked meat. Joe doesn't mess about with his words and, boy, are there lots of them.

'At TRNSMT Festival last year, the organisers told me I needed to have a sign. So, they came back the next day and I'd put a sign in the tree above my stall. They told me to take it down, for health and safety reasons, in case it falls. I told them it wasn't me that put it there … then they came back to check if I'd made a sign, and all I'd done is find a massive blackboard and written on it "Fried chicken and shit". That became a bit of a tagline for a while.'

Behind his stall, Fatboys, you'll find Joe and perhaps a helping hand dressed in flamboyant,

multicoloured patterned shirts that you'd presume were borrowed from *The Fresh Prince of Bel-Air* cast.

'This one photo of me keeps doing the rounds,' Joe says. 'I was wearing a sleeveless plaid vest, with a patch from a child's *101 Dalmatians* bed-set sewn onto it; everyone ripped me for that get-up.' He laughs.

Fatboys is rustling up a menu laden with American and Jamaican treasures, like 'cowcain' brisket sandwiches, 'f*cking clucking' fried chicken sandwiches and 'Nug life', which are jerk chicken nuggets inspired from my first encounter with Joe at Meats & Beats Festival in March 2018. I was full of Barney's Beer and Joe had just run out of chicken wings; naturally I sassily demanded that he deep fry me a chicken thigh instead, and it's been on the menu ever since.

Joe's menu boasts as many terrible puns as it does incredible flavours. At the 2019 Scottish Street Food Awards, he took a food that everyone knows, pulled pork, but used ingredients that the average punter might turn their nose up at.

'This is my crispy pig head crubeen bun with white BBQ sauce, smoked apple ketchup and pickled red onions,' he says. 'I've smoked and braised pigs head, then pulled it, rolled it and pressed it into a sausage, sliced it into patties and breadcrumbed it to fry.'

It melted on our tongues beautifully, eliciting instant respect for an animal part that might typically get wasted. Next up he served us his most popular dish of jerk chicken with coconut rice and peas, scattered with a pineapple salsa, ginger beer and coffee BBQ sauce, and a coriander and scotch bonnet salsa. If that doesn't

sound complex, wait until you find out that his flour is seasoned with allspice, ginger, cinnamon, thyme, clove and nutmeg. The Jamaican green seasoning atop of his jerk-marinated chicken is packed with spring onions, ginger, garlic, coriander, parsley, scotch bonnets, lime, and a few other secret ingredients. When it's Joe's food, it should go without saying that the chicken was crispy and moist in all the right places and the flavours combined to form a loud and happening party in our mouths. He left us with the words: 'It's fresh, flavourful and spicy as f**k – enjoy!'

That's why, after five years of working at the Lake of Menteith Hotel, Joe just had to leave. 'I couldn't really play around with food up there, it's a very touristy crowd and mostly they're much older, too,' Joe explains. 'Obviously, there's the odd person that's up for eating some weird

stuff but I'd struggle to do my own style of cooking, and if I did it, I'd have to word the dish in a way that would make it desirable. Gumbo and dirty rice would have to be creole chicken, chorizo and prawn stew with Cajun rice, and that just isn't what it is. I'd have to name it in a way that someone would say, "Oooh that sounds fancy."'

His creativity was curbed by crowd-pleasing menus that he'd been handed to follow verba-tim for three months at a time. He once made a terrine out of a pig's head for the staff, and even they wouldn't touch it – 'But, oh, they'd eat hot dog made of pig tails, toe nails, arseholes and bollocks, wouldn't they. Sometimes I think it would be better to just not tell people what they're eating until afterwards, and be like, "Oh by the way, that was an ear."' He laughs. People

will eat anything so long as it's packaged in the right way, but convincing the kitchen team and their guests to overcome that psychological hurdle seemed difficult. Joe soon fell out of love with food. 'Any job where it's creative, if you're not allowed to express that creativity, it's like asking an artist to paint in a different style. It's the thing you enjoy doing but it's not the way you enjoy doing it.'

When Joe quit the hotel, he headed out to North Carolina to stay with family and eat BBQ food in the hope to reignite his passion for cooking. It worked.

'That's where I realised what I should be doing,' he recalls. Holidaying in the birthplace of jazz, his idea of pairing food and music emerged. 'You can hear a song and it takes you back to a specific place, food does the exact same.'

Now, whether it's at the Pitt in Edinburgh, Dockyard Social in Glasgow where Joe first debuted in a street food environment with 850 covers across three days, or anywhere in between, you'll hear Joe's stall blasting out the music of New Orleans brass brands, intermingled with a little reggae. He'll never cook without music, so why should eating it be any different?

It's rare to find Creole or Jamaican street food in Scotland, but Joe's is hitting all the right notes (if you'll pardon the pun). Shortly after launching, he was snapped up for a pop-up in a citizenM hotel, and in March 2018 he bagged himself a residency at Sauchiehall Street's live music venue, Broadcast. Though that wasn't all it cracked up to be:

'In residencies, you have no right to complain at the infuriating staff, because you're not the one paying them. But when I'd been there for over three months, and they were still unsure of what each dish was, I was like *come on*! They didn't want to do their bar jobs, let alone serve my food too.' It all ended a little sour when Joe was on holiday, returned to Glasgow after a fortnight's holiday to find he'd been permanently replaced.

But the experience has made him more determined to reach that end goal, of owning his own place. 'I've got an image in my head of what I'm looking for, and I'll decorate it how I want. Broadcast was good but I didn't have any control over the staff or how the place looked. So, as much as it was my food, it still wasn't one hundred per cent me.'

Joe's restaurant will be, in every sense, him. 'I just need to have the money first,' he explains. 'That's what's so frustrating about restaurants;

people with lots of money don't know what to do with it, so they open a restaurant that's rubbish, but guys like me with the knowledge and experience, could open somewhere epic, but just can't afford to.'

Joe wants to 'cut through the crap' – from marketing stunts on a menu to having to dress up to eat out, and even stuffy service where customers are concerned that they'll be kicked out after an hour because the staff want to turn the tables around. 'I don't want that; I just want people to come and have fun. A place that you go for the night which has more of a party vibe. People will come, eat, drink, dance. I don't want a place that's just for dinner, it needs to be more of an experience,' he tells me.

Of course, Joe will still be involved in the street food scene and he's hoping to upgrade the stall to a truck too. 'Speaking to someone who is passionate about something, if you're talking to them about that passion, you'll never have a better conversation. It's the most enthusiastic you'll ever find someone.'

From talking to so many traders, it's clear that one of the best bits about street food is chatting to customers and fellow traders who are interested in the ingredients used and what inspires each recipe. It's a shared passion that excites us all.

'GUMBO IS MY FAVOURITE THING TO MAKE. IT SUMS UP CREOLE COOKING TO ME, WHICH IS HEARTY FOOD WHICH DELIVERS A PUNCH IN THE FACE OF INTENSE FLAVOUR.'
– JOE PEDEN, FATBOYS

GUMBO

Joe says, 'Here's a mighty vat of gumbo to feed the crew.'

....

INGREDIENTS

2.5kg chicken thighs, diced
750g chorizo, sliced
500g prawns
24 garlic cloves, minced
4 large onions, diced
5 green peppers, diced
12 stalks celery, diced
1 cup Worcestershire sauce
3 litres water
Good amount of beef stock
1 large tin of chopped tomatoes
12 spring onions sliced
1 bunch flat leaf parsley, diced
Creole spice

METHOD

1. Brown chicken with creole spice, remove from pan.
2. Fry chorizo with creole spice, remove from pan.
3. Sauté veg with some creole spice, add Worcestershire sauce and parsley and reduce.
4. Add water, stock, chicken and chorizo. Bring to the boil and simmer for 40 minutes.
5. Add tomatoes. Simmer for 1 hour. Add spring onions, prawns, parsley, salt and pepper, and extra creole spice to taste. Then add cornflour to thicken. Enjoy!

GINGER & CHILLI

I was pretty certain that I was Ronan's biggest fan. That is, until I met Joe at Fatboys. 'He has such knowledge and passion for the style of food he makes,' Joe says. 'It really shows. No one else puts so much effort into how a stall, and all of the dishes served, looks.'

Joe continues, 'If you get something off Ronan, it'll have ten different toppings that all work so well. The flavours of the actual curry are nice and subtle but it's once you pair it with everything else, like the almonds, or coconut chutney, or pomegranate seeds, once that's all on there, this subtle dish becomes like the largest party of flavour. You look at him and you don't expect that's the kind of food he's doing, let alone how mind-blowingly good it is.' Okay, Joe, you win.

When passers-by see a restaurant is filled with diners who might originate from that cuisine's culture, it reassures them that there's a chef tucked away inside who knows exactly what he's doing. In street food it's no different. At the 2018 Scottish Street Food Awards a man

of Asian heritage strolled up to Ginger & Chilli's bright yellow trailer, Joe from Fatboys tells me, and declared, 'If my mum knew I was getting a curry off of a ginger Irish man, she would not be happy.' He returned ten minutes later to announce, 'Man, that's some of the best food I've ever had, where did you learn to cook like that?' The answer is, of course, Glasgow.

Ronan Vallelly grew up in Derry during the Troubles and moved to Glasgow in 2000 to undertake a business and information systems degree at Glasgow Caledonian University. He was big into his DJ-ing – back then he ran Off The Record at Glasgow's techno den Soundhaus and, even now, he's got his own studio at home. While becoming involved in flyer design and

web development, choosing to take on a master's degree in multi-media communication, Ronan was also getting swept up in Glasgow's food scene.

'I became so inspired by South Asian influences, and Glasgow played a big part in that. There are so many great restaurants, a delicious legacy of the city's Pakistani population,' Ronan explains. By 2014 he'd hung up his headphones and was increasingly working away over the stove. 'Living in Scotland, it soon became clear why so many view this wonderful country as one of the world's best natural larders,' Ronan says. 'Whether it's langoustines from the West Coast, pork from Bridge of Orchy or venison from Roy Bridge, I was recognising the possibilities this produce offered when fused with the Asian food that captivated me so much.'

Cooking became another creative outlet for Ronan and, being a glutton for punishment, in May 2015 he decided to cater for his own wedding, held at the picturesque *Trainspotting* location of Corrour in the Highlands. Seriously, Ronan, as if you weren't stressed enough! After providing memorable food for the wedding party over several days, Ronan realised he could really make a go of this. Enter stage right Ginger & Chilli.

'GINGER & CHILLI IS THE MOST AUTHENTIC INDIAN FOOD YOU'RE EVER GOING TO GET, AND IT'S FROM A GINGER IRISH MAN.'
– JOE PEDEN, FATBOYS

Ronan's love of cooking stems from baking soda bread with his granny in a wee kitchen in Northern Ireland, but now Ronan spends his days strolling down the aisles of Glasgow's SeeWoo Chinese supermarket or Halal butchers and greengrocers, like KRK in the West End or Strawberry Garden in Southside, in search of unusual ingredients to make his dishes pop.

'In one night, you can expect to travel from Sri Lanka to Penang, via Kerala, Phuket and Glasgow, without a plane or train in sight,' Ronan boasts. And his aromatic dishes always contain those two vital ingredients: ginger and chilli. For me, Ronan's the king of texture. He takes freshly steamed squishy bao buns and gives them an Indian makeover, loading them with fried paneer marinated in a gorgeous spice mix of achar and mango powder, Ronan's own garam masala, cumin seeds, raita and a classic Indian green chutney. Then it's topped with Asian slaw, pickled cucumbers, spring onions, more green chutney (lots of coriander, mint, ginger, garlic and a little cumin), and Ronan's mango and jaggery chutney, a piquant sweet and sour combination of mango pulp, star anise and lemongrass. It's served with a fresh herb garnish and Ronan's homemade Bombay mix – yes, he even makes his own sev (crunchy chickpea noodles to you and me). Outstanding.

Every dish Ronan creates incorporates that careful balance of sweet, sour, saltiness and spice, delivered through dozens of homemade ingredients. They're often vegetarian or vegan to encourage more sustainable choices and to prove you don't need meat to achieve deliciousness; and Ronan's poured his heart into every bite.

In many ways, he's now a victim of his own success. 'There's only one of me and, honestly, I struggle to keep up,' Ronan admits. 'I'm the brand and it's hard to find people you trust to deliver that same passion. I do everything:

accounting, marketing, social media, hiring and managing staff, running the business and cooking it all – the workload isn't sustainable.'

Ronan's made huge sacrifices in his personal life to maintain Ginger & Chilli; like a duck, he looks calm on the surface but underneath he's paddling furiously. That's the bit no one sees and it's important to address the impacts on mental health the street food industry can have.

'We can all get lulls; sometimes I feel so low I struggle to decide what to have for dinner. Between the dips in creativity, long hours serving alone and the lack of confidence from having your food constantly judged, it's hard, and it's the same across the whole industry.'

There's currently nowhere for hard-working chefs to seek help, so it's important to take time out and focus on themselves. This year Ronan's been on a ten-day silent retreat to take care of his health; though as far as his cooking's concerned, there's no need to worry. I'll say it in writing, Ronan – for you to read in moments of doubt – your food is out of this world.

Here's Ronan on the recipe that follows. 'It's a take on one of my favourite chefs, Rick Stein. I replaced the chicken with short rib of beef and bone marrow. Beef works really well and the bone marrow adds a rich depth. You could use brisket, but if you haven't tried a short rib then it's a must for beef lovers. It's a delicious cut, which we sadly underuse in the UK. For vegetarians or vegans you could substitute the beef with paneer, veggies like potatoes, peppers, cauliflower and lentils. If you don't like it spicy then use less chilli powder and omit the cayenne chillies. Seasoning your dish at the end is vital. Salt, sugar and vinegar are your friends and help transform a decent dish into an amazing dish.'

SHORT RIB OF BEEF & BONE MARROW SRI LANKAN CURRY

SERVES 4

Preparation time: 30 minutes to 1 hour
Cooking time: 3 to 4 hours

....

INGREDIENTS

FOR THE ROASTED SRI LANKAN
CURRY POWDER

1 tbsp uncooked long grain or basmati rice

50g coriander seeds

25g cumin seeds

25g fennel seeds

7.5 cm piece cinnamon stick

1½ tsp fenugreek seeds

½ tsp cloves

½ tsp cardamom seeds

½ tsp black mustard seeds

1 tsp black peppercorns

3 dried red Kashmiri chillies

CURRY

2 tbsp coconut or vegetable oil

15 cm cinnamon stick, broken into smaller
  pieces

10 cardamom pods, bruised

10 cloves

350g onions or shallots, thinly sliced

40g garlic, crushed to a paste with the
  edge of a knife

25g fresh root ginger, peeled, finely grated

2 tbsp roasted Sri Lankan curry powder

1 tsp Kashmiri chilli powder

1 tsp ground turmeric

200g canned chopped tomatoes

20 fresh curry leaves

4 x 4 cm pieces pandan leaf (available from
  Asian grocers)

1 fat lemongrass stalk, outer leaves removed,
  cut in half, lightly bruised with the edge of a
  knife

2 green cayenne chillies, split lengthways

1 tsp salt, to taste

1 tsp sugar, to taste

400ml canned coconut milk

750g–800g short rib of beef (or brisket)

200g bone marrow (optional)

1 tbsp freshly squeezed lime juice

salt and freshly ground black pepper

TO SERVE

Steamed rice and roti

RECIPE CONTINUES ON THE NEXT PAGE

METHOD

1. For the curry powder, heat a heavy-based frying pan over a medium heat. Add the rice and cook for 2 to 3 minutes, shaking the pan regularly, until the rice is toasted and pale golden-brown. Transfer the rice to a large mortar or spice grinder and leave to cool.

2. Repeat the dry-frying with the spices, then tip into a bowl and leave to cool.

3. Repeat the dry-frying with the chillies, tip into a bowl and leave to cool.

4. When the rice, spices and chillies have cooled, grind them to a fine powder. The curry powder can be stored in an airtight jar for up to three months.

5. For the curry heat the oil in a large, heavy-based casserole dish e.g. Le Creuset. Make sure it's got a lid. Add the cinnamon stick, cardamom pods cloves and curry leaves, and fry for 15 to 20 seconds until fragrant.

6. Add the onions or shallots and fry for 4 to 5 minutes until softened and pale golden brown. Add the garlic and ginger, stir well, and fry for a further 2 to 3 minutes.

7. Stir in two tablespoons of your curry powder, the chilli powder and ground turmeric and fry for a further minute.

8. Add the beef ribs and piece of marrow bone and quickly fry on all sides to get a bit of colour on the meat and bones.

9. Add the chopped tomatoes, coconut milk, pandan leaf, lemongrass stalk, cayenne chillies and salt. Cover the pan with a lid and bring the mixture to a simmer over a low to medium heat. Simmer for 3 to 4 hours until the beef is tender and starting to come off the bone. Keep an eye on the curry to make sure it doesn't dry out. If it's becoming too dry add a splash of water

10. Stir in the lime juice and remove the pan from the heat. Serve with steamed rice, coconut chutney and a roti.

SMOKEY TROTTERS KITCHEN

There are burgers, and there are burgers. Robert Lorimer's are the latter. They're the kind that'll put greasy patches on your chin and sloppily disintegrate on that short journey to and from your mouth, leaving behind remnants of crumbled black pudding or perhaps circles of pickled cucumber on the plate. Don't even try to eat them in a dignified or sophisticated manner, cutlery has no place here. Plunge in head first and surrender your chances of a second date with that hottie sat opposite you. It's the only way.

Venturing into street food wasn't the easiest task for Rob. 'The positives are you get to meet all your customers, the negatives are . . . you get to meet all your customers,' he laughs.

Before launching Smokey Trotters Kitchen in 2014, Rob had spent years working as a head chef in a county club hotel. 'I took on the job before I was ready for it,' he confesses. 'I started teaching myself from scratch and began by getting full animals in and butchering them – it was a good learning curve. I got thrown in at the deep end and, yeah, I blagged my way through it.' By the time Rob was ready to leave – equipped with enough skills to rustle up a mean à la carte of French and British fine dining staples – he'd become well and truly accustomed to working cruel hours with no customer interaction. 'Doing street food events, I realised very quickly that you need to smile all the time, and I really wasn't used to that. I'm used to being locked in a basement kitchen and leaving the waiting staff to do the chatty bit. Yeah, it was a challenge.'

Even outside of the kitchen Rob would rarely get the opportunity to meet new people. 'In most kitchens you work in, because of the rota and hours, you never get to see anyone.

For a chef to speak to people, it's really unusual. It took a little getting used to, but I do genuinely enjoy it now, it's good to get out there.'

Rob's Smokey Trotters uniform, a black branded tee printed with a rather unnerving bearded pirate wearing a chef's hat, features the endearing line 'Don't be skerd eh the berd' – that's Rob welcoming punters over to order his food and have a blether while they wait. He's a natural now, and Dockyard Social – of all of the Glasgow street food markets – is probably where you'll find him.

Given the opportunity, Rob might still shy away to the kitchen. It is his natural habitat after all. Between popping up in McChuills on the High Street, the East Village-style speakeasy Chinaski's, the Record Factory in Partick, Linen 1906 in Shawlands, Ginger Browns Gin Joint &

Kitchen in Rutherglen and – breathe – in 2019, the Dirty Duchess in Finnieston, Rob's become something of a kitchen-takeover specialist. It's a partnership that works both ways. Handing over the kitchen keys to a burgeoning street food trader allows a pub to offer more than pork scratchings and peanuts to their punters, while the managers can channel their energies into rotating beer taps, or wacky seasonal concoctions. Meanwhile, the trader bags themselves a prime location with regular income on top of sporadic events.

'It's great because the people who would typically come and find us at festivals and street food events, now know exactly where to find us on a regular basis and still get that street food experience but inside,' Rob explains. Of course, having a permanent roof over his head,

'Everyone wanted to track me down and taste the burger that won.' It brought Rob a whole new loyal burger brigade, who'd line the pub waiting to get their paws on *that* bucky-soaked beauty. Buckfast gets a bad rap in Scotland – okay, it's proven to be a young offender's drink of choice prior to committing crimes – but when that syrupy fortified wine seeps through tender pork shoulder its effects are magical.

Rob named it the Banh Mi Fae Buckfast; combining the Vietnamese word for bread (from Seb & Mili bakery, a handful of doors down from the Dirty Duchess) with a handful of meats from longstanding G.H. Davidson's butcher to create a dirty stack of chicken liver pâté, hoisin and Buckfast pulled pork, cheese smothered beef patty, garlic mayo, sriracha and pickled slaw. It's Smokey Trotters Kitchen on a plate; a hefty portion of unrestricted comfort food, maxing on the freedom that street food brings by taking inspiration from Asian, American, Korean, Indian and, of course, Scottish cooking.

'The ability to mix it up on a daily basis is epic,' Rob explains. His menu might feature everything from Korean sliders to a majestic mound of loaded fries laden with haggis, mature cheddar, peppercorn sauce and crispy onions. Even a little Mexican flair shines through; his moist yet crispy fish tacos, battered in vodka and lemonade with *pico de gallo* and sriracha atop, have a habit of making anyone's hands look small. Nae bad for a man who started off as a pot washer and got thrust into covering a commis chef when he phoned in sick. 'From that moment I was obsessed with cooking,' Rob tells me. You know what they say, if you can't stand the heat, get out of the kitchen . . . Rob's been in there ever since. Nae bad at all.

with a secure space to prepare for outdoor weddings, can be a godsend in Scottish weather conditions too.

There's no denying the potential street food has in increasing a pub's revenue. Often customers will come for the food and end up washing it down with a couple of pints; that's before we get to Smokey Trotters Kitchen's own pull. In 2017, Rob battled some pretty fierce competition, bringing home the winner's snazzy glass trophy from the 10th annual Glasgow's Best Burger Awards, only to have it accidentally smashed by a customer a few weeks later in Dockyard Social. But it still counts.

'The competition wasn't on in 2018, so technically I'm the reigning champion,' Rob laughs.

BANH MI FAE BUCKFAST

MAKES 12

Cheeseburger, pâté, Buckfast and hoisin pulled pork, garlic mayo, sriracha and pickled veg. This is a recipe for 'Scotland's best burger'. You can make the pulled pork a day in advance, and simply reheat it when you're burger-ready. There's enough here for a proper party – so invite your pals round, or pare back the quantities.

....

INGREDIENTS

FOR THE PULLED PORK
2.5kg boneless pork shoulder
500ml BBQ sauce
2 tsp smoked paprika
2 tsp ground cumin
2 tsp pepper
2 tsp brown sugar
1 tsp garlic powder
1 tsp onion powder
1 tsp salt
250ml hoisin
1 bottle Buckfast

FOR THE BURGERS
2kg chuck mince, 20% fat
   (formed into 6oz patties)

FOR THE PICKLED VEG
300ml white wine vinegar
50g caster sugar
2 carrots
2 red onions

FOR THE GARLIC MAYO
300ml mayonnaise
4 crushed cloves of garlic

FOR THE CHICKEN LIVER PÂTÉ
200g butter
2 shallots, finely chopped
2 garlic cloves, crushed
A handful of thyme leaves
400g chicken livers, roughly chopped
50ml Buckfast

RECIPE CONTINUES ON THE NEXT PAGE

METHOD

PULLED PORK

1. Mix together the smoked paprika, ground cumin, pepper, garlic powder, onion powder, and brown sugar, plus 1 tsp salt. Rub over the boneless shoulder of pork.
2. Put the pork in a big casserole dish, skin-side up, and pour in the Buckfast.
3. Cover with a lid and cook in the oven at 130°C/gas 2 for anywhere between 4 and 8 hrs until falling apart. Check every few hours in case it gets dry – if it does, add some stock or water.
4. Take it out of the oven and put the meat in a big dish, leaving the liquid in the dish.
5. Cut the skin off, then shred the meat using two forks. Toss away any fatty bits and skim any excess fat off the surface of the sauce.
6. Add 500ml good smoky BBQ sauce and the 250ml hoisin to the casserole, mix it in, reduce to a nice sticky consistency.
7. Put the pulled pork back in the casserole with the juices so it stays moist. Season to taste. .

PICKLED VEG

1. Heat the vinegar, add sugar and dissolve. Allow to cool. Grate the carrots, thinly slice the onions and add both to your pickle juice. Allow at least 2 hours in fridge.

CHICKEN LIVER PÂTÉ

1. Put 100g butter, shallots, garlic and thyme in a pan and fry gently for 7 minutes.
2. Add the chicken livers and cook gently for another 5 minutes.
3. Add the Buckfast and cook for a further minute, then tip it all into a food processor.
4. Blitz until smooth, season, then add the remaining butter and blitz again. Sieve into a bowl and put into the fridge. Give it a couple of hours to set.

TIME TO MAKE THOSE BURGERS!

1. Season the burgers on both sides with plenty of salt and pepper.
2. Pan fry in hot vegetable oil or barbecue for 2 minutes on each side for medium or 5 minutes for well done.
3. While cooking the burgers reheat your pulled pork in the hoisin and Buckfast BBQ sauce. Do this in a small pan or microwave.
4. Place two slices of mature cheddar on top of each burger and put under a hot grill to melt.
5. Slice the buns in half and toast lightly under the grill. Spread pâté on the bottom half of each bun before placing the burgers on the bases. Top with pulled pork and pickled veg. Then add as much garlic mayo and sriracha as you see fit before placing the lids on top.
6. Get it in yer gub!

BABU KITCHEN

My life up until 27 April 2019 would have been considerably tastier had I discovered Babu Kitchen's naanwich earlier. (Put this book down and run, don't walk, people!) It was on that fateful, overcast day in Paisley when I was first drawn, like a moth to a flame, to the kitsch and colourful yellow trailer, serving up *those* Bombay street food delights. Sinking my teeth into that fluffy herbed-up naan, a cornucopia of flavour exploded in my mouth. 'It's made with twenty-five spices,' the obliging server told me. 'If you're ordering just one thing, it's got to be the naanwich; it's got a cult following.'

Indeed, she wasn't wrong. The couple behind me were visiting from England, and they'd heard they had to sample the one with succulent masala roasted chicken. Others might opt for Shetland haddock masala naanwich, or perhaps the vegan tattie pattie, or indeed forgo the unparalleled sandwich and tuck into crunchy clouds of pakora followed by the growing heat of a chickpea chole, that's served in a roti, garnished with lime, red onion and fresh coriander. It's all superb.

We've already established Glasgow's sultry love affair with Indian food, but our relationship with Babu Kitchen moves beyond that. Each bite evokes feelings that, at least towards food, you wouldn't think possible. There's turmeric, garlic, gently sautéed onions, citrus, sour yoghurt, fragrant coriander, fenugreek, red chilli and that's only skimming the surface; unravelling those layers of texture and spice is a gastronomic journey, one that's likely to steal the limelight from whatever gig you're attending. Rachna Dheer has been pioneering Glasgow's street food scene for years. She started off hustling at

farmers markets back in 2007, though looking at her you'd never guess she'd been around that long. Really, it's shameful I hadn't discovered her sooner. Born in Bombay, now Mumbai, Rachna understands authentic Indian cooking like no other, and truly it's worlds away from what we might find in the Balti House down the road. If you'll pardon the pun, she's streets ahead. This is Rachna's story.

Q&A

WHEN DID YOU MOVE TO THE UK?

I was eleven when I came to London. My parents were classical Indian dancers; Dad taught dancing for the Bollywood movies, they had their own troupe that performed all over India. I grew up in that environment, going to film sets with Dad, dancing around, having fun.

WHERE DID YOU LEARN TO COOK?

I learned to cook from my parents; they were really into food. We used to cook things together and I was the prep chef who peeled and chopped onions, diced the garlic. I would always ask 'What's going in next? And why?' and 'Why does it take so long?' We grew up cooking and eating together. When my parents went to perform, my sister and I were left to our own devices. One day I went to a local butcher, picked up a chicken, marinated it in yogurt and tandoori spices, grilled it and then had it as a snack. That's my first memory of making my own food.

My dad tells a good story about his foodie background. When he was a boy, he was sent to the butcher to get two kilos of lamb and his grandad said, 'Now remember, do not get lamb from two different animals, get it from the same animal.' But my dad, being a child, didn't really care. He brought the lamb home, his granny cooked it and they ate it – after his first bite, his grandad gave Dad a wallop and said, 'I told you not to get lamb from two different animals!'

The same cut from two animals cook very differently depending on how they're grown, how they're cut, how long they've been dead. That's why one will be tough, and another tender: like humans, they're not the same. My great grandad could taste the difference and he passed that palate on to my dad. I hope I've got it too.

My home-style curries and pakora are inspired by what I grew up eating. I use Mum's green chilli and coriander chutney, and my auntie's red chilli chutney is in the naanwich. A lot of my family recipes run through the menu.

HOW DID COOKING BECOME YOUR PROFESSION?

My family and I moved to Glasgow when I was nineteen, and I've always made food for my friends and family here. They used to say, 'You're a great cook, you should open a restaurant,' but you think they're only saying that because they're your friends. Then I met Gail who's a graphic designer; she ate my food and said, 'You know what, your food is amazing. I'm not just

saying it; if you want to do something, I'll design your brand for you.' I was blown away!

I went for it. The smallest risk I could take was to go to Queen's Park Farmers Market – the pitch fee was £60 and I thought, I'll take one empty pot, buy all the ingredients and cook it there on the spot. I bought local, organic produce from the market and I cooked. I told myself, if I don't sell out today, that's the universe telling me, 'Game over, kid,' but if I do sell out, then perhaps I should actually go for it.

So, I cooked a vegetarian dish called Pav Bhaji, my favourite street food dish ever – I grew up eating it on Juhu Beach in Bombay. The best thing is, in Glasgow they make these delicious Morton rolls (morning rolls: crispy on the outside, squidgy inside). In India, Pav means roll and the Bhaji is the curry. We eat the Bhaji with a toasted, buttery roll – so I was looking for the same sort of consistency here. The Morton roll was it! The dish is a great combination of Indian and Scottish, street food roots going back to Bombay but with a Scottish twist. People loved that I was using an ordinary morning roll, in a totally different way. We pan-fry the roll or Pav in butter then serve it on the side of the Bhaji, which is a proper Indian curry made with butter, mixed veg like cauliflower, peas and capsicum alongside chilli, tomatoes, lime, coriander. You use the roll to scoop up the Bhaji, it's delicious. Oh, and I sold out.

WHERE DID YOUR STREET FOOD JOURNEY TAKE YOU?

I stuck to my word and did another farmers market, and the dishes kept on growing – there was an appetite for something different to the usual dirty curry people were used to. Eventually,

I had enough money to open a shop in West Regent Street in 2013. Until I started, there was no such thing as street food in Scotland. There were no markets, street food events or other traders, nobody was doing what I was doing. People now are so lucky; even Glasgow has three regular places for people to trade at.

In the early days, it wasn't easy. There was a constant battle between the food served in Indian restaurants and the food I'm doing. Mine is the sort of food I would make at home — if my mum came and ate my food, I'd want her to be proud of it. I'm creating something real, that we'd typically cook at home and you would find out on the streets of Bombay.

If you want what you get in a restaurant, don't come to me — you'll be disappointed. We make our dishes without oil. People always say, 'Oh, you don't put oil in your food.' No I don't, my food is delicious without oil. 'That's not very Indian,' they'll say, because Indian food is associated with curries floating in oil in UK restaurants. That's not what I'm doing here.

We had the shop for five years but didn't renew the lease. The scene had moved on so much and we had the opportunity to go back to our roots. All the cooking, travelling, setting up, cleaning up, going home to start cooking again: it's crazy but I totally love it. That might change as I get older, but right now it's amazing.

WHAT ARE THE POSITIVES AND NEGATIVES OF STREET FOOD?

People like you, Ailidh, and your reactions to my naanwich! It makes my day to see so many people enjoying my food and running back to tell me how brilliant it is. It's very flattering, but a real negative is people copying you. There's

the physical work: it gets extremely tiring at times.

Thirdly, and this is the big one, the organisers have noticed the increasing demand for street food pitches and so they hike up their prices massively. They're charging far too much, and if this continues I can see people stopping street food and regressing back to rubbish burgers. I'm worried punters think we charge lots because we're greedy, but it's because we have to pay so much to be there. Most of the people I know in street food cook from their homes and it's hard work, but they are so passionate about it and want others to share their passion.

WHAT'S NEXT FOR BABU KITCHEN?

I've done Babu Kitchen for over ten years and now I'm branching out. People have said, 'We want Babu, we love it,' but then at the actual gig, business-wise, it's terrible for me. Forty per cent of people like proper Indian food the rest like something plain, they'll have kids or older people, and often only foodies will take the risk.

So, I want to be able to sell something people will buy straight away, without thinking about it. I'm launching several brands; I want to do a taco truck, and I recently launched Poke Gourmet Loaded Fries. It's a cheaper produce and it appeals to more people; I had to branch out for financial survival — I give people want they want, and I do it really well, with amazing toppings. Poke makes far more money than Babu, that's the reality. I've got another brand called Mucky Face Churros; they go down well. Who doesn't love freshly fried churros?! I'll decide which brand goes to each gig depending on the audience. But Babu Kitchen will never stop, that's my passion project.

GALLUS PASTA

No one cuts shapes like Jules McGuire. Her fresh pasta is a work of art, even when bundled high on cardboard-like Vegware Bagasse plates. Customers line up for slippery pillows of ravioli stuffed with spinach and ricotta that bursts with a perfectly cooked oozing egg yolk, combining with sage butter to form indulgent ochre puddles on the plate. Or there's miles of hand-cut silky ribbons, coated in Jules's eight-hour slow-cooked pork and beef ragu. 'One *taglierini con sugo di carne*,' she'll eloquently announce. It's worthy of being framed and hung in the GoMA.

Getting into street food was 'one big happy accident' for Jules. She was given pasta dough instead of play-doh at her grandad Nonno Leno's house at the ripe age of three, and you could say it stuck. 'I wanted to get better at it, so I challenged myself to make a kilo of dough every day for a year, just for fun' she laughs. 'I didn't expect that over 365 kilos of dough later, I'd be making it on this scale. It's crazy.'

Jules graduated with a degree in accounting, and had recently been working in her partner's tattoo parlour . . . so you can understand why

Jules's dad nicknamed her Gallus Alice; she really is bold enough to try anything! Jules started documenting her pasta journey on Instagram – from intricate culurgiones, scarpi-nocc and fagottini to more familiar shapes like ravioli and farfelle – take a look and you'll soon realise that not a single moment in her daily 18-hour pasta production goes wasted. It's no wonder the team at Platform pleaded with her to open a stall the second they first saw her Instagram account.

'So that's my story; within three weeks of

chatting to Platform I'd bought all of the catering equipment and had fully set up.' She began serving her Nonno's ragu to the good people of Glasgow in August 2018 and six months later mission impastable was completed (sorry, I couldn't help myself). Jules had officially handmade in excess of 365 kilos of dough.

This is proper Italian cookery. It's nothing like the sort you'd find in microwave meals nor the kind typically served in restaurants. Why? Well, Jules is desperate to the keep the traditions of pasta making alive. You won't find tortellini on Jules's menu unless it's served stuffed with Parmigiano Reggiano and the proper mix of prosciutto, mortadella and pork loin, all swimming in *brodo* (homemade chicken broth), as it would be in Bologna or Modena.

'Sticking to regional traditions is the mainstay of Gallus; I could never have carbonara on my menu because it's not a fresh pasta dish, it's traditionally made with dried pasta. That's something I want to drive home – the differences between dried pasta and fresh pasta.'

There's nowhere to hide with pasta; the quality of those two ingredients makes all the difference between miserable, uninviting grey dough, and . . . Jules's. In Platform, her most asked question is, 'Why is your pasta so yellow?' It's because she works with a local Italian supplier to import her eggs and flour.

'Italians feed their chickens with the yolk in mind, they'll feed them things high in carotene: carrots, sweetcorn, and even their own eggs shells for calcium, giving the yolks that vibrant colour and higher fat content,' she explains.

Meanwhile her dough is a mix of Tipo 00 and finely milled semolina remacinata, her meat is from her trusty butcher, Donald's in Uddingston, and her menu centres around the fresh vegetables and herbs found every week in Blochairn Market. 'Beyond those two top ingredients, I just put everything into it. I hate to sound so cheesy, but it's passion. I absolutely love pasta, and I hope that that comes across in every dish.' Yes, it's confirmed. Jules's pasta might be the best you ever eat.

FUJISAN

Ian and Chihara are nothing short of a dream team. They met through a mutual friend at a music festival in Tokyo in 2006. He was teaching in an international kindergarten; she was working as a chef in various restaurants in the capital. They immediately hit it off and years later, after getting married and having a baby daughter, the family moved out to Minami-Yono in Saitama.

Every summer the town centre would come alive for a matsuri, an annual five-day festival flooded with dance, Japanese drumming and carnival festivities, with each side of the roads lined with toy vendors and street food stalls. In 2014, Ian and Chihara were asked if they wanted to do a pop-up and, of course, they jumped at the opportunity. With a very simple set-up – a table under a gazebo with no more than the necessary equipment. Knowing that the festival would be saturated with Japanese fare, they rustled up an Indian chicken curry.

'It was a huge hit,' Ian recalls, 'and we were invited back the next year, and then the following year too. We'd caught the bug for it, so while preparing for our move back to Scotland, we knew we definitely wanted to work together and thought that street food could be the option.'

In April 2017, after jumping through hoops to organise visas, Ian moved the family back to his home turf. Big Feed had just started and, having read about the success of Edinburgh's Harajuku Kitchen, Ian and Chihara realised that it was about time the people of Glasgow got to experience some authentic Japanese cooking, too.

Five years ago, you would have been forgiven

for thinking that Japanese food was just sushi and ramen. It's all Scotland had really known until an influx of Japanese and fusion restaurants popped up. Even now it's still maki- and sashimi-centric, the popping colours of grade A tuna and salmon, intermingled with blobs of wasabi and flying fish roe-topped avocado and prawn tempura rolls, all presented on an extravagant bamboo boat, are just far too pretty not to snap and share on social media. But, beyond the popular sushi porn hashtag, our western palates have been opened up to the likes of yakitori, chicken karaage and katsu curry. We've probably got to thank that overpriced Japanese chain for introducing us to the latter; they rolled out the aromatic panko breadcrumbed dish across the UK, setting a benchmark for Fujisan to surpass.

'It's everywhere now, even Greggs are doing a chicken katsu bake,' Ian laughs. So, when considering their menu, Ian wanted to serve the approachable dishes that he'd enjoyed eating in Japan and knew that the people of Scotland were slowly becoming accustomed to back home. 'I mean our *karaage don* is just fried chicken on rice, what Glaswegian isn't going to love that,' he jokes. There's more to it than that though: these bitesize crispy morsels are topped with their signature tangy lemon and spring onion 'Pac-Man sauce'. The flavours are insane and, judging by reactions I've witnessed at both Big Feed and Canteen, Ian was spot on: the people do love it.

Starting up in a city, without a single contact in its street food circuit, isn't the easiest task. Once Ian and Chihara had purchased a horsebox and found the right people to help them convert it, they just needed to get a foot in the door.

'We got our first job in December 2017 at the arts venue SWG3 and then immediately after that Kyle from Dockyard Social got in touch, so we became regulars there and did the odd pop-up at Big Feed too. In the New Year everything changed from us emailing folk constantly, to us suddenly getting approached for events,' Ian recalls. 'Once other traders heard about us, the support was phenomenal. Everyone looks out for one another and if there's a job going that we think someone else might be available for or more suited to, it'll get passed on.'

Fujisan – named after the volcano and a song the couple liked from a Japanese band called Denki Groove – is now their full-time gig. Three events a month is a good balance between quality time with their daughter and earning a comfortable wage, and the couple have worked out how they can do it all themselves. Quite rightly, Chiharu's incredibly proud of her cooking, with her family recipes passed down through generations.

'It's not that she wouldn't trust someone else to do it, but she'd be worried the quality of the product might not be as high as she wants it to be,' Ian says.

So, what you should you order from the talented chef? The pork katsu curry is Ian's favourite and most recommended dish. 'It comprises both Japanese and Western elements, which mirrors what Fujisan is, representing the street food trailer and the people who run it,' he says. Or you should get their Nagoya-style fried chicken wings, a regional dish from Niigata, with crispy fried wings tossed in a sweet garlic soy and black pepper glaze. It's truly unique. No one else in Britain does it.

PRIME STREET FOOD

All the traders I've met thus far have crafted one singular menu with a handful of dishes, but Scott Gibson of Prime Street Food has almost thirty. There's the vegan menu where a Vegware pot delivers an impressively comforting chick pea and sweet potato stew, alongside more experimental dishes like crispy jerk tofu wings. There's the page dedicated to enhancing beef dripping fries with one portion topped with wasabi sour cream, seaweed and sesame, while another is given the Canadian treatment with chunks of cheese curds and crispy bacon all swimming in unctuous beef gravy; and there's the 'hearty menu' where a pork belly Asian broth joins melt-in-the-mouth beef goulash with sourdough bread – just what the doctor ordered on a bitterly cold, quintessentially Scottish afternoon.

Of course, only one menu is ever displayed at once, that'd just be overwhelming otherwise, but it'll be chosen according to the audience because, as Scott explains, 'Some places in Scotland aren't quite ready for street food. It means that I can create more extravagant menus for the places where adventurous dishes are welcomed, but tone it down in others.'

It's not that he's indecisive. Far from it. Scott has been working in restaurants and four-star hotels since the age of fourteen, and a huge chunk of his career was spent abroad, working in nine different countries, becoming hugely inspired by the global street foods encountered along the way. 'I've managed to sandwich both my passions into one. I travel and I cook; now I get to change up my menus all the time to reflect that,' he says.

You might naturally presume, with such an extensive repertoire, that some corners are being cut along the way. Admittedly, this was my initial assumption until I realised that Scott won't even use shop-bought mayonnaise. 'I catered at the Independence March up at Bannockburn and some guy was complaining about the price of my burger,' Scott recalls. 'I was trying to explain to him that the same product is £15, over double the price, just down the road in a restaurant and he replied, "That's a restaurant, that's why," but I'd actually worked in that restaurant before so happily told him that our burgers were worlds apart. Mine isn't just a burger, every single thing in it is either locally sourced or handmade from start to finish. He shrugged at me and said, "Okay," then walked off. Sometimes in street food I find you've got to explain yourself, when really you shouldn't have to. He bought the burger and did come back afterwards to say it was good, to be fair to him.'

> 'YOU'VE GOT TO PUT PRIME STREET FOOD IN THE BOOK! SCOTT ALWAYS CHANGES HIS STYLE OF CUISINE, HE'S BANG ON WITH HIS CHEFFING SKILLS AND HE'S JUST SO HILARIOUSLY, BRUTALLY HONEST. WHAT A MAN!'
> – FRANCESCO, WANDERERS KNEADED.

Scott will make everything from scratch unless it makes sense to outsource it. 'Perthshire Preserves [who have their own stall at Edinburgh's Stockbridge Market] are unbeatable. If I'm not making the chutneys or relishes, I get them to supply it, they've won sixty or so awards for their marmalades and relishes,' he says – while vessels like the blue corn taco, are best left to the experts in Mexico. Scott loads

them with Ayrshire pork cooked three ways – cured, roasted and confited – brushed with a Gochujang Korean chilli paste, topped with his own pickled vegetables and a sprinkle of sesame seeds. The dish is Mexico-meets-Korea, and it's delicious.

'There's a massive difference with Scottish pork in terms of flavour, texture and even when you're cooking it. It has a different smell – this might sound crazy – but it's not as stressed as the animals you get elsewhere,' Scott laughs. Some traders have confessed to being cooks, but it's undeniable that Scott, on the other hand, is a chef.

After working in Sweden, Canada, Ireland, France, Austria, Greece, Cambodia, Australia and New Zealand, gradually picking up new cooking techniques, Scott returned to Scotland in February 2017 and immediately went on the hunt for a truck. During the time he'd spent in Scandinavia, working as a baker and pastry chef, he'd slowly fallen in love with Swedish fare. So, that was Prime Street Food's original theme.

Scott began with portions of handmade lingonberry meatballs followed by *kanelbullar* (or cinnamon buns to you and me) accompanied by custard. Unfortunately, it just didn't work.

'For a long time, I've been testing the waters to see what people are prepared to eat,' he explains. 'I was selling these pork cheeks with apple chutney coleslaw all over Scotland and no one would eat them. So, I removed the word cheek and just called it slow cooked pork and just like that it became a bestseller. It's funny how they'd forgo a pork cheek and buy a crap hot dog from the trader next door, which is made of 96 per cent of a pig, including the arsehole. So, they'll eat an arsehole but not a cheek. Seriously?!'

At first Scott found the street food scene tough; it's a minefield of good and bad events, and often it's not what you know but who you know. 'I've been at the Scottish Street Food Awards for the past three years, but I normally avoid some of the markets where there can be ten traders and only 500 people. You can't really get profit from that,' he tells me.

So, while he's based in Stirling and often roams between Glasgow and Edinburgh, sometimes travelling up north too, there's every possibility that you could go a whole year without crossing his path. It's bad luck for us, but thankfully the Prime Street Food Facebook page keeps us informed of Scott's whereabouts should you wish to track him down wherever he might be.

'LOTS OF US VENDORS BUY THESE EXPENSIVE, BIODEGRADABLE DISHES AND THEN THERE'S NO BINS PROVIDED FOR THEM AT EVENTS SO THEY CAN'T ACTUALLY BE COMPOSTED. OR SOMETIMES THERE ARE BINS BUT CUSTOMERS JUST THROW THEM IN GENERAL WASTE. BOTH THE EVENT ORGANISERS AND THE ATTENDEES HAVE TO UP THEIR GAME!'
– SCOTT GIBSON

THE ONLY VEGAN MAYO RECIPE YOU'RE EVER GOING TO NEED

These are my words not Scott's –
I made the mayo and it was lush.

....

INGREDIENTS

150ml water from tinned chick peas
1 tsp white wine vinegar
½ tsp wholegrain mustard
2 sprigs thyme, finely chopped
2 garlic cloves
330ml good quality oil

METHOD

1. Apart from the oil, mix all the ingredients together using a hand blender.
2. Add the oil slowly to the mixture until it thickens, then season to taste.

VEGAN & GLUTEN-FREE CHICKPEA BURGER

INGREDIENTS

MAKES 4

240g tin of chickpeas, drained
20g gluten-free flour or plain flour
1 lemon, zested and juiced
2 cloves of garlic, diced
3 sprigs of thyme
1 sprig of rosemary, finely chopped

METHOD

1. Mix all the ingredients together and use your hands to form into a loose ball.
2. Shape the mix into roughly four burgers. If the mix is too wet, add some more flour.
3. Pan-fry the burgers in a little oil, flipping to ensure both sides are evenly cooked.
4. Optionally add vegan cheese or cheddar to each burger, then remove from the pan once the cheese is melted.
5. Serve in a fresh squishy brioche roll. Scott's Vegan mayo goes brilliantly with this.

FLAMING INDULGENCE

Now we're heading south from Glasgow . . . It takes quite a woman to single-handedly fly the street food flag for Ayrshire, wood-firing hundreds of thin and crispy Roman-style pizzas each week . . . let alone a woman who has previously conquered the world on a bicycle. But then, Rhona Quarm, fondly known as the Pizza Lady is not just any woman.

Rhona pays above average for her pizza's vegetable toppings, including curly kale, fresh basil and courgette, from the Auchincruive walled garden. The community allotments there are supported by Gardening Leave, a charity that uses horticulture as therapy to support veterans experiencing PTSD. Rhona always pops a few extra coins in the honesty box to show her appreciation for their hard work. She's pure salt of the earth.

When Flaming Indulgence first took off, Rhona's mum was mortified – 'Pizza? You're going to sell pizza on the streets?' – but just a few bites later Margaret was convinced otherwise.

'She'd had a stroke and her speech wasn't brilliant,' says Rhona. 'The van didn't have any graphics back then, so she kept saying "Rhona, when are you getting the hieroglyphics?" When she passed away it felt only right to dedicate the van to her. It has "In loving memory of Maggie May" written on both doors – I guess the van's called Maggie May.'

Support for Rhona's new venture came thick and fast. After a holiday to Tasmania, which escalated into helping out at a friend's tavern, Rhona's passion for wood-fired pizzas was ignited.

'I was Cordon Bleu trained a good thirty years ago and have my own traditional catering service called Pure Indulgence. But in just one week I was so attracted to the idea of going back to basics and cooking on wood that, after lots of research, upon returning to the UK I met up with a man called Jay at Bushman Wood Fired Ovens.'

Named by the *Daily Telegraph* as 'the wood fire oven guru' – and for good reason – there are few British pizza enthusiasts who Jay hasn't kitted out. Instantly, Rhona was introduced to renowned traders from all over the UK including Birmingham-based Bare Bones who willingly shared years of experience and advice, before offering Rhona a shift in their mobile pizzeria.

'Mike was great about the set-up of his van,' she explains, 'and even pointed out things that were wrong. He said do this, don't do that. I'm hugely grateful; thanks to them, my van is laid out really well; there's a perfect work flow.'

Meanwhile, back in East Lothian, Chris of the Big Blu pizza van who's years ahead on the street food scene, constantly passes on to Rhona events that he can't make. They're practically competitors and yet his website's contact form reads, 'We generally take bookings throughout the East and South of Scotland. For bookings on the West Coast please contact Rhona Quarm of Flaming Indulgence.' If ever an example was needed to demonstrate the sheer camaraderie of the street food community, then look no further.

So, since 2016, Rhona's been challenging South Ayrshire's presumptions of takeaway pizza from a van, and as the only longstanding trader in the area, she's probably changed quite a few prejudices about the freshness and quality of street food too. Though, in more recent years, it's Rhona who's been surprised.

'I typically work all year round,' she says, 'and then take six weeks off at the beginning of the year, when it's cold and dark, to go travelling. I never thought that people would keep coming to me in the winter, but then there was a sudden influx of messages asking where I was and when I'd be back trading. When it's baltic, people will even jump in the car and drive to wherever I am, pop out to order, and then sit back in the warmth of their car to eat.'

In March 2019, Rhona broke her leg mountain biking in New Zealand. 'Thank goodness,' she says, putting on a brave face, 'imagine just tripping over a pavement and denying the people four whole months of pizza! At least I've got a decent story.' The sick leave has been nerve-racking at times, though ultimately it's given Rhona the opportunity to properly reflect on the future of her business.

Letting go of the reins is possibly one of the hardest milestones for a trader; it's the only time the business will double in size overnight. But since Rhona's rushed off her feet at both her Maidens and Ayr Racecourse pitches, with weekend wedding requests filling up her inbox, it's time to expand!

'It's the perfect opportunity to get a second van that's purely for weddings, like a beautiful vintage van. That was always the dream but you've got to find a compromise between practicality and aesthetic; Citroën H vans are lovely but it's amazing how many people have told me the problems they've had, the engine failures, the breakdowns on the way to gigs ... but for local weddings it wouldn't need to travel too far.'

A second van, focused entirely on private events, would mean that the current oak-lined Peugeot Boxer can attend a third or fourth midweek pitch; and, thanks to South Ayrshire's flexible stance on trading, that's perfectly plausible.

'It's such a shame because there's massive pitch fees for any events here that are unaffordable for small businesses. I'm not mass production, I'm quality and service. The council aren't hugely encouraging of small businesses. So, I'm best off trading on the streets, though there are still lots of rules. I'm not allowed on the main streets or within the centre of towns, and you've got to be careful on certain junctions in terms of where's safe to trade, plus there's a limit on how close you can be to the beach.'

Little does Rhona know that South Ayrshire council are more progressive in their views on street food than most other areas in Scotland. The ability to rock up and trade on a street is golden. But what about the staff? A second van will require a whole new team.

'I've got to the stage now where I need to train up more people to run the vans as it's currently only me that drives ... I didn't think I was a control freak, but perhaps I am. It's because I put so much into trading and I'm so passionate about it: I worry that part-time staff wouldn't have the same passion. And it'll take a while to find the right person who can also be great to the customers. When you're flat out serving a huge line-up, juggling 25 jobs each, maintaining that customer interaction is so important.'

This is arguably Rhona's unique selling point. It explains why customers will venture out into the blistering wind, driving past warm restaurants, to eat her pizza. Of course, it goes without saying that they're the real deal. The pizzas are topped with Mutti pasata, beautiful Bonnet goats' cheese from Dunlop Dairy and sausages, haggis or sometimes even meatballs from Dalduff Farm. But it's the way Rhona chats to customers, taking a genuine interest in how they are, working tirelessly with a smile on her face and still finding time to pop up cute Facebook videos for her followers. Really, it's no wonder Rhona's developed a name for herself in the community.

'What I love about street food is the interaction with customers; obviously if you're a chef you're always hidden in the kitchen and struggle to ever see a customer. That side of Flaming Indulgence will always be very special.'

Ayrshire's street food scene is looking a little thin on the ground, but if Rhona's worked out that 'street trading is a simpler formula that means you don't need to do 50-hour weeks' then the rest of the county will surely catch on. 'Ayrshire's street food scene is about to take off. It's about to explode.' I certainly hope you're right, Rhona.

SHAWARMARAMA

There's a joke in my family, which probably stems from that time Dad picked me and my friends up from a party, and I badgered him to take us to a kebab house on the way home. I'm famed for my late-night donna escapades. Even now I'll plot my nights out according to which kebab shops are in the vicinity and, yes, I am prepared to leave a bar early if it means getting my greasy chicken and garlic mayo fix prior to hitting the hay. I've got a kebab radar and Glasgow's Shawarmarama have been on it for a while.

Actually, it's almost insulting to compare the divine juiciness of a Shawarmarama kebab to the ones I've been known to consume at 3 a.m. There's cumin-spiced brisket, which might just be the most succulent strands of beef that'll ever glide across your tongue, elevated by the fiery heat of 'Yemenite Dynamite', a fresh and bright homemade zhug loaded with coriander and garlic. Vegetarians and vegans might opt for the falafel wrap. Not the beige balls of death that get lodged in your throat and often propel you to snatch a drink out of the hands of an innocent passer-by (look, I'm a drama queen, okay?). No,

these are delightful cauliflower and pea bites wrapped in proper Lebanese flatbread – from the Baker's House – that has been generously smeared with a roasted pepper, coriander and walnut muhammara.

If you were to lock me in a room, with a tub of that chunky Syrian dip and a spoon for company, I'd be a very contented woman. I'm making it all sound very simple. There's also bucket loads of intense flavour, delivered by fresh spices straight out of Glasgow's Strawberry & Spice Garden and Babylon, to mirror a genuinely authentic Middle Eastern experience.

Louise Olivarius knows, quite literally, the recipe for street food success. 'A business must be that wee bit different and it needs to serve something for all dietary requirements, like vegan and gluten-free,' she explains. 'I think the healthier the food, the more attractive it is, and crucially the whole thing must be exceptional value for money.' Shawarmarama caters for Glasgow's diversity with halal chicken, and she's not messing on that last point. It feels like their shawarmas weigh more than a human baby; you'll want to hold it protectively in your arms and show it off to your friends.

Shawarmarama is more than an outlet serving dense and delicious kebabs, it's a culmination of smart business decisions. Louise and her husband Chris ran the well-known Finnieston pizza pub, Firebird, for seven years. During that time, they'd watched street food flourish in London and realised that, with a few contacts

from Louise's days of working at festivals, they could take the Firebird pizza product outdoors to events. With the freedom of a Piaggio Ape and Firebird's head chef, Thomas Preston, in tow, they hit the roads, catering Tiree Music Festival and the posh tepees at T in the Park. Needless to say, it was almost too much of a success; other entrepreneurs had cottoned on to pizza's profitability and Scotland's street food arena became a little too pizza-centric for the trio's liking. So, what could they do next? Well, before meeting Louise, Chris was executive chef of the Bar Soba group; between that and travelling, he was an expert in Vietnamese, Thai and Malaysian cuisine. Bingo, Nom Nam was born. It's like nom nom nom, the sound of enjoyment echoing from a mouth full of tasty food, but with a little Nam thrown in, naturally.

As purveyors of South East Asian delights (on top of pizza), they rocked up to the

Edinburgh Fringe in 2017; the year the street food in George Square suddenly got good. There were trays of sweet potato and aubergine curry, glowing from the silky turmeric and coconut milk sauce, vibrant Vietnamese pork shoulder *bahn mis* and piping hot pork, ginger and chive gyozas; a huge step-up from previous festival fare.

'But then everyone else caught up, and we noticed lots of new traders doing that style of cooking,' Louise explains. 'We go to London once or twice a year to see restaurants, eat street food and be influenced. We go to cities like New York, places where these ideas develop long before they make their way up to Scotland.' After a particular visit, Chris and Louise realised that Middle Eastern food was taking off on the streets. They'd been regulars at Dockyard Social and had done the odd stint at Big Feed, but they were yet to muscle their way into Platform, because Platform do their own pizza and already had a South-East Asian stall. 'We gave some real thought as to how we could get into Platform; it's on every weekend and we wanted to be there.

'As no one else was doing it, Middle Eastern street food was just the ticket. Iron Man speaks my language when he says, "You ever tried shawarma? There's a shawarma joint about two blocks from here, I don't know what it is, but I want to try it." That's Robert Downey Jr's line as he's saving the world in *The Avengers* – is there ever a wrong time to think about shawarmas? So, Shawarmarama, its name inspired by that iconic scene, took off in July 2018.

While their street food brands were evolving, Louise and Chris's restaurant and pub weren't doing so well. 'It was a depressing time for hospitality businesses,' Louise tells me. Giving up their bricks and mortar was daunting, but they stepped away from Firebird and passed the keys on from McPhabbs. 'We'd gone from employing 35 people to it being me, Chris and our business partner, Thomas. I'm operation-focused, Chris is kitchen-focused and Thomas is the perfect mix of both; without him, we'd spend our time arguing,' she laughs.

It's gone from strength to strength. Firebird Al Fresco rebranded to Nomad Pizza (yes, that's the wood-fired sourdough at Big Feed), and they joined forces with Rachna of Babu Kitchen to rent a railway arch unit. 'Doing street food out of domestic premises isn't the easiest; you've got to have space to cook, store and refrigerate the food. We once offered our peers Fujisan a big event and they had to turn it down for lack of room to prep; so, what comes first? The chicken or the egg? We knew Rachna was in the same boat and we took the plunge together,' Louise says.

There's no exact science to it. Some traders use street food as a stepping stone into bricks and mortar while our trio revel in the freedom it brings. They'll continue to expand their offering and pioneer Glasgow's scene according to consumer trends: the beauty of street food is there's very little holding them back.

'We kept our trailer plain with changeable branding so we could use it for either Nom Nam or Shawarmarama, but we've also got a tent set-up. So much has changed since we bought our pizza van in 2012 – people are willing to travel out to Govan, where there's nothing to do except eat street food. We used to accept every gig we were offered including pizza parties for a handful of people. Those are such time wasters. Scotland tends to be four seasons in one day and that can be a challenge, so we go to events where there's a guaranteed number of people, and we know how many other traders will be there, so we can make an educated guess on how much we're going to sell. That's much better than turning up without a guaranteed footfall,' Louise explains.

The trio are booked out every weekend for the forseeable future, with jobs for each of the brands, but there'll always be Louise, Chris or Thomas at the helm. 'It's important people know we're a husband, wife and friend team; that they understand our story and taste our personalities coming through the food. That's so crucial and we'd always want to maintain that relationship.'

What's next for Glasgow's street food scene? Louise is convinced street food will continue its take-over. 'Interestingly, I was on a panel of experts talking about how shopping centres were changing their food halls to become more like indoor street food markets,' she says. 'It was hosted by Threesixty Architecture, and I met a chap from Market Halls, who have three down in London and are looking to introduce the proposition to Glasgow.'

That might have a huge impact on the likes of Platform, but it's another opportunity for keen cooks, who don't have their own premises, to try their hand in this thriving climate. Market Hall's website reads 'pull up a chair and enjoy the buzz of a new era for British dining', so I guess we'll have to wait and see . . . in this fast-paced industry, I doubt we'll be waiting long.

SHAWARMARAMA SEASONING

Here's all you need if you're slow roasting lamb, beef or chicken and want to zhuzh it up with a little Shawarmarama flair.

....

INGREDIENTS

5 cardamom pods

3 cloves

¾ tsp fennel seeds

10g coriander seeds, toasted and ground

20g cumin seeds, toasted and ground

¼ tsp dried chilli flakes

¼ tsp ground pepper

18g table salt

25g soft dark brown sugar

2 tsp cinnamon

¾ tbsp ground ginger

1½ tsp ground turmeric

METHOD

1. Combine ingredients together in a bowl. This recipe makes 150g, so it'll go a long way! You can store it in a screw-top jar.

FIFE & ANGUS

_____

I'll never forget my road trip venturing across the shiny new Queensferry Crossing with my best friend, Heather, in search of the unmissable traders who are making a name for themselves in the unexpected pockets within Fife & Angus. The Kooks were playing full blast and the sun was beating down on a deceptively sunny March day. Then we passed that majestic 'Welcome to The Kingdom of Fife' sign, complete with an overarching rainbow. Glorious.

While I'm conscious of lumping Fife & Angus into the same chapter, I feel it's right to do so because the upcoming traders frequently roam between the two. As the peninsulas that sandwich Scotland's fourth largest city, Dundee, their similar geographical features lend the area a bounty of produce, be it beautiful seafood from the small harbours to award-winning meat, fruit and vegetables from the inland pastures.

These regions have a lot in common. Fife is famed for its quaint fishing villages of Anstruther and Leven, dotted between the golden beaches of Elie and West Sands. On a kind weather day, this picturesque coast makes a convincing argument for renaming the county the Fife Riviera. For others, it's predominantly known for golf whose birth, legend has it, occurred in the ancient university town of St Andrews, in the 15th century. Across the Firth of Tay, the region of Angus supplements its coastal villages with rounded hills and long glens that run into the Grampian Highland scenery beyond. With a backdrop like this, you'll never be short of a scenic picnic spot, nor locally sourced delights for your hamper. The fertile soils provide rich grazing lands to nourish the livestock and offer exemplary growing conditions for each harvest.

It's a delight to wander around Fife & Angus, sourcing exceptional raw ingredients from individual suppliers and farmers. However, if time's not on your side, a more convenient route might to visit the hubs at Bowhouse and Balgove Larder, both of which have been instrumental in the birth of the area's street food scene.

Bowhouse, on the Balcaskie Estate between Elie and St Monans, is a market which hosts monthly food weekends. They bring together producers, street food traders and shoppers to replace the missing link in the local food chain. Toby Anstruther, founding member of Fife's Food Network explains, 'I was struck when talking to one local chef who said, though he was very keen to use local ingredients, he ended up sourcing his vegetables from the Glasgow veg markets or even from Holland, because, despite seeing the vegetables growing in Fife's fields all around his restaurant, there was no way to connect those fields to his business. Bowhouse is intended to be part of the answer to this challenge.'

Meanwhile, further north, on the outskirts of St Andrews, I'm convinced I've died and gone to heaven. Balgove Larder bulges with a plethora of goodies from throughout Scotland. In 2013 they sought to adapt their car parking space to stage an inviting night market for street food vendors to assemble. It's an opportunity to meet the makers and see their produce transformed into delectable dishes, served by esteemed traders. Held on the first Tuesday of every month from April to September, it's a jovial affair with live music, well worth clearing your calendar for.

SCREAMING PEACOCK

It's taken Guy Wade three years to hone his business strategy. 'On one of our first events in summer 2016, we lost £600 over the weekend,' he says. Guy could have walked to an ATM, withdrawn a wad of cash, then literally thrown it in the bin and saved himself a lot of effort. But that wouldn't have been any fun. 'That £1,200 pitch fee really screwed us over, but over time you learn which events are good and which aren't. You brush yourself off after the bad ones and justify it as "good promo". But genuinely, if I put out a stack of flyers and they all go, often enquiries for private events and weddings will flood my inbox in the following weeks.' Of course, even after an unprofitable event, when no one will book you to cater the most important day of their lives without trying the product first, the exposure always helps.

Now Guy has realised that absence really does make the heart grow fonder. If he can't be pinned down, then when his gourmet burgers are finally available the demand goes through the roof. 'We go to St Andrews Student Union one Wednesday a month, and the mentality is, "Oh my God, they're here, let's get a burger cos they won't be here tomorrow!" The students will always take advantage of the opportunity and buy lunch or dinner from us that day. For them Screaming Peacock is a treat once a month, but for me it's just another day in the office. If I had a regular pitch, they'd be like, "Oh, let's go today, actually no tomorrow, hmmm I'm busy, let's go next week instead!" People won't drop everything to eat your food in the same way.' If Guy can secure more customers like the Student Union, one for each day of the week, then he'll be set for life.

There are some nineteen-year-olds who

spend the summer after their first year of university in Magaluf or Ayia Napa, finding out the hard way that their alcohol tolerance really isn't that high. But not Guy; he's always had a serious entrepreneurial mindset. After the first year of his business management degree at Northumbria, he sought a way to make use of the waste product of his father, Steven's, business.

'Dad takes clients out wild deer hunting across Fife, Tayside and Highland Perthshire and brings back the full animal to butcher it. The quality cuts like venison fillet, tenderloin, haunch meat, diced back legs and shank steaks get sold fresh, or in sausages and pies, through his company Woodmill Game. But I use the shoulder – a less premium cut that's absolutely fine when minced up – in Screaming Peacock's burgers. They're made with twelve ingredients in total and it's all gluten-free; we use rice and gram flour instead of wheat flour and that acts as a bonding agent, so we don't use eggs either.'

It's a real father–son collaboration; Steven's thirty years of game bird experience also lends to Guy's second product, a pheasant burger. They've researched and refined the recipes together; beef fat combines with red peppers to complement the darker venison meat, while chicken fat is mixed up with yellow peppers in the pheasant burger.

'When the animals are both very lean, we like to use fat from similar animals, it's like keeping them to their own species,' Guy laughs. The result is moist and juicy patties that are nicely charred on the outside and offer a lingering smoky aftertaste. They're topped with bacon, melted cheese, fresh salad and Guy's own tangy tomato and BBQ relish; the earthy venison meat is more robust and works well with thin slithers of raw onion. It's accompanied by his rather good double cooked skin-on rosemary fries (first fried at 130°C then later at 190°C). It's a real burger van experience, made that little bit gourmet.

When it's slim pickings on catering vans and street food vendors in Fife, it's unsurprising that Guy's been asked to cater for parties and just provide beef burgers. 'My response will always be no,' he states. 'I'm not here to heat up someone else's food, and I'm not about to buy a cattle farm. I'm in this industry because I'm passionate about what we do. The priority is the product and I'm a specialist in game. Provenance and traceability are huge for us, I know exactly where the burgers have come from and how they were made.'

He could write an essay on the psychology of a pheasant burger, and I've witnessed the unusual customer reactions first hand. 'Immediately they'll decide they don't like pheasant; it's for posh people with lots of money who go shooting, and they're not one of them. Then there's the contemplation of what even is venison, it sounds like an intense flavour that they may not like. But, then they say, "Oh, it's a burger and we love burgers."'

Guy's job is perhaps a little harder than other traders: he needs to convert potential customers by persuading them that the two phenomena can co-exist and be delicious. And once that hard bit's over, then he needs to convince them to part with £6.

'In a way, we're encouraging a greater demographic to enjoy something that is associated with pure negativity,' Guy explains. The problem with the pheasant shooting industry is that

those involved aren't consuming most of it; it's shot for fun and then wasted. 'We tick the ethical responsibility box for landowners and gamekeepers by offering to transform clients' birds after their shoot, into a more accessible burger form for them to cook at home. People love that fuzzy traceability stunt.'

In such a loud blue and green trailer, Guy is literally peacocking. 'It's a dangerous thing to do; if you've got a bad product people will remember you for it and you'll never lose that reputation, but if you've got a good product, you'll stand out from the crowd and develop a following.'

Guy's mum was the influential force behind the wacky idea and the branding. 'When people ask, I always refer to an amazing burger joint in Newcastle, called Fat Hippo. The name isn't desirable or elegant, it's a bit absurd and bordering on repulsive, but everyone loves it and it sticks with you.' Guy's Screaming Peacock adopts the same idea, and he's happy to play with puns like 'feeling peckish' and 'burgers worth screaming about' to market the business.

By April 2018 he'd realised that the one trailer wasn't enough; private bookings were coming in thick and fast, and Screaming Peacock needed to expand. 'Now we're in our fourth summer and I've finally figured out what it takes to run one unit (let alone two!). Over the winter we scraped some things together and trialled the gazebo. I needed to realise I could let my peacock go to someone else for a day. It felt like such a massive step; your mentality is "Only I can do it right, only I can do it properly," but you've got to try and change that. The light bulb moment for me was that sudden realisation of, "Of course someone else can do it, it's not rocket science; we're flipping burgers, for God's sake!"'

THE
MUCKLE
BACKIT OVEN

'Everyone always asks where the name comes from. Our house in Auchmithie (ahem, the Naples of the North) is called the Muckle Backit, and the Waverley Hotel that overlooks us is where Sir Walter Scott wrote the *Antiquary*. While staying there he would have looked down on our house, which was occupied by fishermen back in the 1800s. Every day the wives would carry their husbands, fathers and brothers through the waves to their boats, so the men didn't have wet feet for the day. They developed rather strong backs, so were known as muckle backit women. Scott celebrates them in his book, and since our trailer has an almost hump-backed oven protruding from it, we thought we'd call it that too.'

Stumbling upon Muckle Backit Oven with its warm roaring fire is nothing short of a gift from above on a cold Scottish day. Watching Peter Hibbert preparing pizza at his open-air kitchen, tearing mozzarella by hand with mini whirlwinds of flour in the air and the eye-level oven with its contents screaming 'eat me', all adds to the addictive street food experience.

We drove along picturesque country roads to track Peter down. He'd set up a wee spot outside Grewar's Farm Shop in Dronley where locals pick up their weekly groceries of rooster potatoes and juicy Carse of Gowrie berries. Should the farm shop be closed, there's a vending machine filled with Angus onions, carrots and free-range organic eggs for the community to shop from. Here, Peter has an audience of 'support local' enthusiasts who get lured in by the wafting aromas, while the farm shop saves a fortune by not having their own café, which would hardly see a soul on weekdays.

'We did the big events at the beginning

because we thought we had to,' Peter confesses. 'But when you pay £250 to be there, and our maximum volume is 85 pizzas in three hours, we make more money doing pop-ups like this.' There's only so much him and Joan, an art student and part-time employee, can achieve. But that's all Peter is looking for. 'We haven't tried to push it or make tons of money, we want it to be a relaxed venture that keeps us comfy. My wife's a school teacher and I mainly trade on weekends so I can spend time with my two boys.'

Seven years ago, Peter and his family were living down in London. He was a freelance photographer with his own darkroom and did side work for Neal's Yard Dairy at Borough Market while enjoying being a stay-at-home dad. 'We'd watched the whole world of street food kick off down there and we'd enjoyed it. I'll never forget the queues at Brindisa for their famous chorizo rolls with grilled red peppers, rocket and that incredible vinegar dressing.'

When they moved back up to Scotland, trying to avoid the heavy rainfall of their original home in Ayrshire, they decided to give the east coast a go. 'With the rise of digital photography, the darkroom wasn't working up here. At the time I was obsessed with Asian street food but had no idea how to progress it, and pizza is much more viable. I didn't expect it to take off: like, who'd come to the North Sea cliffs of Auchmithie for a pizza? But they did.'

When Muckle Backit Oven began Peter got requests for toppings like pepperoni, ham and pineapple, and chicken and sweetcorn. Meanwhile, he was foraging for pine shoots and serving up bambi on a pizza. Awkward. 'You have to sell what people want but I've been that little

bit more daring as we've grown. In Arbroath, people would happily pick off the fresh basil from their margherita, but now ingredients like wild garlic are better known. That's the most accepted foraged leaf and it goes so well with Great Glen Charcuterie's venison salami.'

I don't think I've met a trader who talks about his sourcing as passionately as Peter. It's about replicating the simplicity of Italian cooking – things that grow together, generally taste good together – while using small-batch British produce that tastes extraordinary and, ideally, doesn't come with a carbon footprint. He sought to find a middle ground with his customers and sourced a great British pepperoni by Blackhand Charcuterie; it joins garlic, oregano and his own chilli honey dressing to form the Guilty Pleasure. 'It's based on those frozen Chicago things from the supermarket. If the boys and my wife are away, I might sneak one in,' he admits. Otherwise he's playing with meats from Peelham Farm, Piggery Smokery or Great Glen Charcuterie. 'Their bresaola is pretty expensive but slapping that on a warm pizza straight out the oven is out of this world.'

His mozzarella is from Delicatezza in London. Living in Auchmithie, delivery can be tricky if you haven't vigorously pre-planned, so Nife Is Life (Nice Italian Food Everyday) is a great backup option. There's Isle of Mull cheddar, corra linn, shaved ewes' cheese, too many local cheeses to name, and as for the vegetables, Pittormie Farm has the best around, so whatever's in season will be involved. Then there's asparagus. With Angus's unrivalled growing conditions, it's understandable that Peter's eyes lit up when we discussed the season of vibrant green spears. Asparagus, béchamel, mozzarella,

blanched nettles, garlic and lemon zest: a zingy spring pizza I'd demolish in a heartbeat.

It all sits on a fresh yeast, Neapolitan-style pizza base (flour, water, yeast, salt) made from Mungoswells in East Lothian, blended with two Italian flours. It sounds straightforward, but the elements can play havoc with the dough. Peter says, 'The wind dries it out the second it comes out of its cosy box. It will crack and doesn't cook as well. You've got to think about how hydrated the dough is, how long you've got to prove it and how long before the event you can make a dough ball.' It's not the easiest thing to work with, and that's before we confront Peter's dairy and gluten intolerance. Proving the dough for 72 hours helps with this, but in the interests of good food, Peter tends to turn a blind eye anyway.

You'd think his boys would love the stuff, but after years of being Dad's guinea pigs, they're fed up. 'They always leave the crusts, but I turn leftover bases into focaccia with garlic and rosemary, which is practically a giant crust and they love that!' That's where a portable Ooni oven comes in handy. 'When it takes hours to get the Muckle Backit going, and a good bit of wood, they're great for trialling one new pizza and experimenting with toppings like wood-roasted vegetable fennel.'

I could eat his pizzas for ever; mine was a take on the Lahmacun Turkish flatbread that Peter used to wolf down after a London night out. It's scattered with the growing heat of lamb mince, a mix of peppers, parsley, pomegranate molasses, cumin, red onion and sumac, then finished with a local feta, mint and yoghurt sauce.

For Peter, street food is like freelancing, in that he only needs to worry about the next job. His trailer and 400°C oven have paid off in dividends and will continue to do so in their new Glasgow home – the city in which Peter grew up and where the family are yearning to return. In fact, they may have already done so by the time you read this.

LATE-NIGHT NONSENSE
LAMB FLATBREAD PIZZA

SERVES 6

The best thing about these moreish pizzas is their super-easy bases, made with shop-bought flatbreads. Make sure you have plenty in!

....

INGREDIENTS

PIZZA TOPPING

500g minced lamb shoulder
2 tbsp cumin seeds, toasted and
  ground in pestle and mortar
2 tbsp cayenne pepper
½ tbsp cinnamon
1 tbsp pomegranate molasses
1 tbsp sea salt
½ red and ½ green pepper
1 small red onion
Large handful of chopped flat
  leaf parsley

PIZZA SAUCE

San Marzano tomato sauce
100g feta
200g Greek yoghurt
Large handful of mint

TO SERVE

Flatbreads, at least one per
  person

METHOD

1. Finely chop the onion and peppers together then put in a muslin cloth and let it sit a while so you can squeeze as much juice out as possible so as not to make the pizza soggy. (You can keep the juices for marinating chicken, or to add to vinegar for a salad dressing.)

2. Once nice and dry, mix it with the spices into the mince and leave in the fridge overnight to mingle nicely.

3. Take it out the fridge so it's at room temperature before using.

4. Preheat the oven to 200°C.

5. If you're using a wood-fired oven, shape the mince into large golf balls (each one is enough for a 8" pizza), and bake for 8 minutes so slightly cooked. You don't need to do this if you're cooking with an ordinary oven.

6. To create your pizza, spread the flatbread with your tomato sauce (optional), then sprinkle it with the lamb and a drizzle of olive oil. Bake in the oven for 8 minutes or until browned nicely.

7. While it's in the oven, whizz together your feta, yoghurt and mint.

8. When the pizza is baked, finish with the yoghurt sauce, chopped parsley and a squeeze of lemon, and serve.

MEZZALUNA
ITALIAN STREET KITCHEN

When I told Chiara di Ponio I was headed up towards Dundee on a one-day street food expedition, she panicked. They weren't trading that day and she didn't want to miss the opportunity to share her rich Italian history and authentic cooking with the world. In the spirit of Italian hospitality, there was only one thing for it, they'd host us in their family's garden, with an intimate street food experience fit for queens. 'We couldn't just do one dish, we had to feed you properly!' And so, we feasted . . . on the five-dish spread featured here.

1. FOCACCIA – the spongy chunky sort that's fully loaded with glugs of quality Italian olive oil, fat salt crystals, sprigs of rosemary and fresh garlic. Chiara's recipe lends itself to personal preferences; she kneads the dough until it's nice and springy, before letting it rise and spreading it out like a pizza. That's the way Chiara likes it: she wants thick slabs of comforting bread, not the thin crusted pizza-style version.

2. SPINACH AND RICOTTA CANNELLONI – Chiara's grandad, Mario, taught her to make fresh pasta. 'He lives in the house right there,' Chiara tells us, pointing to a door ten metres away. The process typically spans two days; they'll make the dough on day one, let it rest overnight and then roll it out the following afternoon. Traditionally it's rolled by hand, Mario would do it no other way.

But demand for Chiara's pasta is such that she's had to invest in an electric pasta roller. The thin pasta sheets are rolled into tubes used to house the marriage of spinach and ricotta, striking in its simplicity.

3. LASAGNE – but not as we know it. The sloppy kind that's laden with creamy béchamel sauce is found in the north of Italy, and indeed in the UK. But Chiara explains that lasagne recipes differ from region to region. Coming from Belmonte Castello, a small village in the mountains between Naples and Rome, hers is made to her grandad's recipe, which has been in their family for decades. It combines their secret *sugo* (Italian tomato sauce), minced beef from Dundee's The Butcher The Baker, fresh parsley, mozzarella and parmigiano, dotted with chopped boiled Grewar's Farm eggs. Without the béchamel, it's a much drier dish, so cutting into it reveals perfect layers of pasta – a structural masterpiece.

4. BEEF MEATBALLS – this recipe is from Chiara's maternal grandma. Balls of minced beef, parsley and garlic are bound in egg then rolled in breadcrumbs, shallow fried and smothered in *sugo*. These are so delicious it's hard to believe there'd ever be leftovers, but when there are, Chiara enjoys them cold in a crusty ciabatta.

5. ALFREDO – the grand finale reaffirms my belief that there's no such thing as too much cheese. In this theatrical showstopper, encountered on holiday in Sorrento, Chiara coats her fresh tagliatelle ribbons in a creamy sauce before swirling it around a giant wheel of hollowed out Grana Padano. The steam off the pasta gently melts away at the walls, imparting a rich, complex flavour to create a gooey bowl of pasta. It's a hug in a Grana Padano bowl, and it's well worth the upkeep. 'I have to sanitise the wheel every second day by flambéeing it with brandy. I set it on fire then remove the top coat to keep it fresh. If you don't, it'll get dry and crack, and as it's imported from Italy you want to look after it properly. Really, it's like a baby that demands constant attention and love. After a couple of months, once it's getting that little bit too dry, I'll cut it all up and vacuum pack it to use later for sauces or grated Grana Padano on other dishes.'

Chiara is accustomed to setting up shop in her driveway: that's where she launched in February 2019. She'd completed her geography undergrad, only to dive straight into a master's with second thoughts. Her goal was to be her own boss; that's what her family had been doing for years with their string of Silvery Tay fish and chips shops, but no one in the area was offering authentic Italian street food. Pizza yes, but fresh pasta? Impossible to come by. Chiara was resolute in changing that and trialled her offering to curious neighbours who, while enjoying the pasta, were relieved to hear Italian street food wasn't literally launching on their doorstep.

The demand became overwhelming. For their first event Chiara positioned the elegantly converted box outside Grewar's Farm Shop, assured that fifty portions of pasta would be plenty. It wasn't. She ran out in the first hour, and in Italian culture not enough food is a sin. The family rallied together. Grandad was making pasta at home, Dad was driving it up to the farm; it was frenzied and chaotic, but Chiara couldn't let her first paying customers down. 'Always bring extra. That's what we've learned!'

What might be just a bowl of pasta to us

(nothing from Mezzaluna is ever 'just' anything), is in fact a bowl of crafted passion steeped in family history.

'My grandad, Mario Di Ponio, grew up near Monte Cassino, an hour south of Rome, on the family farm. Here, alongside his four siblings, he learned to make pasta from his mum. This would typically be fresh egg tagliatelle and lasagne sheets. From a young age, all he wanted was to go out and play with his friends – but not until the pasta was made, his mum would command. Midway through the process, she'd always chat away with family and friends, slowing down the day. Grandad realised the only way he'd ever make it out to play was to keep making it himself. He learned quickly because he needed to get the job done, and reckons she did that on purpose as an incentive.' With humble beginnings, it was all *cucina povra*, meaning making the most of limited ingredients, and Chiara lives in the same way: 'a little bit of this and a little bit of that', with everything made from scratch.

When her grandad moved from Italy to Dundee in the late 1950s, the pasta making didn't stop. Together Mario and Chiara's mum, Maria, ensured that Mezzaluna boasted the family's centuries-old recipes. 'They're by far the best cooks I know; I could go to a Michelin-starred kitchen and still think that. Dishes like the lasagne would only ever be for special occasions. At my parents' wedding, my grandad and Mum catered the pasta course by making twenty trays of it . . . I didn't even do a pasta course at our wedding, which my family considers a crime. Yeah, I've got regrets about that.'

Chiara's hitting the ground running with a diary packed with events and, honestly, I'm expecting great things. From bottling up her *sugo* to catering weddings with impressive antipasti boards, or doing something with all those egg whites – pavlova with vanilla poached pears, dark chocolate and crushed amaretti biscuits? – Chiara is brimming with enthusiasm and ideas. 'You don't need to be a trained chef. I'm not! If you're passionate about something you can do it. So, I think you'll find that now the ball's rolling, a lot more people will pop up with street food in this area.' Watch this space.

FISH & FRITES

So . . . you might have heard tell of a big blue van that Pizza Box drove into at Gleneagles? That's Fish & Frites, the East Neuk of Fife's answer to a chippy out on the streets. Sarah and Jordan Black trade out of a beautiful 1966 Citroën H van called Brian, lovingly named after Jordan's dad who passed away sixteen years ago. The engine and driver's cabin are original, while the rear has been fitted with a custom-made fryer that's capable of high output to reduce the long wait time at events. Thankfully, after a little body work to repair the damage done in the crash, it'll live to fry another day.

In the 1970s, Sarah's great-grandfather was the first person in Leven to go out on the roads and sell from a van. 'He got his fish from the harbour at Anstruther and peeled his own potatoes,' Sarah says. 'He was a revolutionary; it was a lot more difficult to do then, than it is for us now.'

Sarah and Jordan started off in 2015 with a frozen yogurt trailer, which they'd bought to attend festivals on top of their day jobs. Here, they spotted a gap in the market; there was insipid flesh bullied into thick oily cardboard-like batter, which had clearly come straight from a freezer. But, bizarrely, no one seemed willing to source and treat quality fish with the love it deserved. Sarah and Jordan quit their day jobs and took up that mantle, only to find out that Sarah was a descendant of a Fife street food legend. Even the mother of one of my mum's friends fondly recalls heading out on the streets for a fish supper from the vintage Bedford van driven by Sarah's great-grandfather. 'When we found out, it felt like we've come full circle,' Sarah says.

Alongside popping up at local Fife farmers markets, the Edinburgh Fringe and catering for Murrayfield's 67,000 ravenous rugby fans, the couple have committed to a regular fortnightly pitch in Leven to pay tribute to Sarah's great-grandfather. And, like him, they're working hard to channel Anstruther's quality seafood reputation. 'All of our supplies come from within a five-mile radius. The fish comes from local merchant G & J Wilson in St Monans, who are supplied by the fishermen of Peterhead near Aberdeen, and fillet the fish for us. Our meat comes from Minick of Cupar, who have shops dotted throughout Fife.'

Seventeen-hour days are strenuous, but Sarah's determined to find the time to make their own chips which will join their homemade tartare sauce and mushy peas in accompanying the haddock encased in Jordan's family's secret-recipe batter. It's incredibly crispy and, once fried in vegetable oil, doesn't leave you with that rancid waxy-mouth feel that fish fried in beef dripping would. You know, when the roof of your mouth feels unpleasantly greasy after caving into your fish supper cravings? At Fish & Frites it all feels good for you. Not that you need an excuse to get stuck in.

THE
CHEESY TOAST
SHACK

In their first year of trading, *The Scotsman* thrust them into the limelight with the title of 'the best place to eat at the Edinburgh Fringe 2016'. Then Radio Forth, STV and the BBC swiftly caught on, and within months they were trading at Glastonbury. Now, there aren't many vendors who get to experience such a prestigious festival after just one year on the road. But then again, the Cheesy Toast Shack, helmed by Kate Carter and her partner Sam Larg, isn't just any vendor. In 2017 they were finalists at the Scottish Street Food Awards and in 2018 they were awarded Street Vendor of The Year in the Menu Food and Drink Awards. But it's just cheese toasties, right? What's all the fuss about?

No, these aren't just any cheese toasties. The Cheesy Toast Shack is home to some of the best in the world. They're gourmet in terms of their fine Scottish ingredients – St Andrews Farmhouse cheddar which can be found at I.J. Mellis, sourdough from Wild Heath Bakery in the village of Comrie or Lochaber Farm in St Andrews, chutney from Trotters Independent Condiments in Kirkcaldy, and meat and seasonal produce from Balgove Larder – but they're also

utterly filthy, greasy and delicious in all the right ways.

'We're not shy about giving that extra quantity of filling,' Kate tells me. 'We want it to be disgustingly gooey with cheese, so we tell our staff, "If you're making a toastie and think to yourself *Have I put enough cheese in?*, the chances are you probably haven't, so add a handful more for good measure."'

When you cut a toastie in two before

serving it, the blade naturally forces the melted cheese to recoil back into its own half, leaving a customer's first bite that little bit less satisfying. For Sam and Kate that won't suffice. They've created 'the weld'. If you linger near their stall long enough to warrant loosening a notch on your belt, you'll probably hear their staff joking, 'Make sure you do the weld,' and 'You've got to do the weld.' That's the all-important extra layer of cheese sandwiched down the middle between the two halves. If there's room for air, there's room for cheese. 'We're not trying to trick anyone, there's still enough cheese in the toastie to sink a battleship, we just want that instant gooey first impression. We're making big fat proper Instagrammable cheese toasties.'

Who would have thought a holiday romance in Bali in 2015 would bring a carpenter from the Inner Hebrides and a teacher from Dorset together, to embark on one hell of a delicious journey? After a long-distance relationship (over 600 miles apart) they soon met on neutral ground and moved to St Andrews to set up shop and start building their impressive empire. 'We had little money, perhaps a couple of grand, but decided that we didn't want to work for other people, so in 2016 we bought an old (but hardly used) burger trailer from Gumtree. It was just a plain box trailer, but with Sam's carpentry skills we transformed it – we gutted it, got it vinyl wrapped, cut down old scaffold boards for cladding on the bottom half, tiled the interior and built old-style shelves. We'd realised street food was just taking off in Scotland and we wanted to be part of that journey; but first, we needed a decent stand-out trailer.' They even got inventive and used cheese graters for lampshades.

Between them Sam and Kate had little formal experience of cooking, but what they did have was the determination to share their love of cheese with the world. 'It's the ultimate comfort food. You've had a bad day, have some grilled cheese. It's cold outside, have some grilled cheese. You've been on a diet all week and it's the weekend, have some grilled cheese. It's the answer to everything, or always has been in our lives!'

After storming through their first year, applying for every possible event and promoting their street food through a strong social media presence of irresistible cheese porn, the couple vowed to reinvest every penny of profit back into growing the business. They've since launched their own permanent kiosk with the stunning backdrop of East Sands in St Andrews, and in 2019 boasted three Fringe stands for a second year running, positioned at Pleasance, Underbelly and within Gilded Garden.

'Scotland is now a destination for street food. You used to see it in European cities like Copenhagen and Amsterdam, but now tourists actively seek it out in Scotland.' Their street food success is testament to what you can achieve if you don't skimp on the ingredients, but Kate's realised that it's not just down to the top-notch toasties. Rather, it's about their brand, work ethos and the way they hand pick their staff. 'Sam and I have created the company and the brand, people who work for us are personable and like to have a laugh. We make the food fresh to order, so it can take a little longer, so we try to create an environment where everyone is having fun and bantering while they wait.'

That sounds a little contrived, but it's true. Even at 2 a.m. during the Fringe, when the rest of Edinburgh has decidedly had it with the tourists, the Cheesy Toast Shack will be brimming with energy and laughter, ready to grill up a camembert and balsamic mushroom toastie, with blackcurrant mayo and wild rocket in organic wood-fired sourdough. Heavenly.

These are the good times. The bad ones might involve trading at an event where the power supply provided wasn't strong enough and the grills kept blowing every few minutes. Or that time in Glasgow, during the early days, when Kate was sold a pitch with the promise of thousands of attendees: 'I got totally misled on numbers, the whole thing was awful.' Inflating ticket sales and deceiving traders seems to be common practice, but they soon get wise to it and know which events to avoid.

Kate and Sam have come a long way since their first event at the Balgove Night Market in May 2016 and have plenty of plans to expand further. In the meantime, it's not just the business that's grown. In August 2018 Kate gave birth to a beautiful daughter, who I have no doubt, will be raised on cheese toasties, laughter and love. What a lucky girl!

THE ARBROATH SMOKIE GRILLED CHEESE TOASTIE

SERVES
1

INGREDIENTS

½ Arbroath Smokie, flaked

A very big handful of good
  quality, extra mature cheddar

½ an onion, finely sliced

Splash of white wine

2 cloves of garlic

1 tbsp double cream

1 knob of salted butter

1 free-range egg, hard boiled and
  sliced

Salt and pepper to season

Parsley, a couple of sprigs

2 slices of sourdough bread

Full fat mayonnaise

METHOD

1. Fry onion and garlic with butter until softened. Then add white wine and reduce. Once wine is reduced, add the cream. Remove from heat and set aside.

2. Lay out sourdough bread, layer up with cheddar, flaked Arbroath Smokie, sliced egg, and the onion, garlic and white wine mix. Season and top with a little parsley.

3. Lightly spread a layer of mayonnaise on each side of the bread (outside) and grill. This can either be done in a contact grill, or on a flat griddle, on a low to medium temperature, to allow the cheese to be melted on the inside, and the bread to be a nice golden brown on the outside.

4. Don't forget to cut it in half on the grill and add a mature cheddar weld if you're feeling super naughty.

ABERDEEN

When it came to Aberdeenshire, the nuggets of intel I'd planned to squeeze out of my friends over a Bloody Mary just didn't exist. They were scraping the barrel, scrambling for anything that could prove useful for my adventures – 'Does the Highlander Bus count?' and 'Don't Food Story own a truck?' Finally, we resigned to the fact that there's a really long list of hog-roast caterers. Crackling enthusiasts rejoice! But where on earth were all the street food traders?

The Granite City is known for its lucrative off-shore jobs in oil and gas, grey skies that blend into the architecture, and harsh biting winds. Its coast features the world's most powerful wind turbines, but back on land – at least in street food terms – there's no sign of a revolution.

Quite bluntly, it's a little thin on the ground. In Aberdeenshire's defence, the further north you travel from Scotland's central belt, the more street food traders dwindle. Perhaps the trend's just naturally taking more time to filter through. But surely, I thought, someone must be an Aberdonian street food pioneer? And then I struck gold. Let me introduce you to Scott Miskelly.

THE
STREET FOOD
SYNDICATE

A quick glimpse of the Street Food Syndicate's logo and Quentin Tarantino fans will understand what Scott Miskelly is trying to achieve. It riffs off that famous *Reservoir Dogs* image, but with three suited figures, instead of six, now all donning a toque blanche. Spoiler alert: there's no blood and they're not robbing any banks. But the Street Food Syndicate are all about strength in numbers . . . and perhaps there's a touch of rebellion in there, too.

'Up in Aberdeenshire, it's not that easy for people to buy into your ideas,' Scott explains. 'It could take a few years for things like street food to properly catch on. I've spent time in London, in places like Kerb at Camden, where it's already thriving. I wanted to bring that up to Aberdeen and thought the best way to do that was to start a syndicate.'

While Scott was completely new to the street food scene and hadn't yet traded under his brand, Maço, even he had noticed the lack of markets and public events in his county. At the start of 2019, he reached out to two other fresh faces on the scene, Smoke & Soul and Pizza Box,

and together the three founding syndics sought to create their own street food event.

'We wouldn't just turn up and pay a fee. For Maço's first event we'd run it, doing everything from the seating, to the power, to the licensing and the food. Though the latter was by no means an afterthought . . . yeah, I guess we don't do things by halves.'

They began in their home town of Inverurie, just north of Aberdeen, where there was every indication that street food would be well received. 'We've got so many great local producers, butchers and greengrocers up here; the quality at a street food market would be amazing,' Scott says. 'And look, I'm 34, I don't want clinky clunky music and a candle on the table; I want something bouncier to have a bit of fun with.'

Scott was aiming to emulate that vibe, already so successfully achieved by the likes of BrewDog. But, unlike restaurant groups — where if cuts are made the food quality is the first thing to go — the Street Food Syndicate would always make delicious food for the local community a collective priority.

After months of jumping through hoops with the council, Scott convinced them to close the public car park on Market Place in Inverurie. 'Their biggest gripe was that they were losing revenue on the parking spaces — we calculated it, and that equated to £127 for an eight-hour day; I'm at a loss knowing that's what we were arguing over.'

Still, in an intimate town where people tend to know each other, the trio were quickly established as local heroes. In just three hours on the Saturday afternoon, when the event was supposed to last until 8 p.m., all three traders had ran out of food despite thinking they'd overestimated the attendance. 'We brought 500 people into the centre of town. Inverurie hadn't seen those numbers before; it was unprecedented.'

Scott likes a challenge and isn't afraid to ruffle a few feathers in order to improve the area. This one greatly paid off. 'I think a few local eateries were scared of it . . . but then after the hugely successful first event, we got signatures from businesses and cafés to encourage more syndicate pop-ups,' he says. 'Street food really works for those who don't want a ninety-minute lunch. People embrace the fact that they can do two, three, four things at once while eating an amazing meal cooked by someone who cares. It doesn't need to be McDonald's in a bag anymore.'

The Syndicate are all incredibly passionate about food: 'We're no £4 burgers!' Where possible they'll help artisan producers. Mark of Singularity Sauce (hot sauce homemade in Tarves) attended a Syndicate meeting and left with a deal to make three bespoke sauces to complement the dishes of the three members. If an avenue for three new contacts opened up from attending a ten-minute meeting, think what the Syndicate can do for other local businesses.

According to Scott, 'The worst thing about street food is the naivety — people don't appreciate the passion and hard work that fuels it; the time, effort, quality and standard of street food.' Together the Street Food Syndicate are working to correct that. Given that the whole is greater than the sum of its parts, they'll only go from strength to strength. Inverurie's prosecco van Art Deco Prosecco and traditional ice cream supplier, Tricycle Catering, have already signed up for a piece of that successful syndicate pie.

MAÇO FOOD FUSIONS

The food Scott makes is inspired by his life experiences. Once, his flight to Florida was diverted in a storm, leaving him stranded in Philadelphia. Of course, when in Rome and all that, so Scott made the most of an unfortunate situation and beelined for Geno's, famed for the best cheesesteak in the city, served twenty-four hours a day.

'In West Philadelphia born and raised, on the playground where I spent most of my days, chillin' out maxin' relaxin' all cool' . . . Scott created the 'Fresh Prince' to make us all drool. See what I did there? The 'Fresh Prince' is a white corn tortilla filled with tender flank steak, smothered in jalapeño-infused nacho cheese and garnished with fresh herbs. 'It was the most incredible thing I'd ever eaten – I just had to put it in a taco!'

During Scott's first family holiday to Phuket, Scott's taxi driver took them on a day trip to a waterfall. On the way, the driver stopped off to deliver fresh mangoes to his wife's street food stall. She kindly gave them her Thai prawn salad,

and it's stuck in Scott's mind ever since. It's called 'Mr Song's Shrimp Salad' on Maço Food Fusions' menu and replicates all the authentic, aromatic flavours of that Thai street food dish, delivered through infused prawns, crunchy red slaw and a satay-style sauce, as instructed by the Song family's original recipe.

'There wasn't a food hygiene certificate, market operator or health and safety inspector in sight. It was more real than anything you'll see here: the food was out of this world.'

Back in Scotland, Scott's 'Black Betty' plays homage to the tried and tested combination of pork belly, black pudding and apple. It took him hundreds of attempts to hone the pork's

moistness, shredability (totally a word) and the thickness of the crackling, so it could hold its own next to the quality of Speyside black pudding and tangy Aberdeenshire apples. When married together in a taco, the whole thing is a knockout.

It sounds a little meat heavy, but vegetarians are catered for in a nod to Britain's favourite cuisine. The 'Shakaree Cheese' is a mix of gentle Tandoori-spiced paneer, onion relish and green hari yogurt, served in an authentic chapati that's cut in uniform size to the shape of a taco. Essentially, regardless of origin, if it's delicious globally inspired food that could plausibly go in a taco, then Scott will do it.

I have a confession. I've never been a 'fusion cooking' fan. For me, fusion on a menu always translates to *confusion* on the plate. It's for chefs who are trying to be too many things to too many people, or trying to mask poor quality British ingredients with typically Asian spices. Maço Food Fusions is an exception to the rule. Scott's son is called Mack, and 'maço' means bundle in Portuguese. It turns out that 'maco' without the cedilla in Catalan means handsome. And these are some good-looking wee bundles.

I suddenly get it. Scott isn't trying to create anything too pretentious or refined; until setting up his street food business, he'd never cooked in a professional kitchen. In fact, he's confessed that some of his recipes come from just 'winging it on Google'. But the buoyant vibe of street food markets and the sense of community created at every pop-up, that feeling for Scott makes it worth giving up his career as a property renovator and project manager. 'Now I just do what I need to, to fund my street food venture . . . standing at the hatch serving

my food, smiling on a sunny day – I don't think there's a better job.'

Scott bought an old ambulance in November 2018, and had the skills to convert it, adorning it with sunshine yellow *el dia de los Muertos* skulls, thistles and fleurs-de-lis, hinting at what customers might expect to be served.

'Ambulances are brilliant for street food: they're well kitted out, insulated, they've got power and heaters, air con, head room to stand inside, and are built to clock up the miles,' Scott says. 'My ambulance has seen a lot of life – and no doubt death. It's got character. We wanted to create rustic, characterful food, and this is the perfect vehicle.'

Maço Food Fusions is Aberdeenshire's fourth emergency service; these tacos could be genuinely life-saving when suffering the after-effects of a big night out. But they're not just greasy comfort food. Far from it.

'When we started, I said we'll have no ground beef or flour tortillas in our van – that was rule number one,' Scott says. His soft corn shells are imported from Mexico and the fillings are all sourced from local butchers and greengrocers. He opts for a 5 a.m. wake-up every day, to prepare his 48-hour marinated Mayan Bird (Yucatan chicken, mango lime salsa and Mexican crema on a yellow corn tortilla), before taking his son to school and walking the dog.

The secret to achieving a successful street food business while maintaining a dreamy lifestyle is to manage your time and have a clear understanding of what tastes good. The buck stops with the trader and that's what Scott loves. 'The joy of me and my ambulance is that I am the staff and I make the food; if I don't like it, it doesn't go out the window.'

SMOKE AND SOUL

Having launched in September 2017, Smoke and Soul are the longest standing members of the Street Food Syndicate. Corey is the typical hardy Scot: he'll barbecue regardless of the weather. His fiancé, Lindsay, has a degree in business; she manages the marketing and day-to-day organisation of the whole Smoke and Soul operation. Together, they're pioneering Aberdeenshire's first and only wood-fired, slow-smoked meats menu. This is no-holds-barred comfort food and it's naughty in all the right ways.

Corey sources brisket from Quality Meat Scotland-certified Millers of Speyside, while the Scottish pork comes from his family butchers H & S Milne & Sons. His late grandad opened it almost thirty years ago and, keen to keep it in the family, recently passed the butchers down to his uncle. The meats get smoked over cherry or oak wood pellets, imparting flavour from within Cory's pride and joy, a Traeger smoker. It results in moist loosened cuts that fall apart willingly, often before being prompted by a knife. They're then either generously piled into a freshly baked Inverurie-based Bread Guy roll or popped on a perch of creamy, luscious macaroni cheese. Both enhanced by the tang of Sauce Shop's mustardy South Carolina BBQ sauce. It doesn't get much better than that in my book.

These dishes are exactly what the Scots word 'coorie' means to me; it's food that provides a comforting cuddle, a much-needed cosiness on a cold wet afternoon. They're the kind of dishes that you crave in front of a roaring fire in the depths of January; they're good for your soul and they're perfect for Scottish street food.

Unbelievably, Corey's never trained as a chef.

He's fully self-taught, solely through watching YouTube videos. Perhaps these have also inspired the couple's Facebook posts. In a recent mouth-watering video, a juicy picanha rump cap is seen rotating on the spit with its flavourful fat dripping in slow-motion to entice you in. It's then effortlessly sliced in front of the camera, revealing a tender pink inside, that's almost still mooing. It's the kind of video you stumble upon on the Instagram discovery thread and deeply wish was available in Scotland. Well, it is, and I'm salivating at the thought.

The couple share this food with the rest of Aberdeenshire because it's the exact kind they enjoy eating.

'Corey and I have always wanted our own place, a proper restaurant,' Lindsay explains. 'But it's a big dream, and, unless you have a lot of money saved or can get a bank loan, is hard to achieve. So, we thought, why don't we start a street food venture that we can do part-time,

and then we can grow the business until it's feasible to quit our day jobs.'

They aimed for four to five events in their first year, but thanks to an astonishingly receptive audience, ended up doing twenty-eight. 'It grew incredibly rapidly and almost overwhelmingly in the first year. We weren't happy in the jobs we were in, there was lots of stress and anxiety in the downturn of oil, but Smoke and Soul's success gave me the confidence to take voluntary redundancy in December 2018.'

Corey joined Lindsay, giving up his oil and gas career in in April 2019. They've since found their calling in the craft beer industry; juicy pulled meats go down delightfully with rare hoppy IPAs – who'd have thought? When Smoke and Soul were asked to join the renowned BrewDog AGM line-up, typically dominated by the big players from London, Newcastle and Edinburgh, Lindsay was shaken up. 'I can't believe our little Aberdeen business made the cut,' she says. 'It

was an amazing opportunity and we were just feeding folk non-stop. It really gave us an extra financial cushion.'

They've since secured a full-time residency at six°north, in Aberdeen city centre. For venues like this, street food is a no-brainer. Operators with no capital or inclination to pour money into their kitchen are able to keep punters happy with more than a bag of crisps or a bowl of nuts while quality cooks, who care about their brand like Corey and Lindsay do, get to experience a professional kitchen set-up and a permanent spot for their loyal following to find them. 'It's going to be challenging, but six°north will be invaluable in preparing us for our own venture later down the line,' Lindsay says.

In the meantime, while leading the county's street food wave by example, the couple are keen to use their platform to encourage the use of biodegradable packaging wherever possible.

'We want to encourage more traders to be environmentally conscious, and equally make customers aware of what they're throwing away. The street food industry is very disposable. Hours go into making the food and setting up to trade, but within minutes rubbish can be tossed on the floor and a trail of destruction left behind. When we're dealing with so many customers at our events we wouldn't feel right if we were serving in polystyrene bowls with plastic forks that were all going to landfill – and I know the rest of the syndicate feels strongly about this too.'

A lot of their dishes require a smoker, so here they've shared their super tasty Mac & Cheese recipe, that anyone can make at home.

SERVES
4

SMOKE AND SOUL MAC & CHEESE

INGREDIENTS

35g butter
35g plain flour
500ml whole milk
500ml double cream
125g red cheddar
125g mature white cheddar
125g Parmigiano Reggiano,
  grated
420g macaroni elbows (dry)
Salt and white pepper to taste

METHOD

1. Bring a large pot of generously salted water to the boil. Add macaroni shells, stir, cover and reduce to simmer for 7 to 10 minutes, before draining in a colander.

2. Melt butter in a pot, add flour and stir for a minute to lightly cook the flour. Add milk and double cream and whisk until smooth.

3. Once mixture comes to a simmer add in cheese and whisk again until fully combined. Add salt and pepper to taste. Add cooked macaroni shells and stir.

4. This is now ready to serve, but can be baked in an oven or smoker topped with extra grated cheese: bake at 180°c until cheese is melted and golden. For a Smoke and Soul twist, top with smoked brisket and Sauce Shop Korean BBQ sauce.

PIZZA BOX

Grant Garden is a character. He has plenty of thoughts on why Aberdeenshire's street food scene is lagging behind, but admittedly the rest of our conversation was brimming with humour. At not yet thirty years old, he's proud to confess that's he's always been 'an avid pizza muncher'.

We talked about the pitfalls of the street food industry: the weather, his vintage horsebox, which is like a sweaty, claustrophobia-inducing pig pen and naturally there's all the times he's forgotten to bring the food. Sorry, what?

'Oh yeah, there's been numerous occasions when we've gone to an event and just forgotten all of the cheese,' he laughs. 'Our checklist for events is so long; it's ridiculous how much stuff you've got to cart around, especially in summer when it's super busy. We could be doing a lunch event, early evening event and separate night event all in one day. We're always scrambling around with twenty kilos of this, five kilos of that . . . then the penny drops and you're like

"Oh bugger, I've left all the dough at home".'

Grant doesn't take himself too seriously and his ability to make light of an unfortunate situation is infectious.

'Not long ago I managed to push the trailer into the front of a beautiful blue vintage Citroën H van. How it happened I really don't know . . . we were supposed to be set up on the complete opposite side of this massive hall at Gleneagles, but then somehow pushed the trailer all the way across the room, smashing into and doing a fair bit of damage to the front of this van. I mean, luckily the pizza box is in one piece . . . it's made of sterner stuff,' he laughs.

When offered the option of voluntary

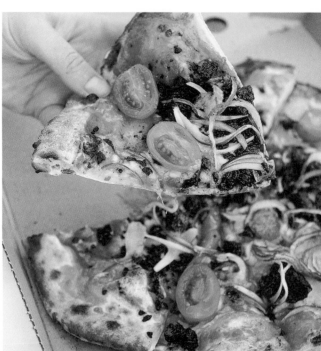

redundancy from his job in oil and gas, Grant seized the opportunity to start Pizza Box. 'I'm just a food lover who wanted to try something different; the job I did wasn't the most exciting. I guess everyone aspires to eventually do a job they have total enjoyment and passion for.'

Ever since his South of France family holidays as a young teenager, where they'd visit a boutique French pizzeria, serving crispy thin crusted pizzas out the back of a wee bus, Grant had visualised his adult life as a pizza chef on the roads.

'They might have been French, but they did make a cracking pizza,' Grant assures me. 'Oh and I've eaten pizza in Rome as well! I'm not a fraud.' Then in April 2018, he made his pizza dreams a reality.

Grant's aim is to deliver decent Italian pizza, made with Scottish ingredients that you'd possibly not expect to find on classic pizza dough. The Double B is a meaty number containing Piggery Smokery's signature bacon and Stornaway black pudding with jalepeños, while the Pulled Pork Perfection parades Davidsons of Inverurie pork shoulder, which has been slow roasted with Asian five spice, scattered with pineapple chunks and drizzled with sriracha

sauce. (I'm a closet pineapple-on-pizza fan, lock me up!) These are all concocted from flavours Grant loves, while involving the odd unusual topping to steer Aberdonians away from their set ways of margherita and pepperoni pizzas.

I must say I was surprised to see an electric pizza roller in the horsebox. I want to watch my dough being meticulously hand-kneaded by gentle fingers that know not to overwork the gluten, before it's romantically flung up in the air as if it were the pizza chef's treasured childhood frisbee. But, from a pragmatic business standpoint, that's not always possible.

'You can't make pizza quick enough at big events to justify doing it,' Grant explains. His electric roller takes a matter of seconds and that can really make the difference between quick efficient service or long queues of grumpy customers and confined, exasperated staff. Hand tossing pizza dough in the air, while working on top of one another, with the intensity of a 400°C oven blazing at you, just would not work. 'That oven is my best friend on frosty winter days though,' admits one of Grant's pizza chefs, Justine, at their Stonehaven Feein' Market pitch.

While up in Aberdeenshire sampling the scrumptious wares of the syndicate, I just had to seek out three more phenomenal traders who are all well worth mentioning. The truth is, I'm an obsessive Instagram scroller. Any downtime in my day merges into an incessant hunt for the latest trends. I sit gawking at tantalising dishes served up at distant hotspots, and if I ever make weekend plans, they're invariably structured around eating these tantalising foods. It's unhealthy. But it did lead me to the next three traders (you're welcome). Truthfully, I've been drooling over their photos for years, so when Michelle Russell, director of North Hop kindly bought them to my attention, it was with a big satisfied sigh that I knew I finally had an excuse to track them down. Let's start with Melt.

MELT

Mechelle Clark is the queen of cheese toasties. After ten years of working in the oil and gas industry, she was made redundant in 2014. She endured eight months of interviews and rejections before finally landing a job, only to be made redundant again a few months later. (Hang on a minute, anyone else spotting an Aberdeenshire trend here?) Well, you know how that familiar proverb goes: when life gives you lemons, make cheese toasties and leave everyone wondering how you did it.

Melt will celebrate its fourth birthday on the first of March 2020. It's a hugely accomplished business now boasting two premises, the Melt Mobile and a street food stall. It bends the rules of my book – does Mechelle's unconventional timeline of bricks and mortar before an outdoor stall disqualify her from the classification of street food? Perhaps. But are her grilled cheeses of such a high calibre that it would be a crime to walk past without joining the queue for them? Oh, most definitely.

The toasties are thick heavenly doorstops containing your week's recommended calorie intake in each half. They're filthy things, loaded with stringy mozzarella and robust cheddar to create the most Instagrammable cheese pull – if you're of that ilk. The pulled pork, haggis, ham and smoked bacon come from Aberdeenshire Larder in Ellon. It's all sandwiched between bread from the Breadmaker in Aberdeen, who are, 'A not-for-profit bakers that employ special needs staff and put profits back into the local community.'

In one shop, Melt gets through a whopping 150 loaves a week, creating toasties like the oh-so-popular Bruiser that has hangover cure written all over it. It's a marriage of macaroni cheese with a three-cheese blend, haggis and smoked bacon and, as a top secret off-menu perk, if you ask for a 'Bruiser Bru', Mel will gift you a pity can of Irn Bru to restore you back to full health. You didn't hear that from me. Scottish rapeseed oil does a marvellous job of crisping up the outsides of the toasties and Mel chooses to cook with big flat top grills and cast-iron steak weights to give the customers a bit of a show.

The shop itself transports visitors back to their childhood. 'The Breville toastie maker came to the UK in 1973, so the design brief was your nan's living room if it had been designed by Wayne Hemingway,' Mechelle says. And 'Mrs Melt' looks the part. Mechelle's style has strolled out of the 1950s with her headscarf, pristine eyebrows, winged eyeliner and 'MELT LIFE' tattooed on her knuckles, which she paid for in toasties to the artist – now that's seriously cool.

One February Monday, a newspaper reported that a passer-by kicked one of Melt's bakers in reaction to them being closed. Heaven forbid anything should get in the way of a hungry woman and her toastie. But the community hasn't always been so … welcoming. Let's rewind.

'When we opened the shop, we had dreadful press. It was faddy, it was fickle, it was bread and cheese: "How dare they charge £5 for what we can do at home?"' Melt was up against it. 'Aberdonians are so fussy and simple with their taste. You work with it or you fight it. I learned very quickly that if you dare to charge Aberdonians £5 for what they deem to be bread and cheese, it better be the size of a house.'

She ran the shop for a year before venturing into street food, and it soon became pivotal. There were only burger vans in industrial estates, fuelling lunch-break workies when she started up, but it gave her business the road it deserved. 'Up here the palate's a little limited. I could go to an event in Glasgow or Edinburgh and use San Francisco-style sourdough bread, that comes out chewy and sticky. In Aberdeen, unless it's a farmhouse loaf, you'd struggle. They don't appreciate specialist cheeses either. I tried to do trendy drinks and got met with resistance from people who just want Irn Bru!'

At times Mechelle's creativity was limited by her audience, but by trading at hundreds of events across Scotland, she could experiment with her produce and then reel customers back in for more. 'People now come to me because they've seen my stall at pop-ups and festivals. There's no better advertising than getting out there and doing it.'

Aberdonians might have simpler tastes, according to Mechelle. But once she's converted them, they're loyal. 'Almost four years on and my customers are incredibly protective of me; we've established a cheese cult!' There are no regrets here.

THE BRUISER

A very Scottish toastie comprised of macaroni cheese, haggis and smoked bacon

....

SERVES
1

INGREDIENTS

2 slices of sourdough bread
50g béchamel sauce
100g mozzarella, grated
50g strong Scottish cheddar
Rapeseed oil
50g Marshalls macaroni, cooked
2 rashers of grilled smoked streaky bacon
100g haggis, cooked

METHOD

1. Lay your bread out and generously spread your béchamel sauce onto both slices of bread.
2. Shower one slice of bread with both types of cheese and sandwich together.
3. Oil a hot pan, a skillet is ideal, and place the sandwich into it at a high heat.
4. If you have a heavy pan press this on top.
5. Lift the underside after a few minutes to check it's browning, adjust heat accordingly.
6. Once browned flip over and cook the other side. When you're happy it has browned and the cheese has melted put the macaroni and meat inside and continue to heat through for several minutes.
7. Take off the heat and enjoy.

THE STORNOWAY TOASTIE

Stornoway black pudding as it should be, smothered in cheese

....

SERVES
1

INGREDIENTS

2 slices of sourdough bread
50g béchamel sauce
20g apple sauce
100g mozzarella, grated
50g strong Scottish cheddar (Mrs Melt likes Montgomery)
Rapeseed oil
50g Stornoway black pudding, cooked

METHOD

1. Lay your bread out and generously spread the béchamel sauce onto one slice, spread the apple sauce on the other slice.
2. Now you need to follow the same steps as the Bruiser, for steps 2. to 5.
3. Once browned flip over and cook the other side. Once you're happy it has browned and the cheese has melted, sprinkle the cooked black pudding inside the toastie and continue to heat through for several minutes.
4. Take off the heat and enjoy.

THE
BAY FISH &
CHIPS

In a review of one of Edinburgh's better fish and chip shops, my idol Jay Rayner dishes out some truths. Chips are often treated as an afterthought, a beige nest in which to prop up the limelight-hogging haddock. But I'm not here for the fish. Yes, it's got to be good, but I'm looking for something extraordinary on the chip front. I want homemade misshapen things, with fluffy inners and golden crispy outers, something my favourite aunt (ahem, Bessie) couldn't rustle up in the oven. As Jay puts it, 'If you're going to eat chips, you need to feel that the calories are worth it: that the potatoes have been fretted over . . . There should be crunch, and the occasional shatter.'

Calum Richardson's chips are exactly that. Made from fresh Maris Pipers and Markies grown in Cambridgeshire, Calum peels and preps his chips every evening ready for the next day. His attention to detail, commitment to sustainability and focus on finessing the quality of our fish and chip experiences are exemplary.

'I like to work with floury tatties that have the right balance of natural sugars, so the chips won't brown too much or too little. If you think your choice of tattie doesn't make a difference to your chips, experiment at home and you'll see a vast difference in the finished product.'

Like Mechelle at Melt, Calum's got his own permanent premises. In fact, *Lonely Planet* has ranked tucking into fish and chips, while sat on the Bay's sandy doorstep at Stonehaven Beach, as one of the world's top food experiences. But when the number of awards under Calum's belt are this staggering – and include Britain's best independent for fish and chips – his On The Road van needs to be tracked down.

Q&A

Calum and I caught up, and I quizzed him on what makes his travelling chippy so successful.

HOW DID IT ALL START?

I've lived in Stonehaven all my life. When I was sixteen I joined the Navy as an engineer, because that's where my skillset was suited. After nine years, when I had the opportunity to leave, I retrained and got into cheffing. I managed a fish and chip shop, and then an opportunity came up to buy my own. The shop was bankrupt, so it was fairly high-risk. But I thought, if I give it my full focus, it'll excel. I did that for six years, and I won Young Fryer of the Year for the UK. That was a big pat on the back. It made me realise there was a career in this.

WHEN DID YOU OPEN THE BAY?

When I was younger, Stonehaven beachfront was a real vibrant area. But over the years I've visited a lot and could see it declining. I knew it was a gamble being on the beachfront because of the weather, but there's parking and someone needed to make the area work. That's what got me buying the Bay property and converting it into a fish and chip shop in 2006. My aim was to win Fish and Chip Shop of the Year: a great accolade to put me on the map and drive business. We won it for Scotland in 2012 and 2013, then won it for Britain as a whole in 2013.

WHAT'S YOUR FOCUS NOW?

The biggest thing for us is sustainability and the environment. We're right on the beachfront, so we see the damage done with thrown rubbish.

That's how we got into using Vegware. Every bit of packaging in the shop and van is Vegware, absolutely no plastic. We've been doing that for about ten years. We were ahead of the time, but we did it because we *wanted* to, rather than we had to. Now, there's a moral pressure. It's the same with food waste: I was composting it well before it became law in Scotland. The shop uses 100% renewable energy, 100% renewable gas. I'm reducing our carbon footprint.

HOW DO YOU SOURCE YOUR INGREDIENTS?

Oh, it's a crucial part of the business. I need to know the story of every product that comes in. How it's made, what it's fed, how it's looked after, is it Red Tractor, is it organic . . . I never compromise on the product.

All our fish is caught in the North Sea and we were the first UK fish and chip shop to gain Marine Stewardship Council Chain of Custody to sell Scottish North Sea haddock on a menu. Our squid and langoustines come from

Harvester in the nearby town of Gourdon.

When I take a product to test, I never ask the price, I just want to taste it. So, when I found Guy Grieve's scallops from the Ethical Shellfish Company and Guy said, 'You'll never sell them,' my response was: 'You leave that to me!' They were expensive but I tried them without knowing the price, and then I chose them because it was right for the business. If you know the price, you're already disliking it before you taste and then you're buying products because they're cheap. That's short-sighted. The scallops are done on the griddle as specials and sell out every time.

WHEN DID YOU INTRODUCE THE STREET FOOD ELEMENT?

I've always been keen, and I had a table-top fryer so I could go to events and cook. But you're compromising yourself when you work with inferior equipment. A good time to do it would have been when I won Fish and Chip Shop of the Year, but we were too busy. So, I waited.

There's a fine line between success and letting it take over your life. I had a guy working for me who wanted to manage the van, so I was training him up. After six years, he decided this wasn't the industry for him. That was good. It was lucky I didn't grow it too big. I would have created a monster I couldn't control.

I'm approached for weddings and festivals all the time, which is great for the brand and spreading our fish suppers to Scotland's far corners. I used the van for National Fish and Chip day: I parked it up at Aberdeen Airport and dished out 500 free portions of fish and chips. The van gave me the freedom to do that. The staff love it, it's a fun day out of the office.

We've been to London, doing parties for merchant bankers at the weekends. We're always spreading the news of how phenomenal the produce is up here.

DO YOU LIKE LIFE ON THE ROAD?

My nan is a chef, and I remember her telling me about that smile everyone had on their face when she'd cooked for them – especially family. She brought people together. Everyone was happy, everyone was talking. No one was working or on their phones. That's what I enjoy and street food is a great way of achieving that.

HAVE YOU EVER CATERED FOR ANYONE FAMOUS?

One time I was approached by a company who I turned down . . . then I found out it was some folk from *Game of Thrones* getting married. That's unreal! But to be honest, anyone who comes to the hatch deserves the same quality. Half the time you don't know who you're serving. The number of times I've seen a tweet from a celebrity and I'm like, 'Did I serve them?' You're that busy, you're heads down and working away.

WHAT ABOUT – THE FUTURE?

I'm busy all the time now. I supply the Compass Group with my signature batter and fishcakes throughout the UK – the army, navy, air force, oil rigs, schools and hospitals. I took all the colourings and additives out because if you're trying to buy the best produce and the best fish, why would you want to coat them in chemicals? You want to let the product taste of itself, not overpower it; the batter can't be too thick. You've got to look after your ingredients, look after your oil and have a heap of passion!

HOMEMADE TARTARE SAUCE

SERVES
2

INGREDIENTS

2 spring onions
2 tbsp mayonnaise
1 tsp gherkins
1 tsp capers
Dijon mustard to taste
Pinch of fresh parsley
Pinch of fresh chives

METHOD

1. Finely slice the gherkins, spring onions and capers.
2. Chop herbs and combine with the mayonnaise and Dijon mustard to taste.
3. Store in the fridge until needed.

SMOKED SCOTTISH HADDOCK FISHCAKES

SERVES
2

INGREDIENTS

340g natural smoked MSC
  Scottish haddock
6 Maris Piper potatoes
1 lemon
1 tbsp butter
1 egg, beaten
3 tbsp breadcrumbs
1 tbsp curly parsley
Salt and pepper

TO SERVE
Tartare sauce (homemade is
  best!)

METHOD

1. Peel and chop the potatoes, place in a pan and boil.
2. Place the haddock and butter in a tin foil pouch and place in a colander on top of the pan with the potatoes to steam. When the potatoes are soft, remove and drain.
3. Flake the fish into chunks and put to one side.
4. Pour the juices from the pouch into the potatoes and mash. Add the parsley, salt, pepper and a squeeze of lemon juice and mix well.
5. Add the fish to the potato and fold.
6. Use your hands to roll the fishcake mix into equal-sized balls, flatten out and shape. Dip in the egg then lightly coat in breadcrumbs.
7. Pan-fry the fishcakes for colour then put in the oven at 180°C for around 15 minutes to finish cooking.
8. Serve the fishcakes hot with tartare sauce and a green salad, or your favourite steamed green vegetables.

THE
LIBERTY
KITCHEN

Porridge is part of Scotland's national identity; it's in our DNA. We get so hung up on complaining about the inclement weather, we forget it's these conditions that help our beloved oaty crop thrive. In Scotland we've been growing and scoffing oats since late medieval times.

I was raised on the stuff and don't know a single Scot who wouldn't fondly think of home when eating a warm bowl of porridge. It's made a recent comeback, thanks to aligning seamlessly with our modern living ideals: sustainable – tick, healthy – tick, vegetarian and easily made vegan – oh absolutely. What was once just high in fibre, low in GI and proven to lower cholesterol has been made desirable with the enhancement of seasonal toppings. We now dress our oats to suit our developed taste buds. It's no longer cheap fuel that's eaten out of necessity for its slow-release energy – I'll actively go out of my way to track some down for breakfast. So naturally, when there's the opportunity to stroll along Aberdeen beach with a tub full while walking the dog, or having just finished a Park Run, we're going to say yes. Yes, please.

Nikki, the Liberty Kitchen's owner is a traditionalist insofar as her porridge is made with rolled oats, water and salt. 'It doesn't need milk to make it deliciously creamy,' she assures me. But she elevates the humble oat with produce from her dad's allotment at Greyhope Bay. In May, Nikki delights morning strollers with her rhubarb and rose compote on top, while in chillier months she experiments with warm and fragrant overnight cardamom and chia oats. It's all washed down with the hot trickle of Sacred Grounds organic Peruvian coffee, which bursts with notes of cherry bakewell and chocolate, and will double up as a handwarmer in winter.

But nutritious breakfasts on the go aren't Nikki's only forté. Her white horsebox, positioned on the Esplanade, is home to superb vegan fare. There's homemade cakes, like the lemon drizzle or the banana loaf that everyone raves about, and heartier lunch options include her much sought-after vegan chilli.

'The base is made of the usual suspects like peppers and beans, but then I'll spruce it up with whatever vegetables are in season, alongside spinach and kale from the allotment. The chilli is always colourful. It's important for vegetarian food to have a mixture of colour and texture.' Nikki prepares beautiful Buddha bowls topped with her limey avocado cream (think one bowl of healthy elements, arranged in such a way that it *must* be instagrammed before consumption).

Nikki turned vegetarian when she spent a few years in Houston, where the meat was pumped with hormones and chemicals. It started as a health decision, but with the rise in awareness of animal cruelty and the environmental impact of farming, there was no need to go back. It's here that she also fell in love with street food. After graduating in textile designs, Nikki travelled the world only to return to Aberdeen and fall into the oil and gas industry, as Aberdonians tend to do. Ten years later, she relocated to Houston, Texas and got stuck into the food truck scene.

'My favourite was the Eatsie boys – a take on the Beastie Boys – they operated out of a huge converted ambulance, wrapped in metallic gold. They were trading as a partnership with 8th Wonder Brewery at the time – you need to check out their website.'

I did. The intergalactic truck is all about 'waffle fries for the homies' including buttered corn fries with lashings of garlic aioli, hot sauce, a sprinkling of cotija cheese, green onion and

lime. If I wasn't hungry before, then I certainly was now. They've celebrated their eighth birthday and still radiate a zealous attitude: 'Purveyors of good eats, licensed to grill 8 days a week.'

When Nikki's marriage broke down, she returned to Aberdeen and channelled her energy into launching the horsebox venture. She dipped back into the oil industry to raise extra start-up cash, then, in January 2018, the Liberty Kitchen was born. You don't need to be Sherlock to figure out why it's named that! But it hasn't all been plain sailing. Trading on the Esplanade in sub-zero temperatures requires a lot of determination; Nikki will toil away with her mum, Joyce, braving everything the north east throws at them, just to generously serve up these compostable pots of goodness, and all with a smile.

'It's too much sometimes,' Nikki admits. 'I only trade at the weekend, when the weather permits. But some days it'll start off bearable and quickly turn baltic, with what feels like the most ferocious winds you'll ever experience. My licence is up in September and I'm debating whether to wait and just renew it in spring, that

might be easier than letting customers down.'

It would mean that in winter Nikki could focus on her new project Liberty Lifestyle, offering Reiki therapy as a nice weekday earner. 'But I really am in two minds,' she contemplates. Nikki endured such a lengthy, frustrating process to get that pitch from the council: it would be a shame to miss six months of the year.

'All in all, my experience of trading on the Esplanade has been incredible. People down at the beach have been so delighted to stumble upon the horsebox and to be able to eat anything without allergy limitations. It's all gluten-free and mostly vegan, too. This has been my dream. I've worked hard and I've been lucky, people have been so supportive from the very start. I've got some really loyal customers who come every time I'm open and some who will travel to different locations, when I'm doing markets, just to get their coffee.'

For a relaxing weekend beach walk, made memorable with orange brownies, silky turmeric lattes and great conversation, head to Aberdeen's Esplanade and, most weekends, you'll find Nikki there.

RHUBARB AND ROSE PORRIDGE

SERVES
2

INGREDIENTS

PERFECT PORRIDGE
100g rolled oats
700ml water
Pinch of Himalayan pink salt or
   sea salt

RHUBARB AND ROSE COMPOTE
(6 SERVINGS)
6 rhubarb stalks, trimmed into
   1-inch chunks
2 tbsp rosewater
1 tbsp unrefined caster sugar or
   agave nectar

TO SERVE
Edible dried rose petals, seeds,
   nuts, plant-based milk

METHOD

1. Add the oats, water and salt to the pan.
2. Bring to the boil then turn down and simmer for
   5 minutes, stirring until soft and creamy.
3. Meanwhile add the rhubarb and the rosewater to a pan,
   sprinkle with sugar and bring to the boil stirring gently
   to avoid breaking up the rhubarb too much.
4. Cook for around 5 minutes and remove from the heat.

TO SERVE
1. Top the warm porridge with the rhubarb compote,
   sprinkle with chia seeds or nuts and seeds of your
   choice and a little plant-based milk.
2. The compote is also delicious cold drizzled over
   overnight oats or with granola and natural yoghurt or
   plant-based yoghurt.

ARGYLL & BUTE

With a stunning coastline longer than France and 23 islands, inhabited and yet largely untainted by commercialism, for me Argyll & Bute join the Highlands & Islands as some of the world's most naturally beautiful destinations. Between them, I could write a whole book on Scotland's seafood shacks (brace yourself for a sequel), with their freshly landed catch which is best enjoyed unadulterated, served with a little butter and squeeze of lemon at most. But beyond the outstanding seafood from its pure waters, great credit must be given to their other produce: cheese, award-winning haggis, lamb and whisky – great Scottish staples, which have made their way into street food dishes across the country. I've seen Isle of Mull cheddar crumbled atop of pizzas and oozing out of cheese toasties. Delicious!

TOBERMORY
FISH & CHIP VAN

What's the story in Balamory? I'll tell you. Plump, translucent, just-landed scallops cooked to order, overlooking the joyfully painted buildings of Tobermory Bay. It doesn't get much better than that! Best friends Jeanette Gallagher and Jane Maclean launched their fish and chip van back in 1988 to cater to the island's demand.

All year round they're trading six days a week on the Fisherman's Pier in the heart of the town, feeding a long string of loyal locals, hungry visitors and passing cyclists. Perch on the base of the clock tower, or on a nearby lobster and prawn creel, and tuck into the fresh and crunchy battered angel-cut haddock that's come straight off the boats that morning ... though you might find the chips a little disappointing after such outstanding fish. The secret?

'It's cooked and eaten fresh, and the fish quality is like no other,' says Jeanette. Back in 2003, it was deemed 'delicious' by His Royal Highness The Prince of Wales. Well, if it's good enough for Charles ...

OBAN
SEAFOOD HUT

You would have thought the best shellfish in Scotland could be found, after waiting months for a table, within the walls of one our esteemed Michelin-starred restaurants. But no, it's served up in polystyrene trays from an unassuming green hut on Oban's CalMac Pier, for a tiny fraction of the price.

Okay, the polystyrene packaging isn't so great. But its contents of fleshy langoustines atop a medley of seafood, gigantic crab claws with insides that need only a gentle tease from your disposable fork, and creamy oysters at 95p a pop, is all entirely unrivalled.

With a race to the one communal picnic table, most people stand and embrace the sea breeze, which threatens to blow away your garlic butter-sodden napkin. Not that your hands need it; cleaning up the buttery remnants from your scallop shell, which are making their way down your sleeve, is most definitely a job for your tongue.

CREEL SEAFOOD BAR

Siobhan Cameron isn't messing when she says 'from creel to the pan as fast as we can'. This is exactly how seafood ought to be enjoyed, beside pristine waters a stone's throw from where it was landed. In her little hut, that looked like a garden shed until it was painted sky blue in summer 2019, Siobhan fries her homemade skin-on chips until they are deep brown, crunchy and dangerously moreish.

These are a mighty fine enhancement to the main event: smoked Loch Fyne kippers in a warm crusty roll, Inverlussa mussels given the marinière treatment, half lobsters baked in lime and garlic, and traditional fish suppers. There aren't many places in the world where you can find such range or quality, nor pick up a roll teeming with black pudding and meaty scallops to eat on the hoof as you board a ferry to a remote island. But this tiny shack has it all.

THE
REAL MACKAY
STOVIE CO

So, we've cottoned on to the notion that Scottish seafood is some of the best in the world, and from Aberdeen Angus to Belted Galloways, so is Scotch beef too. But what about lamb? It gets bullied to the back of the supermarket aisles by its Kiwi counterpart, when really the lamb on our doorstep is fresher and, to my mind, much tastier. For a while now, I've been on a mission to encourage more Scottish lamb consumption, and some of the tastiest dishes I've encountered have turned up in the most unexpected places.

Now I'll cut to the chase. There's a lot of poor quality fast food churned out at the home of Scottish rugby. On match days, 67,000 supporters make the pilgrimage to the hallowed turf of Murrayfield Stadium in Edinburgh, often beginning in the prestigious watering holes of Rose Street, dipping into the raucous atmosphere of Teuchters, then winding their way past the young pipers, paying them en route. As anticipation and noise levels heighten, Murrayfield reverberates with the skirl of the bagpipes, with 'Scotland the Brave' and 'Flower of Scotland' stoking the patriotic fire within fans' bellies . . . but that's not enough; they'll need to be properly fed too.

It's in these precious moments before kick-off that the canny tartan-clad Scot makes a beeline for a hearty bowl of stovies from the Real Mackay Stovie Co. They'll join the queue for the famously wholesome produce from Argyll before scurrying back to their seat – you wouldn't want to miss an early try. Though, as each mouthful ignites a radiating warmth from within, it's perhaps the only time you don't want Scotland to score, for fear yer stovies could go flying.

So why does this meal outweigh the plethora of burgers and hot dogs on offer? Traditionally the leftovers from your Sunday roast, or your evening meal, would go into a giant pot on the stove to be heated up for the next day. It might have contained crumbled sausage or corned beef, but this one's a labour of love by Rhuaridh and Alison Mackay, who've turned the dish up to a ten on the quality scale.

'We use the whole beast and all the good bits,' Alison explains. 'The lamb's roasted for ten hours at a low heat, with the bones and gigots all diced together, slowly releasing the jelly and goodness out of the bones. That's what gives it the flavour.'

The couple have been tenancy farmers on the Duke of Argyll's Stronmagachan Farm since 1999. That's where their black-faced lambs are born and reared, left to graze on wild grass and heather and roam free on 2,400 acres between Inverary and Dalmally.

Street food was never part of the plan, but when the price of lamb fell so low in 2008, Rhuaridh refused to let it go at the market for such a pittance. That's when they decided to take a punt on the stovie stall. 'Food From Argyll had started up and were hugely supportive of our new venture; in fact, we couldn't have done it without them,' Alison recalls. 'We started attending events like T in the Park, Belladrum Tartan Heart Festival and RockNess. It just took off.'

When they were invited to trade at the 2014 Commonwealth Games under the Scotland Food and Drink banner, it was obvious that they'd make great ambassadors for Scottish produce; as indeed they did. This opened the door to a regular Murrayfield slot, keeping them busy between one-off rural events.

Their menu has since expanded to include freshly baked sausage rolls, haggis, neeps and tatties; the key ingredients sourced from Mark Grant, a specialist butcher in Taynuilt. 'We're pretty basic, we're not cooks, we've learned to make the most of what we've got. Customers like coming to us for a good blether, because we know what we're talking about and the food is freshly made on site.' Gregor Townsend, Scotland's national rugby coach, has even been spotted tackling – sorry, tucking into – a bowl.

HIGHLANDS & ISLANDS

Venturing north from Argyll & Bute you reach Scotland's breathtaking Highlands & Islands. Whether you're touring via the North Coast 500 or choose to relive the *Harry Potter* movie set, crossing the Glenfinnan Viaduct, the scenery is breathtaking. Here the pace of life slows down and if you can find time to stroll along the soft white sands or even bag a Munro, you'll experience a solitude like no other. This is a place to lose yourself in Scotland's natural beauty.

On the move, and often pitched up in Inverness city centre, I've found a superb pit stop for cake and a cuppa, and beyond that it would be a crime to stroll past the laidback village of Ullapool, which hosts an award-winning street food shack. Meanwhile, on the islands, street food is a far cry from what you'd find in Scotland's cities. The gritty industrial feel of our curated markets is traded for a rural environment, and rather than using ingredients or spices and influences from other cuisines, traders here celebrate their local Scottish larder. There's no better place to enjoy fine seafood and maybe a wee dram or two, from one of the region's many renowned distilleries.

BAD GIRL
BAKERY

Before 2018, no street food traders had permission to trade in Inverness, the cultural capital of the Highlands. That is, until Jeni Hardie, owner of the Bad Girl Bakery Café in Muir of Ord, invested in a sleek, retro aluminium caravan and filled it with her irresistible cakes – worthy of a spot slap bang in the city centre, beside Eastgate Shopping Centre.

'When we first drove it through the village, it felt like we were driving the shimmering Coca-Cola truck! People were waving and tooting – we were celebrities,' Jeni recalls. The head-turning monocoque body lends itself to a 1950s design, packed by Rocket Caravans into a stylish-but-strong lightweight aluminium body, purposebuilt to meet Jeni's needs on the road – though nothing will ever prepare you for a harsh winter in the Highlands. 'It's probably ridiculous [not thinking about the winter] given that we live here, but we were a bit naive. I was just so excited, I didn't think about the effects of the weather. But because we bake fresh every day, we're not like other street food traders who can prepare things as they go along. We had to learn very quickly to control our stock levels because if people didn't buy the cakes we baked, they'd go in the bin. When the snow got really heavy, we couldn't even physically drive to the centre, let alone afford the waste.'

But Jeni is no stranger to seasonal peaks and troughs. She supplies all of the National Trust properties in the north west of Scotland, baking each cake by hand, like she does for her own café, delivering them fresh three times a week. If you've ever had the luxury of travelling on the Caledonian Sleeper – experiencing the romanticism of falling asleep in smoggy London and waking up with breathtaking views of the

Highlands – it's Jeni's cakes that you would have tucked into en route. Being such a tourist destination, however, at the end of summer these wholesale figures drop considerably, and that's where street food plays such an integral role in keeping Jeni's business afloat.

'Our recruitment policy is a little unique. We only hire people who aren't bakers, so to invest all our time in training them, only to say goodbye at the end of the summer didn't seem right. That's why we launched our beautiful cake and coffee caravan, to keep our fantastic staff on the books and give them another branch of income throughout winter and spring,' Jeni explains. From attending local events like the Loch Ness Marathon to the largest agricultural show in the north, the Black Isle Show, the caravan has been a business game-changer for Bad Girl Bakery.

'There's something immediate about the van. It's a lovely experience chatting directly to customers, and it's given us real exposure in the city centre, driving custom to our café in Muir of Ord.' What started as a pilot scheme evolved into a product development opportunity. 'We're testing new flavours in a small-scale way on the people of Inverness, before introducing them to our wholesale menu. And we're playing with fryers to make these incredible doughnuts – we've never done deep-fried baked goods before.'

Jeni's the bad girl in all of this. Gosh, aren't we all? The bakery is about treating yourself every now and again, and not feeling guilty about it. Why on earth should you?

'Everyone's got someone in the family who frowns upon you having a treat, if you're having a slice of cake they'd say, "Ooh, you're a bad girl!" So it's just light heartedly poking fun at that idea. Here, we're all about the treats.' Now there's a woman who speaks my language.

There's nothing more disappointing than disappointing cake. So, Jeni's portions are big and generous. It's not just masses of sweet things piled high in a box and slathered with buttercream, there's whacks of flavour and unexpected textures in each bite; a layer of salted caramel here, some crumbled biscuit there – Jeni's resolute in her fight to end the circulation of tasteless baked goods.

'If you don't treat yourself very often, every bite needs to count,' she says. 'You can't think, "Oh God I wasted my calories on that." We're about indulgence and exceeding expectations.'

The caravan's emblazoned with the words: 'Bad girls make good cake', and she's not wrong. But, of course, what was originally just Jeni baking through the night in her own home, has now expanded to a talented team of sixteen (with a handful of men, too) operating in a professional kitchen. 'The street trader's licence is only per individual, so you can imagine, it was quite the cost to set up.'

While street food is a little sparse on the ground in the Highlands, with tens of miles between each village, Jeni says the distance is irrelevant.

'The one amazing thing about the Highlands is that people are really driven by quality; we might make a hundred-mile round trip to go for seafood. We've got people who make a hundred-mile round trip to come for cake. The geography doesn't seem to matter. I'm

from Dundee and the idea of driving to Fife to get something to eat is ridiculous, but in the Highlands it's not unheard of to take a road trip to find something nice to eat.'

So, where should my next stop in the Highlands be? Jeni says the Seafood Shack in Ullapool is unmissable. 'We went on Easter Sunday – they do this amazing tempura-battered haddock in a wrap, my husband Douglas is a big fan of the langoustines and our wee boy who's eleven loves their lobster bisque.' I soon realised that chatting to them was a must!

THE
SEAFOOD
SHACK

If at any moment you've questioned whether a seafood shack counts as street food, then here's your answer: in 2017 the Seafood Shack in Ullapool won Best Street Food at the BBC Radio 4 Food and Farming Awards. Jeni was right when she said I needed to speak to Kirsty Scobie and Fenella Renwick; this is street food that's seriously worth travelling for – some of their customers have driven hundreds of miles for it, the girls tell me. This is an unmissable destination for seafood junkies.

We restaurant goers have fallen into the habit of researching everything in advance. I for one don't seem capable of eating out without scouring an online menu beforehand – there's no spontaneity or surprises anymore. That's unless you're headed to the Seafood Shack where the menu of the day is the catch of the day, chalked up on the blackboard and prepared fresh that morning. It might feature luxuriously creamy lobster mac 'n' cheese, Cullen skink packed with generous chunks of smoked fish or their best-selling haddock tempura wraps smeared with lemon mayonnaise and pesto, but

you won't know until you get there. I've said before that quality Scottish seafood is best left the hell alone, but the exception to that rule is if it's in the accomplished hands of chefs who know exactly which herbs, spices and textures will best complement its unrivalled natural flavour. Kirsty and Fenella are of that ilk.

Though their crowd-funded trailer only opened its hatch to the public in May 2016, they both have extensive years of experience, more than qualifying them to handle seafood. Fenella was brought up around the stuff with her dad being a fisherman and her mum owning a seafood restaurant, while Kirsty had always loved cooking, having previously worked in restaurants and being self employed as a lodge cook. Both of their other halves are fishermen. Kirsty's partner, Josh, provides the shack's langoustines, lobsters and crabs. Fenella's husband Mark, on the other hand, dives for their scallops. Knowing exactly how to tease the maximum concentrated flavour out of lobster shells, tails, claws, knuckles and legs to create an indulgent bisque, that few others could live up to, really is their forté.

The shack was born out of the local lassies' frustration. It stemmed from a discussion while out fishing, when the conversation turned to the serious lack of fresh seafood available in the village. 'Ullapool has around twelve local boats: five prawn trawlers and seven inshore creel boats, with a further two crabbing boats coming in each week and around ten white fish boats that land regularly, depending on the time of year. We're provided with a variety of seafood daily, but where was it all going? Straight onto the back of a lorry.'

Desperate to change this, Fenella and Kirsty wanted to do something different. 'We wanted to watch people enjoying Ullapool's amazing seafood. We wanted to interact with our customers, talk to them and not only provide delicious food but educate them on it, too. Street food has become such a trendy, up-and-coming market, people want to grab their food and go, but most importantly they want it to be of a high quality. We decided this would be perfect for us; to have a street trailer with its hatches wide open, so that the public could come to us, watch us cook and then ask us any questions they have on seafood and fishing.'

With multiple awards under their belt, Kirsty and Fenella have certainly achieved their aim. If you're headed up in that direction, you'll find them cooking up a storm in an unassuming lot, one road back from the shore. It's sandwiched between two windbreaking buildings, with unobscured views of picturesque Loch Broom. When the sun beats down, you'd be forgiven for thinking you were in the Mediterranean. Though in the likelihood of summer showers, there's something really romantic about listening to the rain ricocheting off the tarpaulin above, while tucking into today's catch. And it's all served in biodegradable packaging – hurrah!

HADDOCK WRAP

INGREDIENTS

SERVES 4-6

PESTO
100g fresh basil leaves
2 garlic cloves
Handful of pinenuts
Chunk of Parmesan
Squeeze of lemon juice
Olive oil
Pinch of salt and pepper

FOR THE LEMON MAYO
2 cups of mayonnaise
½ a lemon, zested
½ a lemon, juiced
Pinch of salt and pepper

FOR THE BATTER
150g plain flour
100g corn flour
10g baking powder
Salt and pepper

Fresh haddock fillets, 4 to 6
White tortilla wraps, 4 to 6
Salad
Cut veg of your choice

METHOD

1. Add vegetable oil to your deep fat fryer or large pan. Heat it to 180°C.

2. For the pesto: roast your pinenuts in a pan until golden brown. Pop all your pesto ingredients into a blender. Add the oil while blending until it's a smooth, textured paste.

3. For the mayo: mix all ingredients together until smooth.

4. For the batter: add all ingredients together. Use an electric or hand whisk and slowly add water as you whisk. Continue until your batter has a thick but runny consistency. It should stick to your finger when you dip it in. Make sure this is seasoned well.

5. For the fish: check the haddock fillet for bones. Coat the fish in a bowl full of plain flour. Then dip it in the batter so it gets a good overall coating.

6. Place gently into deep fat fryer (make sure you give it a gentle shake so it doesn't stick to the bottom). Cook until the batter becomes brown and crispy, for around four minutes. Remove and place on some kitchen roll to soak up any excess oil.

7. Time to assemble! Take your tortilla wrap and spread it with as much pesto and lemon mayonnaise as you want. Add salad and cut veg. Place your fish in the middle. Season, wrap and enjoy!

THE
OYSTER SHED

Off the main road in Carbost, a minute from the Talisker Distillery, Paul McGlynn, aka the oyster man, sells his Pacific oysters, grown in the crystal-clear waters of Loch Harport on the west coast of Skye.

The main shed has been converted into something of a farm shop, with Isle of Mull and Orkney waxed truckles, game from the Highlands, local pâtés, seaweed and other artisan delights. It's here that Paul and his team will teach you how to shuck an oyster, which builds up your appetite nicely for the main event: a smaller shed serving up all the goods cooked to order. There's Hebridean crab claws, lobster tails pan-fried in garlic butter, salt and pepper squid, and the majestic seafood platter.

Huddling round a barrel, repurposed as a table, I realise that each disposable tray-full is better than the last – how is that even possible? For the real Skye experience, Paul's more than happy for you to BYOB, should you have been lured into the neighbouring distillery en route.

THE
SCALLOP SHACK

A shack dedicated to celebrating the dog-paw-sized hand-dived scallops collected from the seabed surrounding the Isle of Lewis in the Outer Hebrides – that's got to be bucket-list worthy, surely?

Dave and Julie Smith have been providing the locals of Uig with raw scallops from their eye-catching, shell-decorated hut for over thirty years. They've even got an honesty box system if no one's around to take your money. After plenty of requests, in 2018 they decided to convert a neighbouring shipping container to serve pan-seared scallops straight out of the hatch during the summer months . . . and, oh what a success!

Vegware tubs are loaded with squishy golden scallops, studded with your choice of bacon lardons or black pudding: all entirely dreamy, and the sensation of being perched almost on the edge of the world – with the expanse of the North Atlantic laid out before you – isn't too bad either. It's a perfect setting to contemplate the last stop on our *Street Food Scotland* journey.

THE FUTURE – STREETS AHEAD OR KICKED TO THE KERB?

STREETS AHEAD

In Scotland, street food is big. In fact, if the number of quality traders is anything to go by, it's colossal. We're in the midst of an incredibly exciting revolution; yes, it's finally crept its way north of the border and no, it's not just the taking part that counts; in the street food arena we mean serious business. In many ways Scotland is perfect for it; if you can pop on a raincoat, see past the drizzly weather and get yourself out there to enjoy this beautiful country at its finest, then you'll understand exactly why. Scottish produce is some of the best in the world, and, in the right hands, it's made to sing.

With our food and drink industry steered by the likes of Tom Kitchin, Gary Maclean, Nick Nairn, Neil Forbes, Martin Wishart, Lorna McNee, Tony Singh and the late Andrew Fairlie – to name but a few – as a nation we're developing some rather discerning palates. Even if you're yet to dine in their establishments, the influence of these chefs permeates down through our traders and continues to advance our country's culinary offering.

As a nation, Scots are known for their friendly, welcoming nature. If you're debating that, you only need to attend a wedding with even a single Scot present to be proved wrong; out of the entire party it'll be that one tartan-clad guest who woos their way into the bridal album, makes a lasting impression on the dance floor and forms concrete friendships with every single attendee, including the catering staff. There's nothing we enjoy more than having a blether, even to strangers. So, it's no surprise that street food, with its queue of chatty patrons and the promise of meeting the chef at the end of it, is right up our street.

Beyond that, we're living in bizarre times of technological change and us Scots are yearning for a wee bit of regression. It's the self-service checkouts and the impersonal online booking systems. I don't want to rate my experience on-screen; I want the server to ask if everything's been okay with my visit. Equally, I don't want artificial intelligence to tell me what I want to eat based on my previous spending habits; I'm looking for a real-life human being to recommend a dish they ate the night before, that they think I might love too. That's why our street food markets and events are soaring in popularity; they supply us with buckets full of the social interaction that we so desperately crave.

At the same time, we're a sassy bunch. We aren't afraid to give our opinions or voice when we've been let down by a dish, whether that's by its freshness, flavour or price. I spent a big chunk of my life in the south of England where, believe me, it's staggering how much poor food gets tolerated. In Scotland we know what we like, and we won't entertain food that doesn't meet our high standards. Collectively, we'll weed out the bad stuff. The traders who work tirelessly to deliver original dishes full of local

Scottish ingredients will flourish and those who don't won't be around too long. Street food is still fairly new to us, and it's okay to admit we were late to the party, because by the time it spreads up to the northern cities and round to the west coast where our seafood is landed and our cattle roam free, I know we'll be streets ahead.

KICKED TO THE KERB

On these pages I've celebrated the positives and also divulged some of the plights of our traders. I'm an honest reviewer and I believe it's important for us, the street food munchers, to understand the challenges encountered behind the scenes. It'll make us appreciate the food, and the cooks who've slaved so hard to produce it, a whole lot more. Owning your own business is notoriously tough. From trying to stand out when you first launch, to the long and often lonely hours; hiring staff who are the right fit and feel as passionate as you do, and finding that equilibrium between selling at an attractive price point while making enough profit to survive. That's all amplified in the cut-throat food and drink industry, where you're laid out before gastronomes, ready to be criticised, on a daily basis. (Sorry, I'm one of them!)

'It takes a very specific kind of person to get into street food,' Anna from Freddy & Hicks explains. 'We're the work hard play hard types. You've got to be resilient and determined, but also physically strong, there's a lot of lugging heavy items around,' she tells me. It's not the easiest lifestyle to hack but once you get that recipe right, taking into consideration brand, product, pricing and the right pitches, it can be financially rewarding. In many ways, that's why street food is at risk of ruin; with success comes greed.

We've already started to see the large enterprises muscle their bullish way in. From, the multiple-unit operators who've launched their own food truck in an attempt to camouflage as local, to the supermarkets who've detected its growing popularity and have introduced microwavable ranges inspired by street food to drive additional revenue. In 2019 McDonald's piggybacked on street food's success and took to the roads with their fleet of Chicken McNuggets vans, attending festivals looking for an unprecedented grab of market share. It's all very well wanting a piece of the pie, but eventually these companies will ruin the whole revolution altogether. Street food is cool because it's independent and supports local; the second those money-hungry big players move in with wholesale produce and unethical practices, it'll be time for me to go home.

At the same time, we've got to thrust event organisers under the spotlight. Like the big brands, the pupils in their eyes have been superseded by pound signs. As street food's popularity and demand increases, there will inevitably be more competition for a pitch. In Scotland, our street food traders are paying extortionate rates, because organisers know they can get away with it. It's so uncool. When ingredients are proper and margins are already tight, as I've disclosed on these pages, the independents can really struggle — in fact, some of my favourites have bitten the dust. If such hefty pitch fees continue, the standard of food will slip, or worse the conglomerates will step up to the plate; after all, what's a four-digit pitch fee to them?

You can see where I'm going with this; before we know it, it'll be back to mediocre burger vans. Street food as we know it will be kicked to the kerb. It's food for thought; as street food fans, it's our duty to do something about it!

CONTINUING THE MOVEMENT

Almost every trader I've had the pleasure of nattering to has emphasised the power of the street food community. From passing one another events, to sharing trailers and staff — the camaraderie is unreal. For me, the community doesn't end there. It extends to us, the customers. Unlike restaurants and bars, most street food traders have a very poor online presence; there isn't time for beautifully curated Instagram pages and the whole movement has yet to be recognised by online review sites (admittedly that might be a good thing).

So, it's our job, as passionate foodies supporting the industry, to continue the conversation, online and offline. Let's shout about the traders worth tracking down, and turn a blind eye to the imposters that aren't. Let's take mouth-watering photos of the food and share them, and yes, let's pass on the news and tell our friends, family and colleagues about our street food experiences. Word of mouth is the most powerful marketing tool out there, and I, for one, want to hear all about your journeys through Scotland. You can reach out to me at @PlateExpectations or join the conversation using the hashtag #streetfoodscotland and together let's help our quality traders thrive.

FURTHER EATING

When I started *Street Food Scotland*, my aim was to shed light on thirty unmissable traders. How naive. Almost sixty traders later, Scotland's street food scene is clearly thriving and, given our support, it will continue to expand. There wasn't room for everyone, so here's a little 'further eating'. If you're making a day of it, please seek out these fabulous traders too . . .

TRUCKLE & LOAF, GLASGOW
Gourmet cheese toasties; I like the pear, blue cheese and rocket one.

SHRIMP WRECK, EDINBURGH & GLASGOW
Fish finger sarnies, lightly battered king prawns in a bun and crispy squid 'Bangkok Bonbons'. If you like fried fish, you'll be in heaven here.

HOOKED, EAST LOTHIAN
Expect toasties crammed with fresh crab, panko crusted oysters and moments of genius in nibbles like tempura East Lothian samphire.

PIZZA GEEKS, EDINBURGH
These guys have been crushing it since day one . . . and they've now got a permanent home at 19 Dalry Road. You'll be in safe hands there.

YUCA TACO, GLASGOW
These guys are brand spanking new, I ate their slow-cooked, Achiote pulled pork tacos at TRNSMT. Superb!

BIG BLU PIZZA VAN, DUNBAR
This beautiful Citroën H pitches up at Steam Punk in North Berwick every Friday evening to serve their thin base pizzas – get down there!

FACEPLANT FOODS, EDINBURGH
One for the vegans. Faceplant have mastered the Reuben sandwich, and they even make their own seitan; serious plant-based toasties.

OVER LANGSHAW FARMHOUSE ICE CREAM, BORDERS & EDINBURGH
Operating out of their own Grassmarket police box throughout summer, their whisky and raspberry ripple ice cream is to die for.

SHAWARMA SHACK, EDINBURGH
I tried these new kids on the block at the Scottish Street Food Awards. What flavour. Their grilled aubergine shawarmas will go far.

HONU, GLASGOW
Honu are a West End restaurant who make appearances at Dockyard Social. Their tempura cauliflower poke bowl is very tasty.

SLY FOX, EDINBURGH
Czech food lovers Martina and Kristyna are taking comforting goulash to the next level – and it's all 100% plant based.

GNOM, GLASGOW
Street food traders 'Chomsky' evolved into Gnom. International-inspired seasonal dishes in a relaxed bistro (ahem, get the Turkish eggs).

FIRE & DOUGH, EDINBURGH
There's always room for more pizza. This is 'love at first slice' from a vibrant green horse-box – their pizzas fuelled my Fringe 2019.

TRUSTY BUCK'S, GLASGOW
The latest trader to join Glasgow's offering, serving plant-based Mexican and Indian burritos from kitchen pop-ups and their horsebox.

THE YARD, PERTH
July 2019 saw the launch of Perth's own street food Sunday hang-out, where you'll find the likes of Mezzaluna Italian Street Kitchen.

LEITH ARCHES, EDINBURGH
Set for winter 2019/20, a cool garage space is being converted into a new street food den.

IMAGE CREDITS

ALL PHOTOGRAPHY EXCEPT FOR THE IMAGES ON PAGES LISTED BELOW © AILIDH FORLAN

i, 12, 80, 93, 107, 177, 201, 227, 228 (left), 230 (left), 233, 243 (left) **Shutterstock**

iv, 94 (top), 116, 117, 118, 136 (top), 140, 142 (top), 144 (bottom), 148, 150, 154 (top right, middle left & right, bottom), 162 (top left), 164, 174 (left), 194 (bottom), 195 **Dockyard Social**

vi, 4 (right), 38 (bottom), 41, 79, 244, 246 (left), 250 **Ellie Morag**

6, 52 (top left), 53 **Norelli/ Dagmara Kalicka**

7, 178 (right), 179 **Bowhouse**

8, 16 (top left), 17, 19, 20, 23, 26 (left), 27, 28 (left) **Alix McIntosh**

13, 14 (left), 88 (top left) **Edinburgh Food Festival**

14 (right) **Sameer Dhumale**

21 **Beatrice/@foodspottin**

30 (left) **Emma Riddell**

32 (top left) **Scott Seaton**

35 (right) **The Peruvian**

38 (top right), 39 **Chick & Pea Ltd**

44, 46 **Catherine Balfron**

48, 49 **Rolly's Ice Cream**

56 (bottom left) **Moskito Spanish Bites/Pablo Mosscardo**

60 (bottom) **iStock/georgeclerk**

63 **Harajuku Kitchen/Caroline Trotter (photo)**

73, 74, 75 **Chris Scott**

82 **Nigel John**

84, 87 **Richard Yates**

88 (top right, bottom), 90, 91, 92 **Alanda Black**

94 (bottom right) **Rankine Photography**

94 (bottom left) **Scott Richmond**

97, 98 **Blue Sky Photography**

100 **The Crema Caravan**

101 **StreEAT Events LTD**

104, 106 **Chunks**

108 (right), 154 (top left) **Louise Mather**

110 (top 2 rows) **Big Feed**

112, 114 **Platform**

124 (top), 125 **Christina Riley**

126 (bottom) **Paul Henderson**

132, 134 **Gram Social**

138 **Keith Inglis Photography**

144 (top), 146 **Clair Irwin Photography**

149 **Fraser Craig**

156 **Deanston Whisky**

158 **Gallus Pasta**

167, 168 **Scott Gibson**

171 **Rhona Quarm/Flaming Indulgence**

178 (left, middle) **Balgrove Larder**

184 (top right) **Clickybox Photography**

194 (top) **Fish & Frites**

196 (top left, bottom), 201 **The Cheesy Toast Shack**

206 (right) **Maco Food Fusion**

209 (right) **Smoke & Soul**

209 (left), 210 **Neil Ruddiforth**

212 (bottom), 214 (top) **Marcus Bawdon**

214 (bottom) **Matt Jolly Photography**

216 **Daniel McAvoy Photography**

218 **Martin Chiffes**

220 **Les Black**

224, 225, 226 **The Liberty Kitchen**

228 (right) **MediaWorldImages/ Alamy Stock Photo**

229 (right) **International Photobank/Alamy Stock Photo**

229 (left) **Steve Morgan/Alamy Stock Photo**

230 (left) **David Kilpatrick/ Alamy Stock Photo**

232 **Alison Mackay**

234, 236, 237 **Bad Girl Bakery Ltd**

238 (top) **Mike Guest**

238 (bottom), 240, 241 **The Seafood Shack**

242 (right) **Kay Roxby/Alamy Stock Photo**

242 (left) **Pep Masip/Alamy Stock Photo**

243 (right) **UrbanImages/Alamy Stock Photo**

BACK COVER IMAGES:
Left **Chick & Pea Ltd**
Right **Ellie Morag**

AILIDH FORLAN has a passion for all things food and drink! Based in Edinburgh, Ailidh was a judge for the 2019 Scottish Street Food Awards and the Scottish Thistle Awards Best Eating Experience in 2018 and 2019. She is the discerning foodie behind Plate Expectations, an Instagram page of unbiased, no-nonsense reviews, coupled with drool-worthy food photography. It's here that she champions Scotland's local produce and documents its newest, most innovative dining experiences. As a member of *The List's Eating & Drinking Guide* review team, Ailidh has critiqued hundreds of Edinburgh's restaurants and bars.

THANK YOU!

Writing a book is tough! I couldn't have done it without an incredible support team. Words will never do them justice, but I'll give it my best shot.

One colossal thank you to my parents, Linda and Mike, who've been my taxi drivers, private bankers, therapists, role models and senior editors (you're over sixty, ha). Thanks for raising me to be an adventurous, unfussy eater and for always taking me to amazing restaurants. I hope to make you proud and teach you a thing or two more about good food, and where to find it, in return. Jamie, sorry (not sorry) for surpassing you as favourite child. Thanks for the GIFs and for assuring me that you'll use this book as a drink coaster; may it be the best you own.

Huge love and appreciation to my rock Jonny. Cold meals (sorry, camera eats first), emotional wobbles (me), motivational talks (you) and, hallelujah, it's over. Roll on book two! Just joking. Maybe. Then there's a girl's best friends. Heather Reid, thanks for injecting our journeys with laughter. Liv Ancell, Amy Nguyen, Caoilfhionn McMonagle, Amanda Hatichavadi, Tor Murphy

and many others, thanks for 'checking in' with supportive messages – they meant the world.

As for Scotland's food and drink community, I'm overwhelmed. Huge thanks to Jo Laidlaw and Donald Reid at *The List* for my first break and for sculpting my writing style. To all the phenomenal street food traders, thanks for your time and honesty; you're doing amazing things.

Big thanks to Ellie Morag for taking *the* front cover photo and to everyone that kept me right: Pam Gilmour, Evalyn and Mike Sullivan, Chris Lindsay, Dave Reilly, Michelle Russell, Sarah Taylor, Leesa Souter, Sophia Wiedermann, Monet Brooks, Alice and Stanley Lister, and the women who inspire me daily: Liv White, Pippa Perriam, Ailsa Harper, Kim Steele, Holly Lithgow, Lucy Paul, Jess Van Tromp, and Emily Weir.

Thanks to Jonnie Cook and George Murdoch at Whiskers in Stockbridge and Michael, Mika and the team at 127 on George Street for supplying me with coffee, red wine and Wi-Fi.

Last, but by no means least, thanks to the team at Black & White for bringing my passion project to life. We did it! This beautiful book wouldn't have been possible without you.